10,000
HOURS OF
FEAR

A Memoir

ELAINE HARTRICK

ISBN: Paperback 979-8-218-19787-2
        Hardcover 979-8-9894893-0-5
        eBook 979-8-9894893-1-2

Today, I'm thankful for the mountains we 'get' to climb.

Often it takes getting to the top of a mountain
before we can appreciate the climb, but the climb
is where we get to learn; the climb is a teacher.

When we 'get' to summit something difficult, we often gain
a greater understanding of ourselves; we become more self-aware
and gain greater insights into who we are and what we're capable of.

Arriving at the pinnacle of a difficult mountain brings relief,
often joy, and a place where we can catch our breath to prepare
for the next ascent. It's a place where we can hold up a flag in the
wind and say "I did it. I did something hard and I made it!"

Sometimes I feel like I've had more mountains
to climb, and continue to climb, than the average hiker,
so occasionally I can be an ungrateful student who feels
like the hill is too steep and my pack too heavy.

But when I finally reach the top of yet another mountain,
I am always wiser, kinder, more compassionate, more generous,
more confident, more resilient, and mentally and emotionally
fitter. And the beautiful part about what I gained from that
rise to the top is that after a short rest, I get to take all of those
things with me on the next mountain I'll 'get' to climb.

Most certainly another will be on the horizon.

So I will give thanks for the mountains, for the summits, but most
certainly for the climbs, from which I have received my entire education.

–Elaine Hartrick

DEDICATION

*To every person that kept me from feeling
alone when life really sucked.*

ACKNOWLEDGEMENTS

Thank you to the true heroes of this tale:

My mother—

Mom, everything I am is because of you. Without you there would be no book, no happy ending, no victory. You kept me sane, you made me laugh, you wept with me. You are the most selfless human to have ever graced this earth. Your entire life has been in the service of mine. Thank you is grossly inadequate, but thank you. You are the shoulders I've stood on. And when I needed to tower over my circumstance, you grew taller.

My son—

Thank you for being so strong yet profoundly gentle. Thank you for waking up happy every single day of your life and having an inordinate amount of common sense. You are an immovable rock of strength for me, and for everyone around you. You are a ray of sunshine in the world—your calmness, kindness, steadiness, and loyalty are without reproach. I am in awe of you. The depth of your character shines through in every story in this book. We are mother and son, but I love that we are also the best of friends and deeply connected in a way that only you and I understand.

My daughter—

You are my hero, my inspiration, and one of the strongest people I know. You are brave beyond description, resilient, defiant of explanation, and the embodiment of wisdom and courage. You are wicked smart, fiercely independent, and beautifully tenderhearted. Your compassion and thoughtfulness is beyond compare. I am so proud of you. With grace and goodness you have overcome more than anyone should have to. You fill a room, make the world laugh, and are, to me, the champion of this story.

For their writing and editing contributions, a special thank you to: Arlene Wallace (Mom), Fraser Tingle, Melody S. Gee, and Kira Breed-Wrisley

I believe that unarmed truth and unconditional love will have the final word in reality. This is why right, temporarily defeated, is stronger than evil triumphant.

—Martin Luther King, Jr., Norway, 1964

PROLOGUE

The summit of Mt. Kilimanjaro is near. I can't see it because the gauze of a freak blizzard gives me only a foot of visibility. The headlamp I'm wearing can't cut through the storm. But the summit must be near.

This final ascent, on our fifth day of climbing, goes several hours through the middle of the night so that we can arrive at the peak at sunrise. I pass climbers pulled over on the side of the path, nauseated and hallucinating from altitude sickness or asking their guides to examine them for frostbite. I hear a woman who I know is a surgeon say, "I can't lose my fingers." Every few steps, I stop to catch my breath. I squeeze my hands into fists and make sure I can feel my own fingers. The thin mittens I'd packed have already soaked through and I am wearing a heavy pair of socks on my hands now. Where is Navy? We'd been walking together but now she's gone ahead of me. Or had she stopped again to rest and I've passed her? There shouldn't be snow. A blizzard like this just doesn't happen here. At least, not until I decide to summit.

I pass more people pulled over on the side of the trail. One man sits trying to catch his breath in the oxygen-poor air. I shine my headlamp's beam on his face as I move past him. Our eyes meet for a small moment, and in the howling wind I hear him say, "It's heavy."

I nod. "Yes," I say.

In the dark, my body pushed to its outer limit, I have no energy for thoughts, and yet they won't stop coming. The other times I thought I would die, not from hypothermia or exhaustion, but from his hands choking me. Or the time I thought I would die from never seeing Navy again. My thoughts always return to her, my fifteen-year-old daughter, alone without her mother. I wonder where Navy is right now? I can't count the number of times I have wondered this before. *What is she doing right now? Is she okay?* The questions land with every thud of my heart, with every icy footstep that pushes me toward the top, toward the light I have to believe will meet me when I get there. I need to find her. I need to see the top with her. I need to know where she is right now because when this is all over and we're back on the ground with warm blood pumping to our hands and feet again, she isn't going to stay with me. The next time I ask, *Where is Navy?* I'll have no idea what the answer is.

CHAPTER ONE

When I was five years old, my nanny sent me to buy her more cigarettes. The store was over a mile away and I'd never been that far on my own before. The cars roared past me, larger and faster than I'd ever remembered, like mythical beasts racing by. I got to the store, found her cigarettes, paid for them, and waited for the teenaged cashier to ask me where my mom was. He didn't say, "Why are you alone? Are you all right?" I took the purchase back to my nanny, who held her hand out without looking up, and let me deposit her cigarettes wordlessly. The nanny was fired, but soon after, I stopped holding my mom's hand to cross the street. "I walk on my own," I insisted. It wasn't long until I was watching myself after school.

My mom went back to work soon after I was born, but she hadn't planned on that any more than she had planned on me. She had been twenty-three and single, just finishing up nursing school. At that time, children born out of wedlock were given up for adoption. She thought she could hide both the pregnancy and the birth by moving to Vancouver to nanny for a family, then return home without the stain of an unplanned pregnancy. But when I was born, squalling, red with a shock of black hair and enormous blue eyes, she was surprised both that I wasn't a boy and that she wanted to keep me. I was, she said, the most beautiful thing she had ever seen, the most perfect little child in the world. But how was she going to keep me that way?

She brought me to her parents' home, bundled tight, knowing they would worry that she had made her life infinitely harder. The day she walked in the door with me wrapped in a bundle was the only time she ever saw my grandfather weep. When I was a month old, my mom returned to work full-time. She knew it was up to her alone to build a life for us.

I was fiercely attached to my mother. She was slim and lovely, with long reddish-brown hair, the same blue eyes as mine, fair skin, and an adventurous spirit that she also passed down to me. She was quick-witted and funny even when things were hard. And when hard things came, she never let me to feel sorry for myself, "no pity parties," she would say, a simple, but enduring lesson that would serve me well in future years.

We lived in a section of Calgary, Alberta called Cemetery Hill, which, as the name suggests, is full of cemeteries. They made wonderful places to play. My mom loved to fly kites and we spent afternoons with the sun on our faces, running our kite into the air amid tombstones in the Jewish cemetery directly across from our house. I ran with my face toward the sky, not wanting to take my eyes off the bright red kite as it tore through the clouds. Racing to catch her, my foot caught on a low, flat grave marker and I fell face-first into the grass. I scrambled up, laughing and tearing after my beautiful mother. Her kite bobbed and darted in the wind, dancing with us. It was always just us.

Cemetery Hill overlooked the Calgary Exhibition & Stampede grounds, home of the world's largest rodeo and fair since the early 1900s. For ten days every July, my mom and I stayed up late and watched fireworks explode, taking the shape of flowers, stars, spirals. I liked the sound of the fireworks almost as much as the fractal beauty of their explosions, with booms so deep they resounded in my chest.

Me, age 5

Around these kinds of celebrations and festival days, our daily life was quiet. My mom worked long hours and I had nannies looking after me while she was gone. They heated the meals she prepared for me and stored in the fridge. When she was home, my mom would make traditional Canadian (by way of England) roast beef and Yorkshire pudding with mashed potatoes and peas. She loved to cook. Her meals, especially her pies, were famous. Having come from many generations of women whose "door is always open" for a home-cooked meal, there was always lots to go around. My favorite, which she saved for just me on a cold day or if I wasn't feeling well, was buttery toast sliced into strips and served with hot chocolate for dipping, just like her mother had done for her.

When I was eight, my mom met Alex, a divorced tradesman. He was clean-cut, with brownish, graying hair. I liked him. Every time he came over, he brought me an *Archie* or *Richie Rich* comic book. I loved to read and a comic book was a special treat. My mom adored him. I'd never known my father and my mom didn't speak of him. He wasn't a palpable absence; he just wasn't there. I didn't miss him. My mom and I had each other. I realized when she started dating Alex that I'd never known what it was like to have a father, or even just a man around.

When I was nine, my mom and Alex got married. "I felt like no one had ever loved like this before," she told me much later. "Or ever would again. He loved me as much as I loved him."

My mom and Alex on their wedding day

The ceremony took place in my mom's hometown of Red Deer, ninety minutes north of Calgary, where my grandparents still resided. I stayed with them after the wedding, and as I watched my mom float out the door, radiant and proud, I was flooded with a grief I had never felt while they were dating. I was caught off guard by the intense wave of emotion. It had always been just the two of us, and now this man had taken her from me. I cried inconsolably as my grandmother held me in her arms. It was the first time in my life that I ever felt really afraid. I couldn't feel sure about what life would be like, what my mom would be like, what we would be now that Alex was a permanent part of us. That feeling eventually began to fade, and when my mom and Alex returned, we began life as a new family.

Two weeks after the wedding, while Alex was working out of town, he went out for drinks with a few friends at the day's end. Over the phone, my mom could hear that he'd been drinking, and told him to stay where he was and come home in the morning.

When the doorbell rang, I woke up in a daze. I knew it was too early for the alarm. I heard my mom scream. "No! No! No!" over and over again. The sound was raw and shrill, ripping the air like cheap cloth. I gripped my knees to my chest, terrified.

Alex had decided to drive, not wanting to miss a night with his new wife. He was halfway home when he fell asleep at the wheel. His car careened into a ditch, where he went through the windshield and was killed. After the police had gone, my mom came upstairs and said through her tears, "You don't have to go to school today."

"It's okay," I said. "I'll go to school."

It was hard to see her in so much pain. My mom was twenty-four when she had me, and thirty-three when Alex died. I grieved for her as much as she did for him. I didn't know what to do other than resume my life at school. In truth, my nine-year-old self was secretly happy that, once again, it was just the two of us. Once in a while, she would think about dating again, but I could not bear the thought of it. When she brought it up, I would shut down completely, my anxiety so high that I would have to leave the room. In the end, my mom decided to put my happiness above her own. She never dated again.

* * *

After Alex's death, we moved to the suburbs. She continued to work and by the time I was ten, I'd learned to look after myself. I didn't mind being alone. I could do laundry, finish my homework, and put myself to bed without any supervision. I reheated the meals she prepared for me each day.

My mom, still grieving, was spiritually at sea, searching desperately for meaning, to know what happens after we die. I had been given no religious education at all, but my mom's sister, Anne, had joined a church a few years earlier and believed that her faith could help my mom. She sent missionaries to our home. My mom and I joined her church.

Church was where I met Nicole when we were both eleven. Nicole was Jamaican, Caucasian, and Chinese, and the first thing I noticed was her incredible black hair reaching all the way down her back. She had a fantastic sense of humor and an infectious laugh that I loved. Nicole and I spent all day at school together, then talked for hours afterward on the phone. Her parents became a second family to me. We went along on each other's family vacations, and were comically inseparable. After a trip to Disneyland with Nicole and my mom, spending every waking and sleeping moment together for two weeks, we dropped Nicole off at her house. As she ran to her door she shouted, "I'll call you when you get home!" And she did.

In high school, we traded clothing and dreamed of becoming models, lying on our backs to zip up jeans tighter than corsets, then taking glamor shots as I planned to become the next Brooke Shields. At fourteen, we had our futures mapped out, settling on the sensible strategy of marrying rich. We began to put our plans into action by signing up for tennis lessons, where some magazine had promised you'd be guaranteed to meet wealthy men. Until our rich husbands arrived, there was always Bradley, the cute instructor with blonde hair and crystalline blue eyes. We were both terrible at tennis, always pelting people with balls, but this seemed like a minor obstacle to our ultimate goal. Nicole was, and remains, a deeply loyal friend. The day Tod Beretta, the boy I had plans to marry, tore up my birthday party invitation in front of all our friends at church, Nicole had to be physically restrained from hitting him over the head with a hymn book from a nearby pew.

Our new house in the suburbs

Nicole and I at Disneyland

I loved animals, particularly horses, almost as much as I loved Nicole. In spite of the sacrifice it required from her nurse's salary, my mom managed to buy my first horse, Nugget, when I was fourteen. By the time I was seventeen, I was competing all over western Canada and the U.S. with my first show horse, Boss. I fell in love with Boss at first sight, the day my trainer, Maureen, brought him back from an American Saddlebred show in California. He was a tall, dark bay, deep brown with a black mane and tail, and the longest white blaze down his nose that I had ever seen. I never imagined a horse like that could belong to me until Maureen told me that she had bought him thinking he could be my first show horse. I had always loved to problem-solve and finding a way for me to keep Boss would be no exception. My mom and I sprang into action. I took two after-school jobs, one in an office and the other as a restaurant hostess. My mom and I glued together reindeer ornaments out of clothespins and sold them at holiday craft shows for two dollars apiece. All our hard work eventually paid off and Boss was mine. I was as optimistic as I was resourceful. If I wanted anything badly enough, I believed I could make it happen, no matter how hard I would have to work.

Playing with Nicole

When I wasn't at school or working, I was at the barn with Boss. He was young and bursting with energy, the kind of horse who danced more than galloped, already trotting away before I was completely in the saddle. He could scarcely be held back, and it seemed like a crime to try. Though we only rode in the show ring and stable, it felt like he could run wild and forever, and I could have clung to him as we raced to the end of the world and home again. On Boss's back I felt like we could see everything, go everywhere; especially into the show ring in front of an arena of cheering fans.

Boss and I in the show ring

Had I never found my love for horses, I still would have been working. I flipped burgers at Burger Express, answered phones as a receptionist, and served as an overnight phone operator. There was hardly a moment when I wasn't busy with school, earning money, or at the barn. My sophomore year, on a lark, I tried out for the basketball team. When I didn't make the cut, I became the manager of the boys' team, going to all home and away games. I didn't know what was driving me to stay busy. There was already more than enough to occupy my time between regular schoolwork and fending for myself while my mom worked late nights. I wasn't lonely during those times. My mom always called me on her breaks to check in and see if I was okay. I'd learned to be independent and self-sufficient and enjoy long stretches of solitude. But I was hungry for life, ravenous even, for experiences and challenges, to prove myself capable and excel at whatever I tried my hand at. I believed there was something *more*, something out there that could be mine if I just went for it.

But I did have one blind spot, an old absence that seemed to follow me all my life. I never used to think not having a father left a mark on me. I was too wrapped up in my mother's love and my many activities to notice anything lacking. But what I lacked were any male figures in my life. I didn't know how to talk to boys, or how to act around them. One day when a boy in ninth grade asked me a question in class, my heart stopped. I couldn't believe a boy was actually talking to me, and it didn't matter that he was just asking me to repeat the teacher's instructions. I couldn't believe that he *saw* me. I wasn't like this with girls. I had close friends with whom I shared and listened equally, with whom I could be myself. I was confident with girls in a way I could never be around boys.

And yet, I dated casually like it was a competitive sport, partly because I loved to go out, to get to know someone new, dance, maybe kiss, and enjoy the heady whirlwind of romance. None of it lasted. None of it was serious. I needed an outlet for my gregarious nature, but it never went past a certain level of intimacy. Maybe I was keeping myself safe by keeping myself unavailable. I also strongly believed in my church's teachings against premarital sex, so maybe I wouldn't let myself even get near that possibility. Certainly I was in exploration mode, and never stopped feeling like I knew nothing about boys. I can't say that I ever fell in love, so I didn't know yet about heartbreak or even about the normal ups and downs of romance.

Looking back, I'm struck by my own innocence as a young teenager. I'd learned most of what I knew, or thought I knew, about dating from movies or reading books. What I see in myself from those years is how open my heart lay to anyone who wanted its trust. The world was good. My mom had made sure of that for me, and ours was a community that felt safe and loving. I was, in a word, unjaded. I'm grateful for the shelter and protection. Yet I also see now how naïve I was in many ways.

When I was eighteen, I was hired as a receptionist for a limousine company. My employer, Harvey, was probably in his forties. When he began pursuing me, I was flattered and shocked by his interest, his fancy car business, and large staff. I didn't know what to think of his aggressive come-ons or how to say that this was inappropriate, how to report him, or even to tell my mom. It was like I had been dropped on another planet and didn't know the rules of engagement. We went on a few dates. When he wanted me to be intimate with him, I refused. He fired me. I knew in my core that what he was asking for was wrong, but at the time, I wouldn't have called Harvey a predator, like many would today. I didn't see him abusing his power and authority, pressuring me, or putting me under duress with his attention. The world I came from didn't have people with malicious intentions. How do you recognize something you have no category for?

When I graduated high school my ambitions were to work in the arts. All those hours pretending to be models with Nicole had revealed a real love of art, photography, fashion, and design. I envisioned myself in a chic New York loft, constantly surrounded by beauty and excitement, going out on photo shoots and living life through a camera lens. A scheduled visit to the guidance counselor for a career aptitude test would, I believed, surely confirm my ambitions.

"It says here that you are very resourceful," the guidance counselor began, pointing at my results. "You're good at solving problems and finding solutions to things. That you like it, actually."

"Yes," I agreed. "My friends always come to me."

I wondered what that quality would make me good at someday.

"Well," she continued. "Your aptitude test says you would make a really good general manager of a hotel."

I looked at her with disgust and confusion. What even was a *general manager*? And why would a hotel need one? Undeterred, I continued to hone my photography skills on the small point-and-shoot camera my mom had given me for Christmas. No test was going to tell me that I wasn't going to be a photographer.

In all my dreams, whether my own or the ones ascribed to me, I never thought of myself as a mother. It's not that I didn't like or want kids, but I didn't believe I would ever get married. Who would want me? I couldn't relate to men and I scared most of them off with my confident independence. And what did I care, anyway? I had my mom and Nicole. I had work and my horse and the sheer freedom and exhilaration of riding.

* * *

I saw double one Sunday afternoon after church. An identical red Toyota Celica parked next to mine. It was spring; I had graduated high school the previous June and was dividing my time as best I could between horse shows, work, and trying to make future college plans. As I went to get into my car, the owner of its twin walked up. He looked older than me.

"Nice car!" I said.

He laughed. "Yours too!"

He was sharp-looking, six feet with brown hair and blue eyes. Clean-shaven, fit and in a tailored blue suit and crisp white shirt, he looked like a high-powered executive who had gotten lost on his way to a meeting downtown and somehow ended up at our church. Later, he would tell me he'd had his eye on me for a while before we met. I looked older than my age, tall and mature, and when he saw me one Sunday in a light blue dress and matching hat, he gazed at me all through the service, and wondered, *Whose wife is that?* His name was Kevin.

My Celica

That night, I went over to the house of my friends Karen and John for dinner. Even though I was out of high school, Karen would sometimes invite me over for dinner when my mom was at work. Just as we were finishing our meal, the phone rang. I could hear John saying my name and I eavesdropped shamelessly.

"Uh-huh. Elaine? Yeah . . . yeah . . . I know exactly who you are talking about. Her name is Elaine Hartrick, and she's actually here right now."

John told me Kevin was on the phone for me. "You want to talk to him?" he asked.

I later learned they'd gotten to know each other and John had told him to look up his number in our congregation directory if he ever needed anything.

"Sure," I replied.

John smiled at me when I took the phone from his hand, and motioned me toward the other room where I could take the call privately.

Playing matchmaker seemed to please him.

"Hello?"

"Hi," Kevin said. "I just wanted to say hello to you. It's so crazy that you're right there! Must be fate."

We talked for a few minutes, then he asked me out on a date. I had to think about it. At that time my nights were fully booked: every night that week I had either work or a date with someone else. My Wednesday night date was early, so I agreed to meet Kevin afterward.

Tuesday night, Kevin called. We chatted casually and I began to regret agreeing to our date the next night. Kevin was twenty-nine— much older than I had assumed. He was divorced and had three children. *Not interested!* I thought. As far as I was concerned at the time, only losers were divorced. Divorce meant there was some fundamental weakness in him, some hidden, possibly fatal flaw. I knew that whenever I found someone to settle down with, we would be each other's first everything: first love, first wedding, first intimate experience, first honeymoon, first home, first child. I wanted a shared adventure. I did not want to take the journey with someone who had been there before, someone for whom it would be a do-over and not a discovery.

I believed Kevin was past all these thrilling firsts I could still only imagine. Nothing we would ever do would be new to him. He had already moved on to another phase of life. It wasn't just our age difference, either. He seemed to already be living in a different world than mine. At eighteen, I was chomping at the bit to leap into life, to taste everything for the first time, make choices for myself, and see what the world would offer me in return. Kevin wasn't exactly *done* with life, but he was so much further along than me. Wednesday night was less than twenty-four hours away. *It's only one date,* I thought. *You can always go home early.*

Over dinner, I found myself charmed and surprised. Kevin talked with confidence and ease, unlike the eighteen-year-old boys I was used to dating. Carefree and fun, they didn't know what they were doing and couldn't think past the next party. They didn't know who they were or what they were going to be. In truth, neither did I yet, but I had a sense of ambition and I was looking toward the future. Kevin was different. He was mature and he had manners. He was polished and smooth where the other boys were awkward and flailing. I was intrigued.

Kevin told me he was the top salesman at an insurance company. He took important business trips and won prestigious awards year after year—the kind that only the top 2 percent of salesmen in the country earned. That he had not just a job but a *career* was impressive. Though wealth was never important to me, and certainly of lesser concern in a potential relationship than romantic love, his ambition and drive resonated with me. His life sounded fascinating and exciting, two things I desperately wanted for my own. He talked about the exotic trips he had taken his ex-wife on every year, to places I had only read about in books, staying in luxury hotels and riding in limousines all paid for by his company. I remembered in that moment that Kevin had shared his life with another person.

After dinner, we drove to Banff, Canada's oldest national park, nestled in the Rocky Mountains. We talked for hours and lost track of time. We listened to one another, rapt like we'd never heard such stories before, talking too quickly, as if we could not spill our thoughts out fast enough. I wanted him to know my whole life, my every thought, all at once, and I wanted to know his. I felt so grown up, interested in and interesting to another adult. This was what I had been missing, I thought. If only teenage boys were like this, I would have fallen in love ages ago.

Kevin slowed the car around a curve and looked at me thoughtfully. "You know, I was engaged before you," he said.

I gave him a puzzled look. "You were *married* before me, Kevin."

"No, I don't mean my ex-wife. Here, I'm trying to tell you how much you've meant to me from the first time I saw you."

"Okay, how much?" I said playfully.

"That first time I saw you at church, before I even talked to you in the parking lot, I was engaged to someone else, a girl named Heather Wesson."

I stared at him. "You were engaged when you first asked me out?" My voice was filled with all the outrage my young self could muster. Kevin put up both his hands in self-defense, then quickly grabbed the wheel again.

"No! No, I promise," he assured me. "The day I saw you—I went home that night and I broke it off with her. I said, 'Heather, there was a girl at church today who I think I like more than you and I haven't even met her yet. She's beautiful. I think I could get a girl like that.'"

"You *didn't* say that."

"I did!"

"That is awful, Kevin!" I said. But I giggled.

"What can I say? I was in love."

"That's awful," I said again. *That's so romantic,* I thought.

We left the park and drove the ninety minutes back to Calgary. It was well past midnight. Kevin took me to his condo on the top floor of a high-rise in a nice part of the city. It was clean and organized, the home of someone who didn't depend on his mother to keep his socks picked up off the floor. He had rooms prepared for when his older children came to stay. There was also a brand-new crib. His life, I was reminded again, was so different from mine. But was that a bad thing? I looked around at his impressive home and the signs of his adult responsibilities and softened. Despite the divorce, he had not run away from his family or responsibilities. In that moment, I realized that Kevin was a *man*. He wasn't some kid finding his way into life, he was already living. He had built a home and a family, and when that arrangement didn't work out, he had built this one that I was now standing in.

Before we left his apartment to take me home, he leaned close to kiss me. *This is awesome,* I thought, but the kiss flung me out of my reverie. He was a terrible kisser. Not careful or tender, but greedy and devouring with his very full lips. There was something aggressive about the way his mouth seemed to completely engulf mine. *I can always fix that, though,* I told myself.

Soon, Kevin and I were inseparable. We took weekend road trips, spent beach days at the local lake, and went to concerts. We played softball, went to the movies and church socials, and dined out.

Kevin made me laugh, slurping his Diet Coke from a bottle through a hollow red licorice twist. And he did a million little things for me—ordering for me in restaurants and filling up my car with gas. They were simple acts, things I had always and easily done for myself. But they made me feel cared for in a way I had never felt before by someone other than my mom. He was sweet and affectionate, hugging and touching me whenever we were close, sending me endless cards and letters, even when we were only separated for a few hours. One letter I saved read:

My dear Elaine,

Did I ever tell you how beautiful you are? How smart!? Sweet? I think you have the most beautiful face, your hair is wild! I think you're gorgeous, lovely, magnificent, fabulous, sexy, delicious, very desirable, and I do not have any other girlfriends. I love you and only you.

Love always,
Kevin

My mom, the most important person in my life, liked him. Sometimes Kevin even asked her to join us when we went out. My mom and I had been on our own all my life and I had taken care of myself ever since I could remember. Self-reliance is part of who I am, as is taking care of *others.* I liked that part of myself and took pride in my capabilities. Kevin's favors and sweet gestures didn't take that away from me. They made me feel cherished.

For the first month or so that we were dating, I was casually seeing a few other young men. Kevin knew this, but he couldn't take it for long. About a week after our first date, I went on a date with someone from work. While I was out, Kevin went over to my house, found my mother out gardening, and helped her with the weeding and planting. When I asked him about it, he was nonchalant, as though he had just been passing by.

Then there was my long-planned date with Grant, who lived in Montana and had traveled to Calgary more than once to take me out. I drove down to spend a week with Grant, and while I was gone, Kevin retaliated by asking out my close friend, Jacquie. The whole week I was away, he pursued her intently and convinced her that he wanted to be with her. But as soon as I returned, he cut Jacquie off abruptly, vanishing from her life without explanation. A few days later, Kevin snooped in my room and found a letter from Grant. He read it aloud to me with such scornful mocking that I couldn't stop hearing his voice instead of Grant's. Kevin had gone after Jacquie to make me jealous and he'd mocked Grant to embarrass me. These were, I told myself, signs of how much he loved me, and that he wanted me to be his and only his. They worked. A week after I returned from Montana, Kevin and I became exclusive. I was his girlfriend and we were officially each other's one and only. It felt like a serious step, an adult move in an adult relationship. I had never come this far with anyone before.

Very quickly, Kevin couldn't bear to be without me. He managed to get an evening job at the restaurant where I worked as a hostess, so we would not have to spend those nights apart. When I took Boss to compete, he traveled with me. Kevin had grown up riding horses in a farming community. He had competed in local rodeos and was a proficient horseman. At my shows, Kevin volunteered as Boss's groomer. That way, he promised, he would never have to watch from the faraway stands. Instead, he would be at my side, saddling my horse, brushing his tail, and waiting for me to come riding back to him. He took an interest in every part of my life and in turn made it an interest of his. He wanted to experience the world through my eyes, he said. He wanted to know about everything I did, everywhere I went. He told me he hated being alone because he hated being without me. He asked me to repeat every word of conversations I had without him, with my mom, Nicole, or anyone else. He asked me question after question, seemingly fascinated by every detail and never bored by any of it. Kevin's passion for me was intoxicating. He loved me and I loved how in love with me he was. I felt special, the center of Kevin's world. At the time, I thought this is what it must feel like to be a queen, a goddess even. It reminded me of being the center of my mom's world, only with less space between us.

When I expressed hesitation about not being Kevin's first, he assured me that I was.

"I'm not," I objected. "You've been married. You have kids. I'm never going to be your first anything."

Kevin looked deep into my eyes. When he did, the world melted away and we were in our own universe. All I could see was him. All I could hear was his voice. Even I sort of disappeared and the universe just became Kevin.

"Beth may have been my first wife, but she wasn't my first choice. I had to marry her. Our parents made us."

"How?"

"She seduced me during our church mission in Australia. It's a long story, but we ended up having sex, she lured me in. I didn't want to but I couldn't help myself. You have to understand the spell she could cast on people."

"So, what happened?"

"Everyone found out," Kevin explained, looking full of remorse. "Our parents then pushed us into getting married because they said it was the right thing." He took my face in his hands. "You are my first, Elaine. I'm choosing you. I want you. You're my real first."

My doubts evaporated. I believed him entirely. His voice, his tone, his gaze—they all had the power to quiet any fears and cast away any worries I had.

* * *

About three months into the relationship, a song I loved came on the car radio. Carefree and happy, driving with a man I was crazy about, I turned the volume all the way up and started dancing in my seat, lost in the joy of the moment. Suddenly, Kevin snapped the radio off.

"Why are you being so immature?" He glared at me. "Quit acting like such a child!"

I had never seen him angry before. I suddenly felt eighteen, only eighteen, in the presence of this grown man. I thought it was a strange thing to get upset about, but I also thought he must know more about being mature than I did. I promised not to do that again. Mentally, I added *act mature* to a list I began forming on how to behave.

Sometimes, it was still difficult for me to wrap my head around the fact that Kevin had an ex-wife and three children. Cassie was seven, Miles six, and Jayden eighteen months. Kevin had only ever lived with the two oldest. I wasn't anywhere near thinking about marriage, nor was I worried about being anyone's *stepmother*. But I was secretly freaking out a little. It was a small grain of dread in my gut that I chalked up to my own immaturity and lack of life experience. The kids were sweet and we got along fine when they had visits with Kevin, but they were strange creatures to me. I never really knew how to interact with them.

Far more confusing was Kevin's relationship with his ex-wife, Beth. When we came to pick the children up at her townhouse every other weekend, I waited in the car while Kevin stood on the doorstep. He was not allowed inside, even in pouring rain. I thought Beth must really hate him, and how sad that she punished the children's father right in front of them. I never spoke to Beth, so all I knew was what Kevin told me, which was that things had gotten so bad by the end that Beth had attacked him with a knife.

During work one day, I called my mom like I usually did, just to check in and hear her voice.

"How are things with Kevin?" she asked.

"Oh, fine," I said. "But I think he's too short for me to marry."

At five foot ten myself, I always wanted a guy that was six foot two or more. I started to laugh but my mom interrupted.

"Good. Don't marry him."

"Mom, I was joking. Why would you say something like that?"

"I had a call, Elaine."

"From who?"

"Fern Goodman called me a few days ago," my mom went on. Fern had been my church youth group leader. "She knows Beth. She heard you were dating Kevin so she called to talk to me about him. She said she was scared for you, for your safety."

"Why would she say that?" I asked.

"Because he used to beat Beth," my mom answered quietly.

"What? Why should we believe something like that?" I demanded.

"I don't think she would make that up," my mom replied. "What would Fern have to gain from lying about something like that? I was going to tell you earlier," my mom continued. "But I know you when your mind's made up. We both know how stubborn you are. When you said you couldn't marry him, I was happy to hear it."

I couldn't think of a response so I told my mom I would call her later.

That night I confronted Kevin about the accusation. He looked untroubled. His voice was steady and confident.

"Elaine, she and I fought constantly near the end. Every little bump in the road blew up into a screaming match. We swore and insulted each other. It was ugly. Even the sex got rough, and sometimes violent." I must have looked horrified because he quickly added, "But it was always consensual. Always. Anyway, one night, everything had become chaotic and Beth attacked me like some rabid animal. She was hitting, kicking, scratching, biting. Finally, she grabbed a knife and threatened to stab me. I tried to stop her. I pinned her down and tried to get her to calm down, but the knife slipped and it gave me a good gash. She still called the police on me, and I even spent the night in jail."

Then Kevin pulled down his collar and revealed a small scar on his collarbone. At the time, I had no reason to doubt that the scar had come from Beth cutting him with the knife.

He seemed relieved to tell me, like a burden was being lifted. Later, I told my mom the story, and Kevin even talked to her too, pleading for her understanding. We felt bad for him, being thrown in jail because the police would have assumed he was the assailant and not Beth. Becoming a part-time father because of all this mess.

I looked at him tenderly and said, "That must have been awful."

"It was," he replied.

* * *

One day without warning, Kevin called me at work and said, "I don't want to see you anymore." We had been dating for several months and I was happier than I had ever been. We'd settled the issue of Beth and Fern. We'd just been out dancing the night before. All I could stammer out was a weak, "What?" But Kevin had already hung up. I dialed him back but there was no answer.

I spent the rest of the day in shock, barely paying attention to my tasks. On my way home, as I sat at a red light, I heard a honk from behind me. It was Kevin. What a terrible coincidence that we were both far from our homes and had ended up at the same intersection. He looked surprised for a moment, then smiled and waved. I sped out of the intersection, throwing him the filthiest look I could muster.

He called me at home that night. I was still confused and furious. "What happened? Why did you break up with me for no reason?" I said, not sure if I were about to cry or to yell at him.

"Oh, that. I just wanted to see what you would do."

His voice wasn't just casual, it was *bored*. Looking back, I see that instead of being chilled to the bone that he had wounded me for his own amusement, I shut down. Instead of letting it sink in that he was acting cruelly, like a boy pulling wings off flies, I decided to put it out of my mind. Sometimes, an idea confronts us that is so incomprehensible, so incongruous with the charming, affectionate person on the other end of the line, that it gets tucked into a faraway corner of the mind and heart. It's never completely forgotten, and once in a while will stir from the recesses of the mind and knock loudly on the door of your consciousness. It takes an incredible amount of strength to ignore the insistent pounding noise it then creates in the psyche; a pounding in sync with the beating of your own heart.

Kevin was good at quieting my doubts. He was never not whistling or singing, cracking quirky jokes that made everyone love him from the moment they were introduced. He crouched down to greet and coo over every dog or child he met, giving his full attention to any small creature. He lent his car or his golf clubs at the drop of a hat to anyone who asked. He showed up when your car had died to give you a ride. Like me, he didn't smoke or drink. He came from a good family—pillars of our church community. After church socials, he was the only man who came into the kitchen and went straight to the sink full of dirty dishes with his sleeves rolled up, instead of asking one of the women to fix him something extra. And it wasn't just a show—he could actually clean and tidy up, lightening our load and charming us all with his compliments and his wit. It made sense, then, that women liked him more than men. Women, in fact, seemed to be who he gravitated toward and who were drawn to him.

Thinking about all his attractive qualities put me at ease. *He really cares about me,* I thought. *He just wanted to know if I care as much about him. I can handle a little test. In fact,* I resolved, *I can pass it with flying colors.*

* * *

On November 12, six months after Kevin and I had first met, I found an engagement ring on my dresser. I had come into my room, wrapped in a towel from just having showered, and there it was. I plucked it out of the little box and stared at the ring's three diamonds, one in the center and two smaller ones on either side. I wasn't certain what to make of it. Kevin and I had never really talked about marriage. I gazed at the shimmering yellow gold, mesmerized and perplexed. I could hear Kevin in the kitchen, talking with my mom. I felt slightly hazy. I don't remember thinking that he was *asking me to marry him.* I don't remember asking myself if I wanted to marry him. But there were so many questions. What kind of life would we have together? Would we make each other happy? Would he be a good father? I slipped the ring on. I dressed and stepped into the kitchen and into my future.

Kevin looked at my hand before he looked at my face.

"So, are we getting married, then?"

"Sure," I said.

The rest of that night is a blur to me now, somehow disconnected from reality. I felt as though I was falling. But not just free-falling, I was falling *into* something. Something was happening *to* me. I was walking into a marriage, but at the same time, I wasn't making a choice. I was just choosing not to say no, not to do something else, not to do anything at all. I never asked myself if I wanted to marry Kevin. I just wasn't ready to end things yet. I thought of the stabbing feeling in my gut when he had broken up with me suddenly. I had wracked my brain for something I'd done wrong so I could vow never to let that happen again. Having only dated for a few weeks or months here and there, I'd never experienced the kind of breakup or heartache that makes a young heart believe it will never feel happy again. I hadn't yet learned that a heart can survive being broken. Now I was getting married because I knew I didn't want to feel that heartache again and it seemed as though this was the only other choice.

My mom helped me plan the wedding and drove me to appointments and fittings. She'd say, "Let's go pick out your flowers." And I'd reply, "Oh, flowers. Right." While I had never been a girl who fantasized about getting married by wrapping myself in a white sheet and practicing my walk down the aisle, I had always been a planner. I made big plans like moving to New York to be a photographer and I made everyday plans as a leader of my church's girls' group. When I needed money to buy Boss, I planned out all the crafts I would sell and then I got it done. Somehow, that was all gone now that my own wedding was looming before me. My mom had to remind me that I needed to choose bridesmaid dresses, finalize the menu, and settle on a cake. In some ways, I was nothing more than a teenager and unable to see past the next day, let alone the rest of my life. But this feeling of simply putting one foot in front of the other was the same feeling as when I went to school, watched my mom get married, and moved to the suburbs. They weren't my choices so much as things that happened in life. If you'd asked me at the time, I would have told you I was happy.

CHAPTER TWO

Throughout our engagement, Kevin showered me with romantic notes and letters, just as he had always done. One card he sent me shortly before the wedding simply read, *One month to go!* Another,

Hope you love me half as much as I love you. You're the greatest.

Love forever,
Kevin

Make today a great day!

He always wrote that line about making today a great day and he said it often, too. One day, I unwrapped a gold locket with a large oval face and a long chain. Delighted, I said, "I can put a picture of my horse in here!"

Kevin laughed, equally delighted. He knew that horses had won my heart long before he came along.

I had just turned nineteen and started to feel very much like an adult beginning to build a life for myself and my future husband. I noticed a few friends hesitated to give me wholehearted congratulations. He's so much older than you, they said. There's so much baggage with his divorce and kids, they worried. My Auntie Connie was even more blunt. "I think you're too young to get married," she said. "I think it's a mistake, and I don't think you should do it." She didn't say any more and I let it go, annoyed that she couldn't at least pretend to be happy for me. I was hardly unaware of my own age, or Kevin's.

I was also more than aware of my own sexual inexperience. I had dated a lot but I took my faith seriously and had vowed to save myself for marriage. My choice cost me several boyfriends, once they finally conceded that I actually meant what I said. My virginity was to be a gift for my husband. A month before the wedding, I went to the doctor for contraception. My stomach fluttered. I was about to tell a complete stranger that I was going to have sex. There must be some other way to say it, I thought. Surely there were sophisticated words that would save me from humiliating myself when I asked for pills to keep me from getting pregnant every time I *had sex.*

The triage nurse attended to me first, unperturbed by my reason for coming in. "What have you been using up until now?" she asked, ready to make a note on her clipboard.

"Nothing."

She peered at me over her glasses, disapproving. "And why haven't you been using anything?" she asked sharply.

My eyes widened. "I'm a virgin," I stammered. "I'm getting married next month."

She stared at me for a long moment. Then she said, "Can I come over and shake your hand?"

It took me a moment to process her request, but as she started toward me I held out my hand and she shook it. She congratulated me for having done something unique. I felt a flush of pride.

Shortly before the wedding, Kevin took me on a picnic. Settled on our bench and just beginning to unwrap our sandwiches, he put his food down and looked at me for a long moment.

"What is it?" I asked.

"I have to tell you something, Elaine."

"Okay. What?"

"I don't think I could ever make you happy," he sighed. "You know I would do anything to make you happy." He wore a pleading look. "I'm not worthy to be your husband."

It came out of nowhere. Just like when he had broken up with me. I reached out to reassure him that he *would* make me happy, that he already did make me happy. But before I could speak, he went on, hesitant at first.

"If you want to have boyfriends after we're married, it's okay," he said. "Actually, I would be sort of . . . *into* that."

I was stunned. "What? I'm not interested in . . . that," I managed to stammer.

"This is something I want," he pressed.

"Well, I don't," I said, swirling with hurt, confusion, and disbelief that we were even talking about something I had never even heard of and had no interest in doing.

It was, yet again, Kevin's abruptness that caught me completely off guard. What about being his wife? What had happened to being faithful, to being each other's one and only? I was disgusted at the thought of being with others, whom I certainly would not love. What he was asking me to do was give myself away to strangers and then come back to him, to give him pleasure not with the gift I had saved for him, but with this lurid fantasy. His bizarre request left me bewildered. Kevin brought it up again the next day. He made the request sound so normal, like asking for extra butter on his morning toast. He asked every day, pushing against my refusal, pleading or bribing relentlessly. He nearly convinced me it was just something *everyone* did.

Finally he said, "Do it, or I'll break up with you."

I was worn down and overwhelmed by the betrayal. He hadn't even cheated on me, but this felt worse. What could he possibly want this for?

"Fine, break up with me," I said.

I was devastated. An engagement broken because of his disgusting request. I didn't hear from Kevin for two days. Nor did I contact him at all. During that time, I never actually believed this was real. He wouldn't, I thought, actually break off our engagement over something this sordid, this absurd. It was too ridiculous for me to believe that it was actually happening. I still had my engagement ring. He hadn't asked for it back.

Two days later, Kevin came over.

"You're right," he said. "I wasn't thinking."

"Good. I'm glad you see that," I asserted.

"I want to marry you," he said. "You don't have to sleep with other men."

Although shaken, I was relieved and I felt justified. I loved him, we could still be married, and he would not ask me to do this *thing*. I was so naïve at the time that I had little context for how disturbingly deviant his request was and what it might actually reveal about Kevin.

We married on April 26, a crisp, sunny day almost exactly one year after we met. Kevin's parents returned from their overseas church mission to attend. His father, an imposing man who had been an Australian Commando, got special permission from the high administrators of our church to perform the ceremony at our temple. I was very nervous, but when I entered the ceremonial room and saw Kevin, I felt a swell of joy. We were in love, and we were loved by so many others all gathered in the same room. We were part of something incredible, and we would be together forever, Kevin and Elaine Sykes.

Our reception in Calgary was a three-hour drive from where we had our ceremony in southern Alberta. We took Kevin's car, the very car I had spotted parked beside mine when we first met. The spring air flooded our open windows and I can confidently say that those were the happiest three hours of my marriage. We laughed and talked

My wedding day, age 19

the entire drive. Kevin told me over and over how stunning I had looked in my dress. He had told everyone at the temple that I was the most beautiful bride anyone had ever seen. When someone complimented the flowers, Kevin stepped in and said, "This whole thing was thanks to Elaine. She did it all. She's incredible." We talked about spending our first night in our new home, a charming condo we had picked out and decorated together. All our things were there, waiting for us to arrive and step into our new life.

"I can't wait to go to our new home," Kevin said wistfully. "It's beautiful, and all thanks to you."

At that moment, I handed him his wedding present, a silver money clip engraved with his initials. He took it and admired it. He pulled me into a tight embrace and I had to remind him to keep his eyes on the road.

As a gift, Kevin's parents booked a hotel for us that night. When we finally closed the door to our room, we were alone for the first time all day. Kevin stood behind me, undoing each of the tiny and seemingly endless fabric buttons all the way down the back of my wedding dress. One after another, he unfastened them, releasing me as though we were in an old-fashioned movie. I waited nervously, almost frightened, painfully conscious of my inexperience and my new husband's worldliness. The beautiful, romantic, incredible love-making I had dreamed about didn't happen. It was all right. It didn't hurt. But considering how long I waited, it seemed like less than what I expected. I wondered if this was all it was going to ever be.

We honeymooned in Puerto Vallarta. Kevin planned everything. I went parasailing while he stood on the beach and photographed me high in the sky. We lazed in the sun each day and dined every evening under palm trees, sipping fruity drinks and watching the ocean waves swell and break against the shore. We felt like true newlyweds, our whole life before us and bursting with possibility. I could feel our joy and love as much as I could feel the sun or salty ocean waves on our golden skin.

We had been gone a few days and as I was choosing my outfit for dinner Kevin looked over at me. "I don't want you to wear a bra tonight."

Puerto Vallarta

"Why? I don't want to do that," I protested.

My breasts were too large to forego a bra without attracting attention, but he insisted.

"It's our honeymoon and I want you to turn me on."

Whenever Kevin asked for something, it was more of a command than a request. There was always insistence in his voice. Somehow, he conveyed by his tone that I would do what he wanted, no matter my own doubts, discomfort, or fears. And I would do it, without even realizing that I had a choice. Unwittingly, it seemed as though my only choices were to make him happy or unhappy. I was in love, and unsophisticated in my knowledge of how a husband and wife were supposed to behave. I didn't know yet that Kevin dictating precisely what he wanted from me wasn't necessarily something that I needed to blindly accept.

We left the room and my eyes darted around, watching for gawkers. I was sure people were staring; going out that night made me feel like I was on display, unwillingly exhibiting myself. Kevin loved it. We had befriended another couple, also on their honeymoon, and when we went to meet up with them, I found myself almost unable to keep up with the conversation. All I could think was, *Can they tell? Are they looking? What can they be thinking of me?* I was so embarrassed, and yet, there was nothing I could do but pretend that everything was fine. A few days later, I began just putting my bra back on as we were going out, and hoped that Kevin wouldn't notice. I wondered what he might ask for next.

We had been on our honeymoon for less than a week when we had our first disagreement. It was about something so small it didn't even occur to me that we were arguing as we walked along the beach after dinner. But Kevin became abruptly and inexplicably enraged. In front of several onlookers, he threw our hotel key at my face and took off for the room. I chased after him, begging at first for an explanation. When that didn't work, I offered soothing words and contrition, apologizing even though I had no idea what my transgression had been. The storm passed, but a cloud lingered over us. I had no idea what had set him off. I didn't know what had made it subside. All I knew was that I didn't want it to happen again.

* * *

We returned from our honeymoon to our new little condo in Calgary, our first home. We walked up the few short steps to the front door, and Kevin unlocked it. As I was about to step inside, he grabbed me, swept me off my feet, and carried me over the threshold. I was a brand-new bride. Perhaps not a princess in a castle, but ready for my own fairy tale to begin.

We settled into a pleasant routine, going to work, coming home to each other, and letting ourselves get caught up in the exhilaration of being newlyweds. We stayed up talking all night, woke up late, and made love all day. I worked for Tourism Calgary full-time, was taking some courses at the university, and Kevin and I worked together for the Calgary Flames NHL team part-time in the evenings. We ran our own souvenir booth during all home games, selling team gear and other hockey items. Kevin sent me cards and letters even though we lived together, each one praising my beauty, and marveling that he was so lucky, so astoundingly blessed, to have someone like me. From a business trip to Medicine Hat, a small town three hours away, he wrote from the Travelodge:

Dear Elaine,

Well it's Tuesday night and I'm watching the phone, hoping you'll call. It is amazing how much you think when you're alone. You know, I really think you are wonderful. You are so gorgeous. I never thought I would marry someone as beautiful as you. I really appreciate the way you give to me, and your commitment and love lift me to a new height in my life. I hope I give you as much love and support.

In the envelope he enclosed a piece of paper with the words "I love you" in big puffy letters, and a little picture of himself saying, "And it makes me happy."

I was married and adored. I was happy, too.

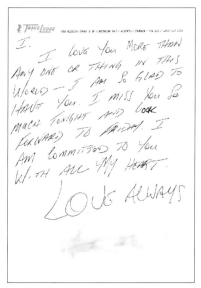

Another letter from the Travelodge

* * *

Our first married summer, we went to my family's Scottish reunion, or *ceilidh*, the perfect opportunity to show off my charming new husband to my extended family. I am many generations Canadian, with distant roots in Scotland, France, and other parts of Europe. We enjoyed celebrating the heritage of my ancestors. At the reunion, Kevin was delightful and affectionate, at ease with my family, and enamored of me. Sitting around the fire one night, I put my coat on against the chill, and a note he must have left for me weeks before fell out of the sleeve. *I didn't enjoy having to hang this up for you, Lover.* Everyone laughed when I read it out loud. He was so sweet, so romantic.

The weekend was filled with Scottish games like the *caber toss*, where men see who can toss large wooden poles into the air and land them the straightest. Or the *welly toss*, where women see who can throw a rubber boot the farthest. We had water balloon contests and talent shows, followed by delicious feasts. By Monday morning,

Kevin seemed to have always been a part of the family.

That August, it was his family's turn for a reunion, and we traveled to Montana for a few days at Flathead Lake. Kevin's siblings were scattered across Canada and the United States, and this was an opportunity for everyone to gather together. We basked in the sun and played in the water. Kevin's children came with us and ran around laughing and playing with their cousins.

Sunday, just before dinner, we left the beach ahead of everyone else and went to our tent to change. It was cramped and low to the ground, and we struggled and contorted into our clothes, unable to stand up. Kevin abruptly sat in front of me, the look on his face strange and determined. Suddenly, just like the day on the beach in Puerto Vallarta, something had changed.

"Take off your clothes," he demanded.

"What? Right now? Here?" I stammered.

"I want to f**k you," he replied.

His entire family was only a few feet away, just outside our thin vinyl tent. It was the middle of the day. People were expecting us for dinner. I tried to give him all the reasons that this wasn't the time.

"Then give me a blowjob," he said, looking at me intently.

"Are you joking?" My voice was quiet. The air felt still and heavy as Kevin's body was in front of me. "No, Kevin. Not right now."

He suddenly bit down on the inside of his cheek so hard his face looked distorted. In a flash, his hands closed around my throat. His face loomed so close to mine that his hot breath gathered on my skin, a bead of his saliva dripping down my cheek. I did not know this face or this man. He pressed down and tightened his grip as I gasped for air. In my panic, with the world crashing down on me, I felt a pebble behind the tent canvas digging into the back of my head. My knee stuck out to the side, slightly out of joint. Instinctively, my hands flew up to cover Kevin's, but it was too late to protect myself.

Then he let go. He stood up and went outside to join his family for the picnic. I straightened my leg, wiped the saliva from my cheek and, not knowing what else to do, eventually followed. We had been married three months.

When we got back to the tent that evening, I asked angrily, "Why did you do that?"

Kevin's downcast face was ashamed and he stood there for a long moment. Then he looked at me with a pleading, desperate sorrow.

"I'm sorry," he said. "I'm so sorry. I was mad. It won't ever happen again."

"Why did you do that?" I asked again, my voice barely a whisper so we wouldn't be heard, even though I felt like screaming.

"You," he began. "You should have just done it."

"Kevin!" I snapped. "It was absolutely not the time."

"No one gets me," he moaned. "I thought you would. I thought you understood me better than anyone. That's why I married you. My whole life, everyone's treated me like shit." He stopped and looked straight into my eyes. "I didn't think you would too. If you knew me better this wouldn't have happened. I thought you did."

Kevin talked fast, spinning my head and my own words. I was still trying to process what happened.

"I don't understand. Tell me this won't happen again, Kevin." I said firmly. "Promise me."

"I promise." His voice was steady and his eyes drilled into me. The words felt bloodless. "I won't do it again."

I thought of all his flowery, expressive notes of passion, of how he used words to both romance and to harm, to confuse and convince. But I believed he was sorry and that it would never happen again. My husband choking me was so shocking and bizarre. I had to believe him—the alternative was unbearable. So I accepted his apology. I told no one, and we went back to our lives as happy newlyweds.

* * *

Kevin's sales job had him on the road a lot, and he wrote to me whenever he was away.

Dear Elaine,

Well, it's been five months. I've never, ever been happier. You have come a long way. How's it feel to be old and married? I hope we can be as committed throughout our lives as I feel we are now. I love you more today than ever.

Kevin

I fingered these notes as proof that Kevin adored me, that he would never mean to hurt me. What had happened in the tent had been an aberration. He had not been himself. Kevin loved me, and I was safe with him.

The letter, written on paper he'd saved from our honeymoon resort

Kevin was a star at work. He made more sales at his IT job than anyone else, and was rewarded regularly with gala invitations and President's Club trips, sometimes overseas with both of us invited and all expenses paid. When he set his sights on making a sale, he would use whatever tools he needed and pursue his target relentlessly. Sometimes it was his charm, but he could also be sweet and vulnerable, hard-charging and no-nonsense, or empathetic and eager to help. He would figure out what worked best on his mark faster than anyone else could and he would pursue them until they were practically begging him to take their money.

At one banquet dinner, I sat at our crystal and silver table catching up with Kevin's colleagues, who had become my friends too. "I'm Kevin Sykes," I heard over my shoulder. Around us, Kevin worked the room. He moved like he owned the ballroom, like he owned the entire hotel. He didn't just shake hands with people, he announced his arrival from several feet away, making people feel like he was blowing off the rest of the room just to spend time with them. He couldn't wait to talk with you, to catch up and hear what you'd been doing with yourself. And he remembered everything—your wife's name, your kids' names, your pets' names, which coworker got on your nerves, what kind of car you fantasized about, which golf course you frequented. As an outgoing extrovert who never found any room full of people too big or too small to enjoy, even I often felt overshadowed by Kevin's personality. I didn't mind, though. He was mesmerizing to watch. I couldn't take my eyes off of him.

As I watched him do his magic, I noticed that people's faces lit up around him. He didn't just talk to the people he knew; he drew their wives in as well. The women in particular were magnetized by Kevin the most. And, I thought, my face must look like that too. I've been under that same spell. I knew the heady, fluttering feeling they were having in their stomachs, the flush of lavish attention just for them. I watched them practically fanning themselves, breathless and giggling like girls.

I heard Kevin talking to one of the women, "Tell me more about yourself. How long have you and your husband been married?"

I turned my head to make sure I'd heard him right. I saw him at the next table talking with a lovely older woman. She seemed caught slightly off guard but unperturbed. Smiling, she said, "Twenty-six years this summer. What else would you like to know?" she asked flirtatiously.

Over the course of many President's Club dinners, I heard him ask women these same kinds of personal questions. *What do you and your husband do for fun? Do you ever fight about money? How many men did you date before you met your husband? You have a daughter in college? You must be so proud of her. Is she dating anyone?* People genuinely didn't seem to mind his strangely prying questions. Somehow, they seemed to draw people even closer to him.

"See those two over there?" Kevin asked when he finally sat down next to me again. "Her husband is ready to sign a huge deal this month. When it happens, we'll make President's Club next year too. It's going to be in the Bahamas."

I was thrilled for him and unbelievably proud. This was my husband, the star of the show. And he was doing all of this for me, to give us a wonderful life full of travel and fulfillment. Maybe I wasn't a professional photographer in some trendy loft in New York, but this life was pretty exciting, and we were in it together.

* * *

One night we were in the living room of our condo, on a rare evening at home after a month of work events and outings. It wasn't yet late, but Kevin told me to come to bed.

"I'm not tired yet," I replied. "I'll be there in a while."

"Come to bed now," he said, his voice hardening.

When I suggested that he could go to bed if he were tired, Kevin snapped into a rage. Again, it was as if someone had flipped a switch. If I could have identified the grenade, I would have added it to my list of things not to say around him. Without warning, he chomped down on the inside of his cheek, and I saw his other face again, the ogre from the tent. He came at me fast, shot out his hand, and grabbed me by the throat, and then my jaw, slamming me up against the living room wall.

"You f**king c**t. You piece of shit!" he screamed. "When I tell you to come to bed, you come to bed, g*ddammit!"

I rarely heard him even curse before we were married. Now degrading and vulgar words, some I barely recognized, came flying at me. Kevin's face so close to mine our noses were touching, his spit flying from his mouth, spraying my face as he choked me. I started to scream out and he covered my mouth with his other hand. Then he let me go. I slumped against the wall and Kevin went upstairs.

Like my mom, I had never had a temper. Though I felt anger, it had never occurred to me to scream or raise my fists. No one had ever hurt me deliberately before. Violence was a language I did not understand. My husband choking me was beyond my comprehension. Yet in that instant, the laws of the universe all changed. Anything I said now could lead to Kevin hurting me. It didn't matter what words I used. It didn't matter if everything seemed fine. What had just happened was now a reality, a possibility.

The next day Kevin apologized. He did more than apologize. He *repented* before me with sincerity. He brought me flowers and fell all over himself to show me how deeply he loved me.

"It's my fault," he sighed. "I was just so frustrated."

"Frustrated?" I asked incredulously.

"You should know what I want when you come to bed. You should have thought about it, made plans during the day, anticipated and prepared to make me feel loved. You should be a student of sex, Elaine. You should study sex books and watch porn. I'll buy you some magazines. Do you think that it makes me feel loved when you don't invest in our marriage?"

"Well, no, I guess not," I said hesitantly.

"Then show me you love me. Other women know what to do for their husbands, so why don't you? I thought that's what I was getting when I married you. You're so much like Beth. We would never have fought if she had just figured this out. I trusted you. I really thought you were going to be different."

"I am," I said. "I'm not her."

"I need you to invest in our sex life. It's the most important part of a marriage, Elaine, and the only thing that matters to me. Don't you get that? You need to be there for me. Don't you want to?"

"Of course," I said.

My head was spinning and my heart felt heavy. I didn't know what we were even talking about anymore. I didn't know what this all had to do with last night, but somehow I knew that I was letting him down; I was failing to help him feel loved after a previous marriage full of neglect.

"Everyone else has let me down. I need you to not be like everyone else, Elaine."

"Okay," I replied.

"You have to take responsibility for it, as my partner. Do you understand?"

I nodded, believing that I did understand, that I knew what I needed to do to fix this problem.

The next morning, I was silent as we got ready for the day. Kevin tried hard to act as though everything was normal, wishing me a great day as he left for work. He called three times during the day to see how I was doing, to tell me he loved me, to suggest we go out to a nice dinner that night. I hesitated, feeling a flicker of fear. And then I thought back to our wedding. Our whole families and all of our friends had traveled to celebrate our union, the life we would build together. They had watched us commit to each other for eternity. To leave Kevin would be humiliating. It would be unbearable. We had only been married a few months. How could I say that this might have all been a mistake? Kevin begged for forgiveness and promised me the moon. I could forgive him or I could walk out of my new marriage with disgrace and heartbreak, and as a failure.

Slowly, Kevin revealed stories about his upbringing, and I went from wanting to forgive him to wanting to save him. Kevin told me that when he was five years old, his father punched him, close-fisted, in the face. I saw a terrified little boy crouching before the attacks of a grown man who was supposed to love him. Kevin's mother had done nothing to protect him, and her willingness to stand by was to him a far worse betrayal than his father's cruelty. In hushed tones, as though he feared being overheard, he told me that his sister's fiancé had lived with the family for several months, sharing a bed with Kevin when he was a young teen and sexually abusing him. He then told me more about how Beth had lied throughout their entire marriage to anyone who would listen about what a terrible person he was.

I was devastated for him. My heart broke over his painful past and all the details I had no reason to disbelieve. Suddenly, his anger made sense. Finally, I thought I understood. *No wonder he is this way. He's been through so much. No wonder he's on edge. The kind of anger he must be holding onto, the pain and fear and betrayal.* I tried to imagine my own mother hurting me or standing by while I was hurt in front of her eyes, and the thought was beyond reason or comprehension. I too would have a few scars. And yet Kevin managed to exude such charm and confidence. He was affectionate and expressive and doting. What an incredible feat, I thought, that he could overcome so much and come out the other side a good person. That was more than anyone should be asked to do.

And here I was. His wife, whom he adored and had opened up to. He needed me. I felt compelled to make up for all the injustices inflicted upon him. I could heal him with my love, my purest, most generous and selfless love. And then everything would be fine.

Love, pity, and the power to rescue is an intoxicating blend. Maybe I should have known better. But I hardly knew a thing. My mom didn't have a marriage for me to watch and learn from. There had been no men in my life, good or bad, from whom I could have learned how to be in a relationship. I grew up bonded tightly to my mom. The more Kevin exposed his old wounds to me, the more determined I became to care for him, to out-love his demons. I had come up with solutions to every problem I'd ever been asked to solve before, and this would be no different. I would take away his pain even if it meant taking it on as my own.

* * *

For a while, we returned to those first days of dating, when our love was brand new and anything seemed possible. But the pattern showed itself quickly. Everything would be fine, and then out of nowhere, he'd bite down on the inside of his cheek. One night, Kevin's attack was different from the first two. There was a stranger on top of me, forcing upon me those most intimate acts which I had saved for only one person—the man who loved me. But this was the same man, aggressive, hostile, and disconnected as he assaulted me. I fixed my eyes on the ceiling, counting the cracks, focusing on anything but what was happening. The man I married was gone but he was still hurting me. I felt tears slide down my face and thought, *I must be crying*. When he was done, Kevin rolled off me without a word and went to sleep. I stayed silent, too afraid to move, to think. And then I heard his breathing deepen into a rhythmic rise and fall. *You ruined everything,* I thought, looking at his slack form. Every touch before and after would now be stained with this act. I could not stand to lie beside him, but I was more afraid to leave the bed.

The following day, he once again offered lavish apologies, gifts, and promises. He expressed remorse and begged for forgiveness. This pattern repeated itself. Dark marks where he had torn off my underwear and where the elastic waistband left burn lines on my skin faded and were replaced by new ones. Once a week, I found myself in this grim, well-rehearsed dance. First it was choking, then he would squeeze my jaw so hard that my teeth would cut the inside of my cheeks. When I screamed he would cover my mouth so I wouldn't be heard. He would spit venomous curses and it always ended with him forcing himself on me. Except that wasn't the end. After he'd expelled whatever vile desires moved within him, he would fall asleep, and I would cling to wakefulness for as long as I could. I couldn't sleep because I couldn't bear waking up, that first bleary moment of oblivion, still half-bathed in dreams, with the world not quite real. But always, as light streamed in and I became aware of my surroundings, the dream world receded, and memory returned all at once: every moment, every wrenching, fearful, nauseating instance, slamming against me with the force of a tempest. In that single second I would remember, *this is my life*.

I would go to the bathroom with my eyes down, avoiding the mirror with a sickening dread of what I might see. I couldn't bear to look at the bruises on my body or my swollen lip, evidence of the abuse I had suffered. When I finally forced myself to look, I focused on the practical task of rinsing my mouth with Listerine, dreading the painful burn from trying to heal the canker sores caused by the cuts from my teeth. I'd hide the bruises with clothing or makeup, though there were rarely any on my face because Kevin was so very, very careful.

Once, riding the train to work, I ran into my friend Karen, who noticed a hand-shaped bruise on my neck I had not concealed well enough. She asked me what happened.

"My horse got a little rough," I said with a small laugh.

The words came fast and easy. I watched her with anxiety: the unique shape of the bruises might easily have given away my lie. But she accepted my explanation, smiled, and got off at her stop. At that moment, I realized that anything I could not conceal could be blamed on my horse.

I went to work desperate to detach from reality for a few hours. But Kevin flooded my office with cards and flowers the morning after every horrific night. More flowers and other gifts would be waiting for me at home. My love of flowers was becoming ruined. In their bright faces all I could see were shades of bruises, the shape of hollow apologies, the reminders of pain. My coworkers were envious of my thoughtful, effusive, and generous husband. It was like a trap, all of this public display. A way to get everyone else's view of Kevin to contradict mine. A monster wouldn't send me love notes at work. An abuser wouldn't leap up to clean after a party in someone else's home. With every public gesture, I was immobilized an inch more. The fallout, shame, and shock grew to overwhelming proportions, until the idea of leaving him simply felt impossible.

Looking back, I can see when he pushed my boundaries. Just a little at a time. Asking for a little more, moving in a little closer, acting a little more unreasonable. He moved fast, and I let him. He toyed with my commitment, and I let him. I said yes to every escalation and started to believe our problems were my problems. My environment changed by the slightest degrees and I willed myself to grow accustomed to the rising heat.

* * *

"Please don't leave me in the morning," Kevin pleaded.

"I won't leave you," I said.

"Please, Elaine, promise you won't leave me."

"I promise."

This was part of the new pattern. Each time Kevin abused me, he'd roll away and quietly beg me to stay. And another new pattern: my leaving. Sometimes I waited until he left for work in the morning. More often, I only waited for him to fall asleep. Sliding slowly off the mattress, I would slip out of our room noiselessly. I would look back to see if Kevin had stirred, wondering what he would do if he woke and found me leaving. I don't know how many times I performed this dance of sneaking out without waking Kevin. These were the most frightening moments I'd ever experienced, even more than when he was abusing me. In the storm of the abuse, I never fully believed Kevin could kill me. But creeping out of the house, knowing that the slightest jingle of my keys might wake him, or that a clumsy move might jolt a piece of furniture and send Kevin flying out of bed after me—these were the moments when I felt the most afraid.

Please don't wake up, I would chant, all my senses on full alert and my body coursing with adrenaline. I was often only half-dressed, but could not stop to put on a bra or sometimes even my shoes. The most important thing—the *only* thing—was not to wake him. *Just get out.* Sometimes the house itself betrayed me with a shriek of a door hinge and my heart would stand still. Then it would pound wildly as I sat in the car with my knuckles white on the steering wheel, waiting for the garage door to lift high enough for me to get the car through before Kevin could burst in and trap me with the press of a button.

True terror has its gifts: the moments when, even in the midst of true, immediate peril, your mind is purely, almost painfully clear, your body reacting fast and precise as if you have rehearsed your every move. When every fiber of your being is dedicated to one purpose: *run.*

Many nights, I drove blindly to a hotel. Even with the doors bolted, even though Kevin had no idea where I was, I couldn't turn off the fear that overwhelmed all reason. I would fall in and out of sleep, lurching awake throughout the night as if he were standing over me. In my mind, he could appear next to me at any moment. A few times I didn't bother going to a hotel and slept upright in my car in the back of an empty parking lot, waking stiff and sore, but in one piece.

I made so many plans to leave for good. I dreamed of going somewhere new, finding any job, and rebuilding a life without terror. I would only tell a few people where to find me—and that's where my plan would fall apart. Who would I tell and what would I say? There was no leaving Kevin without exposing our secret, my shame, my failure. The fear of humiliation seemed to hurt more than the places Kevin had grabbed me. My body throbbed harder from fear than my actual bruised flesh.

Sometimes, alone in a sterile hotel room, I prayed. I asked God to fix what I myself could not fix. I would plead to Him to help me find a way to heal Kevin's wounds so the abuse would stop. Sometimes I let myself sob so hard I could not catch my breath. I wondered who would even believe me if I told them. Not Kevin's colleagues, who saw only a shining sales champion shot through with charm. Not our friends, who saw Kevin's outgoing and sweet side. Not our church community, who saw a member of a prominent, high-standing church family.

"I want to come get my things," I said into the phone one night, in the early dark hours from yet another hotel.

"I'm sorry, Elaine. I'm so broken."

"Tell me when you'll be gone so I can come by."

"I'll go to counseling. I'll sleep in the guest room. I'll do anything you say. And we can just live together, like friends, until I'm worthy of being your husband again."

"Kevin, I don't know."

"Don't leave me. Please. I need help. I need you to help me."

It became our dance. We both knew our parts. His was penitence, profuse apology, remorse, and promises to be better. Mine was hope and belief that none of this was his fault. He was sick and he needed help. What kind of wife would abandon her husband while he pleaded for her?

"You're my only chance, Elaine. I can't do this without you."

I was, I believed, the only one who could save him. No one else understood him like I did—not his parents, not his brothers or sisters, not his coworkers. I knew him best and so I could fix this for us. He was willing to show me his pain, all of it. How could I let him handle it alone? Hurting me was a sign of how much he was hurting. What kind of person would add to that by leaving?

I returned home and I was the one who slept in the guest room. For a while, life was calm, but I didn't know how to come down from a state of high alert. I constantly prepared for the next time. I oiled the door hinges and checked the location of my keys before bed each night. I stashed underwear and toiletries in my car. I made plans in my head. Planning for the next incident oddly took precedence over actually leaving. The tape in my head continued to play on a loop: Kevin was sick and I needed to find a way to help him. It was much louder than the small voice that said I needed to save myself.

I began to live for the times in between. They were the only things that mattered now. Once the horror had passed, I could return with relief, knowing things would be good for a while. I held my breath between these respites. I could put up with the beatings and escapes because we would be *us* again for a while. Socializing with our friends, dinners out, church activities, travel, dancing, and laughter again. I think about how much we talked and enjoyed our conversations. Or going shopping together, and how he always wanted me to pick out his clothes for work or something special for our house. It was Kevin's charm and humor at game nights, his winking compliments, his stream of praise and adoration. It was dinner every week with my mom. It was Kevin's playful side that pushed us to go-karting and mini golf and his mischievous childlike nature that turned an evening with friends into a game of adult hide-and-seek. It was our shared love of horses, the hours we spent together in the barn and traveling to shows. I could almost reach back to when we were first dating and how excited I felt about our future. I thought about our wedding constantly, of all the hope and joy and expectation we felt in that ceremony, of how we were sealed as one before God and everyone we knew.

The storms began to change. Before, they had come on like a lightning flash followed by a deluge. Now I could sense them brewing in the air long before the storm broke. The build-up began first with his language. The sweetness and compliments faded and his tongue turned profane. Now his physical assaults began first with grabbing—at my breasts or between my legs. While I was making dinner or watching TV, he would suddenly reach over and wrench at my flesh or slap my buttocks so hard the sting would linger for hours. His hands clenched fiercely, all of his fury channeled into his fingers pressing into my private parts, but his affect was idle and bored. I was at hand, at his disposal, there to absorb the darkness he could not contain. And then he would grab me and force himself on me. And I would know that the storm had finally broken and the skies would clear for a while.

Kevin's version of the abuse had already won. It wasn't his fault; it was everyone who had hurt him. It wasn't his fault; it was that I wasn't loving him enough or trying enough not to be like all the others. Why did he keep hurting me? Because I was like everyone else who had hurt him. I began to feel like one of his clients, smoothed over with a handshake and good eye contact, drawn into his charm and his need to sell that somehow became my need to buy. I was convinced that what he wanted was what I wanted.

There were times I would begin to say something utterly mundane, like why I wanted to cook dinner instead of getting takeout yet again, and by the end of the conversation, the thing I had wanted seemed so far away and ridiculous in the first place. We both work hard, so why would I want to go to all the trouble of making an elaborate meal? Didn't I deserve better? Didn't I think *we* deserved better? And just like that, our plans were his plans.

I began to doubt my own mind. After screaming obscenities in my face, his next breath would be so mild, his words so contrite and loving, that I found it impossible to believe he had been viciously raging at me just a moment ago. My voice began to shrink while his grew louder and more convincing—always right, always having considered things more than I had, always knowing that, in the end, I would come around to see what's right. He had the ability to speak so soothingly that not listening to him felt actually crazy.

In some ways, this twenty-year-old me was ready and willing to doubt my own eyes and ears and bruises. I had grown up in a cocoon of my mother's love and safety. I was raised in her generosity, and loyalty. We were good people and good things happened to us. Even though my mom had lost Alex so quickly and tragically, wasn't it because *he* had made a very poor choice? I didn't want to believe that the same world in which I experienced deep goodness could house hardness, cruelty, viciousness, and lies. It didn't seem possible to have both.

From the outside, our life appeared pleasant and ordinary, in some ways even enviable. We had good jobs, a good home, and a seemingly romantic marriage. Maintaining this appearance became vital to me. But one night, Kevin's temper betrayed us. Our friends Wendy and Jim invited us over for a game night. We'd had a lovely dinner, then settled in to play. Kevin lost several hands in a row.

"I'm not playing this f**king game anymore!" he screamed.

He slammed the cards down so hard it shook the table and spilled his drink. He walked out into the night without another word. We all stared after him in shock. Mortified, I got up and awkwardly reached for my keys.

"I guess I'd better go," I mumbled.

I couldn't think of anything else to say. I got in the car and started driving around looking for him. It should have been a relief to know that someone else had witnessed his irrational temper flare-up, which put a pall over the room. I should have felt validated to finally have witnesses to his sudden and violent anger. Instead, I was humiliated. He had let slip *our* secret. Suddenly, I realized what I was carrying; what I had taken up as my burden. The thought of someone finding out about Kevin was so awful because it meant they would be finding out about *me*, too. Discovering what he was like meant discovering what I was putting up with. And what I was failing to fix in him. I had always seen myself as strong and independent. I had held down jobs since I was a teenager, while also managing my schoolwork and getting involved in every activity I could. I was—or had been— bursting with life. And here I was, terrified of my husband, and even more terrified of what it would take for me to get away from him.

I found Kevin on the road, already halfway home, and picked him up.

"Why are we even friends with Wendy and Jim?" he scoffed as he slammed himself into his seat. "They're g*ddamn pricks and we are never seeing them again."

I stayed silent, afraid to worsen his mood.

"And you," he went on. "You weren't even on my side. I'm never playing that f**king game again. We need new friends. I'm so tired of our life. I bust my ass all day only to get treated like shit at night?"

At home, Kevin slammed the car door, then slammed the garage door as he stormed inside, still raging about the game and the entire evening. I tried, like always, to change the subject, but just let him finish ranting. I assured him we wouldn't ever have to see Wendy and Jim again, though I knew we would once he calmed down. I knew that if I didn't try to cajole him, the storm would worsen and his rage would continue to blanket our home.

* * *

Since I could not manage Kevin, I tried to manage the world around him, though that didn't always work. It was perhaps the first sign that deep down I'd begun to fear he would not change.

One afternoon, we sat around my mom's kitchen, the conversation drifting here and there, when Kevin started describing a man he'd seen on TV.

"He was dumb. Couldn't speak a word," Kevin recalled.

"Oh, I think that's not a term that's used anymore. I think you mean *mute*," my mom replied.

"No, I don't mean *mute*, Arlene. I said 'dumb' and I meant 'dumb,'" Kevin said. "He can't talk. He's *dumb*."

I could hear the aggression rising in his voice. I glanced at Kevin, next to me, then at my mom, across the table. I knew she was right. I felt jittery and tried to catch my mom's eye without attracting Kevin's notice. She was about to speak; then her eyes met mine and she stopped.

Be careful, I mouthed.

She looked into my eyes for a moment, her face set with confusion. I swallowed deeply. She didn't ask and I didn't explain. Then she calmly remarked, "I suppose you're right, Kevin. So what was it about him you were going to say?"

Her voice was steady for the rest of the conversation and my pounding heart eventually slowed. I sighed quietly in relief.

"Mom," I said later in the kitchen while Kevin lounged on the couch. "You know he was just in a bad mood earlier. Work's been really stressful lately. He hasn't been sleeping well."

"Okay," my mom said.

"You know that's not really how he is," I pressed, needing her to believe this was out of character for my husband.

"It's not a big deal," she replied. She gave me a warm, encouraging smile. "I'm going to get dinner on."

I found my small means of control. I could control myself, my words, my actions. I could walk on eggshells as much as I had to and avoid the tempest. I could get my mom to be more careful. If I couldn't know for sure when Kevin would flip, I could adjust all the conditions around us and try to control the environment instead.

Strangely, as much as Kevin wanted to exert control over me, he was quite careless about so much in our lives. Even though I was working too, the house was my domain, left entirely to me to run in all aspects. Kevin left our purchases, our car and furniture choices, bills, groceries, as well as the cooking, cleaning, yard work, and finances all to me. At the time, it seemed like my responsibility, and I stepped into it like a capable adult. Kevin worked and earned the lion's share of our income, and I cared for everything else.

But perhaps it wasn't so strange a relinquishing after all. Perhaps he was careless about my time and energy because it was less of a division of labor and more like another form of control. After all, if I was in charge of everything around us, then it must be my fault when something set Kevin off. *My* failing, *my* lack of oversight, *my* doing it wrong. If I was responsible for everything around us, then I was always the one with something to apologize for when Kevin was displeased. And what could I ever say I was unhappy about? That would be my own fault, too. Kevin had only to worry about himself while I juggled everything else, and tried to contort every aspect of life, including myself, to keep him calm, content, and good. Regardless, he only cared about controlling one thing: my compliance in our sex life. As long as he held that, he didn't care much about controlling anything else.

He began by telling me he wanted to play some "fun games" to spice up our sex life. He taught me about BDSM—bondage, domination, submission, and masochism—and told me that he wanted to tie me up and blindfold me, maybe spank or whip me.

"We'll have a safe word," he said. "We can stop anytime you want. You just say the word, and it's over. You're *always* in control."

I was hesitant.

"You love trying new things," he said. "You're always the first to try new food, new places; you're never afraid up on your horse!" He pushed and pressured me incessantly until, depleted and demoralized, I complied.

I hated them all.

When I pushed back, telling him that these "fun games" weren't fun for me, he told me that it was the driving force in his sexuality. He told me he could never be sexually satisfied without it. He told me that if I refused, I was refusing something that was at the core of his very being. I was not just rejecting certain sexual activities—I was rejecting everything about him. When I told him that I didn't want to do those things, he found ways to push me into them anyway. The control I was supposed to have vanished as soon as I resisted him. The safe word he had promised meant nothing. He pressed me to try everything that he came across in books and movies, hounding me to play out new fantasies. He read *The Story of O*, an erotic novel about a woman who allows herself to be used as a sexual slave, and he became enamored of it. He constantly badgered me to read it:

"Have you read it yet? Have you read any of it?"

"No," I said. I didn't want to read it; I hated the things he did to me, hated that sex with my husband had become something I dreaded.

"You know you're shitty in bed, Elaine," he snarled at me. "You'd be better at it if you would read this book and incorporate it into our sex life." He set goals for me—ten pages by Friday, or chapter two by the weekend.

I never read the book. Sometimes I would pick it up and scan two pages; sometimes I would lie and tell him I had met his "goal." But in my own mind, I had almost unconsciously set an immutable boundary: I would not read the book. Even scanning it was nauseating—the treatment of the main character, which Kevin found so arousing, sounded to me like torture. *Does he see me that way?* I thought, as I read half a sentence, and closed the book. *Does he want to treat me like that?* Of course, the answer was yes, and as time passed, Kevin became more and more insistent about his wishes, and I became less able to resist. He was shaping me, molding me into a perfect receptacle for his sick games.

"You're so naïve," he told me. "This is what people do. Your idea of sex is childish; you still think like a little girl. "Elaine, this is how people in the world have sex."

"I just don't want to do it," I said. "It all makes me uncomfortable and it's not what I want."

"How can you not want me to be happy?"

"Of course I want you to be happy—"

"Well, clearly you don't, because you're behaving like a child. This is important to me. I told you something was important to me; I shared that with you, and you're rejecting me. You're my *wife*, you're supposed to *want* to make me happy. Why did you even marry me, if you weren't even going to make an effort in our sex life?"

"I did—I want to make an effort, Kevin, but not this. I don't want to do it; it makes me uncomfortable."

"Oh, I see what this is about. God, you're such a closed-minded prude, you're just like my ex-wife! Everything interesting makes you 'uncomfortable.'"

"Wait, what?"

"I should have known from the beginning. 'A virgin until marriage.' You're so f**king religious. You and your f**king religion."

"What? It's *our* religion."

"Well, I'm not the one using it as an excuse to avoid my responsibilities to you!"

"Kevin, I'm not making excuses. You're making this about religion, not me. This has nothing to do with religion, and you know it. I just don't want to do this!"

"You're always making excuses. You're too religious to do this, you're too 'uncomfortable' to do it. Or maybe you just don't love me enough."

"What? Of course I love—"

"You know, I told you about something I wanted, something I needed to be happy, and you're not even willing to consider trying to please me. Do you know how *selfish* that is? You're such a f**king c**t: you marry me, but you don't even love me. Elaine, do you know what it feels like to be rejected like that? Do you even know what you're doing to me? How could you marry me when you don't even love me?"

I was stunned, speechless. It felt as if we were fencing, only his sword was sharp, and probably tipped with poison. He attacked, and I tried to stop him, but he snaked fast and vicious past all my defenses. Every time I managed to answer him, the argument changed; there was no way to win, no way to even play the game. There was nothing I could say that would convince him I was right, or that I even had a right to be arguing. We went in circles, looping around and around, sometimes for hours. Kevin never faltered; he had endless energy for debate, but I was worn down. I was so tired that I was ready to say anything just to get some relief. I just wanted the pressure to stop.

The longer it went on, the more confident he seemed, and the less I could even keep track of my own words. He offered me choice after choice: Are you a bad wife, or will you do what I want? Are you a coldhearted prude, or will you do what I want? Are you abnormal and naïve, or will you do what I want? Do you really love me, or will you do what I want?

One evening I was sitting on our bed, talking on the phone to our friend Murray from church. We were discussing the Sunday school program, and Kevin came into the room, carrying my riding crop that he'd taken from the barn where I kept my horse. He walked back and forth in front of me with a sinister smirk, tapping his hand with the whip. I turned away.

"Oh, really?" I said into the phone, trying to remember what I was responding to.

Kevin moved back into my line of sight and started miming sex acts using the riding crop. I turned away again and forced my mind to focus on the conversation. For a moment, he left me alone, then all at once he came at me with the crop and whipped me so hard on the leg I shrieked, jumped, and banged my head against the headboard so hard I started to cry. I had dropped the phone, and Kevin grabbed it before I could reach it.

"Please just hang it up," I whispered.

"No," he hissed, holding the receiver out at me. "You're going to finish your conversation." I didn't reach out to take the phone, and he held it up to my face so I could not get away. I took a deep breath and wiped my eyes.

"Elaine?" I heard Murray's voice faintly on the other end of the line. "Elaine, are you okay? What happened?"

For a moment I froze. What could I possibly say?

"Sorry about that," I said, my voice shaky. "I hit my head really hard on the headboard. I guess I got startled."

I took the phone back from Kevin, and continued the conversation, trying to sound as if nothing had happened. When Kevin did things like this, when he was rude or cruel to me, I had no idea how to respond. I loved him; he loved me. So how could he behave like this? Rapidly, almost easily, a twisted logic formed in my mind, bending around this new knowledge like a tree growing around a fence.

* * *

The inside of one's head is a strange place to visit. The world would have seen a battered woman, and yet I was in what I thought of as a loving marriage. I would have done *anything* to keep it from falling apart, to keep up my responsibility to solve this problem. At the time, I measured my love by the force of my will. I counted my devotion in the number of ways I tried to keep Kevin from getting angry. My logic went something like this:

I love Kevin, therefore he must be good.

Kevin is good, therefore he would never deliberately hurt me.

Kevin would never deliberately hurt me, therefore something is making him hurt me.

Kevin's childhood pain, grief, and abandonment are making him hurt me.

I need to take away Kevin's pain. If I love him enough, he will stop hurting me.

My thinking wasn't just a logical trap. If Kevin was the broken one, then I was the strong one. I was the whole, capable, abiding one. And yet the truth was, I was helpless to repair him. I couldn't talk him out of the abuse; I couldn't leave; I couldn't make him do anything he wasn't willing to. But it was not in my nature to believe myself incapable of anything. I had never failed at anything before and I wasn't going to let my marriage be my first failure. The stakes were too high and too public. What I knew was that I was resourceful and smart, and had found solutions to everything I had ever tried to accomplish. I had stuck to that paradigm for a long time. It was woven into my identity.

"I know how it looks to the world," a divorcing coworker confided to me. "It looks like I failed at my marriage. I hate it. I hate being another divorce statistic."

I offered her empathetic, supportive words while thinking, *This can never be me. I will not let that be me.* And I was proud. Far too proud to admit that all the voices that had warned me I was too young to get married might have been right. To come crawling back to my family and friends who'd wondered about Kevin's past or whether we were moving way too fast. I thought about Fern's stark warning to my mom about Kevin beating Beth. I hate to say it, but I was so proud that I would rather be miserable than be wrong.

Even if I gathered the courage to tell, who would believe me? *You don't look scared,* I imagined them saying. *You are so self-assured, so capable, so normal.* One friend described me as fearless. But those were not—are not—the traits people associated with someone who would allow themselves to be abused. Kevin was careful. He never gave me a black eye. He never broke a bone. And he was *Kevin.* The man who made you feel like there was no one in the world more important than you. I loved that people believed that about him, and what it made them believe about me. But the more I leaned into his charismatic persona, the higher the wall became that I would have to climb to escape this life.

Here's the other logic that haunted me:

If the secret is told, everyone will know the truth.

If everyone knows the truth, they will think I'm crazy for not leaving.

They will think I let myself be abused. That I wanted it. That I deserved it.

If the secret is told, I will be admitting that I am that kind of woman.

If the secret is told, I will be admitting that Kevin is that kind of man.

If the secret is told, everyone will think about it every time they look at me.

If the secret is told, I will carry it like a scarlet letter forever.

If the secret is told, I will be a failure.

I will be a statistic.

I will be weak and pitiful.

If the secret is told, we won't have our secret anymore.

I could not, would not let that happen. The secret was ours and it bound us together: the lies we told ourselves and each other, to everyone around us—they all twisted together like suffocating vines that from one side might have looked like a shield and from the other a cage.

Me, age 21

* * *

Our outside lives continued to appear bright and promising. Kevin's successes at work seemed limitless. He won prizes for his salesmanship and took us on exotic vacations. Kevin lavished me with presents. Sometimes I came home to discover he had bought me a whole new wardrobe. I bought a new horse, a stunning mare that lived up to her name: Gift. I rode more than ever. All these were badges of Kevin's success—*his* generosity, *his* thoughtfulness. The more luxurious our life appeared, the more luxury he wanted to accumulate and display. We maintained a group of friends who never suspected that behind the veneer, our closely-guarded secret formed whorls and eddies in dark currents, quietly shaping everything we did.

Three years into our marriage, Kevin was promoted and we were on our way across the country, to Toronto. The adventure of a new city thrilled me, but I was equally filled with dread at leaving my carefully constructed and delicate house of cards. In Calgary, my mom was nearby and was a stabilizing influence. We talked most days about everything and nothing. Without telling me their names, she'd fill me in on her patients at work: who was doing well and who was struggling. My mom cared tenderly for every patient and she remembered things about each one. She told me about their lives, about the strength of spirit she would see in them as they fought hard for their recovery. I could drop in for a visit anytime I needed and all the nurses knew me as Arlene's little girl. Often, she would even come on vacation with us, which I knew reined in Kevin's temper. But Toronto did hold one promise: my friend Nicole. We hadn't lived in the same city for over five years, but we'd stayed connected on the phone and saw each other annually, alternating who traveled. I couldn't wait to be near her again.

Kevin's new position was sales executive, overseeing a large team. Soon after we arrived, Kevin's boss introduced me to Craig, the owner of Queen's Quay Cruise Line, a company that hosted corporate events on boats sailing around the Toronto Harbor on Lake Ontario. Craig hired me as his events manager. I would book, plan, and execute over six hundred events a year. Some would be on small twenty-five-person cabin cruisers, others on large mega-yachts for hundreds of people. I was twenty-three, still full of life and gregarious as ever, and I took to the job immediately. I loved being around people, planning parties big and small. I got along with everyone and caught on quickly, which caught Craig's attention. I was a little young to take on this level of responsibility, and that knowledge buoyed me up. I felt confident and good about myself, respected, valued, and for the first time in a while, unafraid. The mental and emotional respite wasn't lost on me.

My other respite was Nicole. We reunited as soon as Kevin and I arrived in the city and saw each other as often as we could. Her mom would invite me to dinner, just as she had done while we were growing up, always playing the part of a second mom to me. Nicole's office and my office were downtown and near each other, so we'd meet up for lunch and she would fill me in on her dating life. Doug was her latest and longest interest, and she confessed how eager she was for him to just propose already. I listened, wrapped in the warmth of my old friend who'd known me nearly all my life, and I couldn't help wishing I could have another chance to meet and date someone. I had been so very young when I met Kevin, though of course I had felt quite grown up at all of eighteen.

"Remember when I first met Doug?" Nicole asked wistfully one afternoon over our salads. "I swore that if he didn't ask me to marry him, I'd leave Toronto, move west and live with you guys."

We laughed at the memory and as I watched her eyes crinkle with humor, I could tell that she was truly in love and that she would wait for Doug. I had a flash of what it might have been like, however, if Nicole had indeed moved in with us. I might have felt safer, knowing that Kevin wouldn't be able to lash out at me as intensely or as often with my best friend living with us.

Nicole at her office

"Well, here we are now," I smiled. "You didn't have to move in with me because I came to you."

I knew it would be only a matter of time before she and Doug were engaged and then married. I was happy for them. I knew Nicole was happy for me—for the picture I painted for her, in any case.

* * *

My success and satisfaction at work only put my home life in an even darker shadow. The part of Kevin that could be romantic and adoring seemed to have disappeared entirely. He grew critical of anything and everything. Other people were assholes or morons. He spat these words behind their backs after seeming gracious to their face. If we spent the evening with friends, his rant would begin on the car ride home and continue for hours. Everyone's flaws were glaring and numerous, and he picked everyone apart with vicious fervor. In turn, Kevin also became increasingly controlling and critical of me. Whereas he once left the home to me completely, he now insisted on telling me what I did wrong—everything from folding towels to where I stored the toilet paper to how I washed the dishes to how I sorted the shoes in the closet. He would insist on telling me how to do things, like folding socks *his way*. His anger flared if I performed any of these tasks incorrectly. One day, as I walked by him, he snapped, "Walk on the balls of your feet, not your heels!"

When I asked what was wrong with my walk, Kevin replied, "Everything you do reflects on me."

He began listening in on my phone calls, especially the ones with my family and friends. He scoured my words for any slip, any betrayal or sign of disloyalty, deliberate or accidental. Even a hint of discord in my voice was enough to call my loyalty into question. I prized my loyalty and Kevin knew this. It was a long-standing character trait that I stuck by people. Once you were in my life, you were in my life forever. To have such a core part of myself doubted by my husband was unbearable. Over and over again I had to prove that I was his and only his—mentally, emotionally, physically. I couldn't be like Beth, whom Kevin had accused of spreading lies about being abused—the ultimate disloyalty. I would never be like that.

I felt my body tightening around him, more on edge than ever before. I began to worry about anything I might have done, said, or forgotten. I checked the house to make sure it was in order, the car to make sure it was filled with gas, and my outfits to make sure they were flawless. He grew more critical of my appearance, once condemning me, as our plane landed after a trip we had taken, for not going to the lavatory and putting on lipstick before we disembarked. I grew more obedient. The episodes where I would sneak out to a hotel were less frequent. So were Kevin's apologies. Abuse and control were becoming the norm, lasting for longer and longer stretches, until there were hardly any of those good times to hope for anymore.

My only reprieve was work, where I was good at my job and people knew it. Colleagues and clients saw that I was smart; they liked my ideas and they listened to me. Without Kevin around, my personality and humor could shine. I should have been able to enjoy this freedom, this cool drink in the desert. But it was another part of my trap. These people, just like the ones in Calgary, would be hard pressed to believe Kevin was anything but wonderful. They would be stunned to know that outside of work I lived in fear, that my days were filled with sharp criticism and derision. It wouldn't align with the person they knew.

And then, one day, Kevin said, "I want you to be with other men."

He held out a local fringe paper with several ads circled: all men who wanted to have sex with someone's wife. I refused and insisted that he stop trying to ruin our marriage with this outrage and humiliation. I thought we were past this. The newspaper personal ads were like nothing he had ever seen before and he would scour them when I wasn't home. He must have felt like he had found a community, like all his deviance had finally found a place to belong. His fantasies were out there, close enough to touch; all he had to do was get me to play along.

"I found one; you should call him," he would say from time to time, and I would be filled with a sudden anxiety. I tried to avoid discussing it, changing the subject, pretending not to hear him, or even leaving the room. Sometimes I came home to find newspapers folded just so, more ads circled in neat red pen, indicating the men he wanted me to meet. I pretended to miss the hints, hoping he would give up if I just ignored him long enough.

He started demanding violent scenarios in bed and brought home belts, chains, and other denigrating props from a sex shop. He continued to use my riding crop as a way to control me, even though I had sold my horse, Gift, when we moved to Toronto. His favorite, however, was a belt, which he used to hit me or would cinch around my neck. He kept everything in a bag under the bed. Trying to fall asleep, praying he would not wake, I would feel the bag beneath me, a malevolent presence, waiting in the dark like a troll under a bridge. My face burned with shame as I thought of someone finding the bag. What if we died and the police searched the house? What if a friend came in looking to borrow a sweater and stumbled across it? Sometimes I took things from the bag and threw them away, convincing Kevin that he must have misplaced them in the heat of the moment. When he decided it was time, he would call me "Lane," not just taking over my body, but renaming me; a different name so that I would be a different woman, a character created just for him.

Even when I slept, I was not safe. He constantly woke me in the middle of the night for sex, and if I refused he became abusive. I learned not to refuse. If I got up to go to the bathroom I did it slow, stealthy and fearful, knowing that if he stirred, I would have to have sex with him or face his wrath. Some mornings I would awaken to his abuse, not because I had failed to respond to his advances, but because I had not woken *him* up for sex in the middle of the night. I had not prioritized him while I was sleeping.

Sometimes, when I watched movies, or heard stories from my friends' loving sex lives, I was filled with a sad yearning. I had only had a few short weeks of a happy, loving sex life. I remember asking Kevin once:

"Could we just be like everyone else? Even once in a while?"

I don't remember what he said.

We never kissed anymore, once the abuse became severe. Kissing is an act of affection, an act of kindness and love, and I don't think Kevin ever felt those things. I had always loved kissing, and it was a loss to have something so sweetly important to me absent from our intimate lives. I believe it rarely occurred to him to kiss me unless we were having sex. When we were having sex, he sometimes tried, but I could not stand it. Sex was almost always under duress, and to kiss someone I was so repulsed by would have turned my stomach. I could not bear such an intimate, loving act from him; no part of our sex life was ever loving. I would turn my face away, and that, at least, he seemed to accept.

As Kevin escalated his abuse of me, along with his sexual demands, he began to take bigger risks, doing things that threatened my precious secret-keeping. He did not seem to fear exposure, probably believing—possibly accurately—that if anything came to light, he would be able to talk his way out of it, making things far worse for me if he chose. He always lied with such unwavering confidence that his stories seemed like the only possible truth; he could convince anyone of anything, or so it seemed, and I was afraid of what stories he might make up about me. In the apartment building where we lived in Toronto, from time to time he would lock me, naked, in the hallway. I knocked and begged to be let in, desperate for him to hear me and take pity, and just as desperate for the neighbors not to see.

Once he did it while we were in Oregon visiting his brother, locking me out and leaving me stranded, naked, in a hallway that his brother or his sister-in-law, or even one of their four children, could have walked out into at any moment. All of their rooms were right beside ours, but by some miracle they did not emerge, and eventually Kevin allowed me back in. It was chilling to think he would have done that to me in front of his own family.

One day at work, I got a sales call; a potentially golden opportunity. The man on the phone wanted to book an event on short notice. He wanted our largest yacht and he wanted to talk to me personally. I told everyone in the office that we had a big sale on the line. "Good luck!" they said as I left.

The man was around my height, clean-shaven, in his forties with a slim build that barely held up his slightly oversized suit. I met him at the dock, where we boarded the company flagship, the Captain Edgar Gold.

"How many people can it accommodate?" he asked.

"This ship can accommodate six hundred people," I said.

He nodded, considering it. "And how long is the cruise?"

"Four hours," I replied.

He looked pleased. "What about the chef? Can he customize a menu for us?"

"Of course. Did you have something in mind?"

"We want to offer fine dining," he said. "I'll be bringing some important clients, and it needs to be first-class."

"We can absolutely do that," I said calmly. In my head I was gleefully adding up the price upgrades.

"Can we bring our own DJ?"

"No problem," I said.

If he'd wanted elephants, I would have told him he could. This would be a dream sale, the kind where everything goes right, the client knows exactly what they want, and is willing to pay whatever it takes. I grinned at him, eager to hear his next request.

"Do you like to wear high heels?"

"I beg your pardon?" I said, unsure if I had heard him right.

"Is that the way you always wear your hair?"

He was giving me an odd look, something not quite businesslike. I shrugged it off. Maybe he just wanted to make sure I would look appropriate for his big event. Then he pointed to the far end of the boat's largest banquet room. "I'd love to see that part of the room," he said.

"Of course," I said.

It was a sunny day, unusually quiet at the waterfront. I looked around and realized there were no pedestrians. There were no cars passing at the moment. He and I were alone in the intimate ballroom of the vessel. "Can you walk for me, down to the end and back? I want to watch you walk."

My confusion over his questions immediately evaporated. I was in stunned disbelief, instantly paralyzed by an unthinkable reality that had just hit me. *I want to watch you walk.* The words cloaked me with dread. This was Kevin. The ads. The men from all those ads Kevin had badgered me with relentlessly. This man, alone with me. My head and the room were spinning now. My entire being felt hunted. Kevin had sent a man to my work, where I had felt safe, confident, and strong. Work was where I did things I was good at, where people treated me with respect. And now it had been invaded. I felt panic come over me.

"I'm heading back to the office," I said. "You let me know if you are ever interested in renting one of our boats for business purposes."

I left as quickly as I could, scurrying down the ramp to my car. As I drove back to the office, I was beside myself. It felt as though someone had taken all the oxygen out of the atmosphere and I was desperately searching for a way to breathe. I pictured Kevin finding this man, prepping him with all the right questions to ask so that I would think he was a real client. What had Kevin told him I would do? I began shaking with rage and adrenaline coursing through my veins. I wanted to confront Kevin. I wanted to scream, *How dare you?* But I was always afraid to show my anger because of his potential for retaliation. At this moment, however, I was so furious that I wanted to force him, somehow, to understand what he had done to me. Beneath my anger was an intense current of fear. Things were out of control. If Kevin was sending strangers to me, after telling them who knows what, I was in serious danger.

"How could you do that?" I demanded that night. Kevin looked unfazed and pretended not to know what I was talking about.

"Do what?"

"Send a man to my job? I was alone with him on the boat! He could have done anything to me. And what were you expecting? That I would have sex with him right then and there? How could you do something like that?"

My anger and volume seemed to take Kevin aback. We were both used to me tempering my anger so as not to set him off. But this time was different. There was no question about how furious I was. I thought I saw something register in Kevin. Perhaps a message had gotten through.

"I didn't think he would really follow through," Kevin replied, looking pleased with himself.

And in that moment, as I looked at his face, I realized that he would stop at nothing to get what he wanted. If he would hire strangers to come to my job, what else would he resort to? I'd learned how to recognize his "tells," the behaviors that preceded his abuse, but what if he morphed into someone even more unpredictable?

The sun was not quite at the point of setting one afternoon in Toronto, and I was standing by the counter, polishing the toaster. I had gotten home early from work that day and decided to tidy up the kitchen. I was holding the toaster in my arms, and the light from our high-rise window shone off its stainless-steel surface. I was intent on its gleam, and I startled when the door opened, clutching the half-polished toaster to my chest.

Kevin strode in and looked into the living room, not seeing me at first, then he looked right at me standing in the kitchen, bit the inside of his cheek, and before I could move or think, his hand was on my throat, and he was strangling me. The toaster fell from my hand and made a metallic crash on the linoleum. Kevin threw me around the room, shoving me up against walls and choking me, and in the back of my head my thoughts were scrabbling wildly around, trying to figure out what was going on: it was the first time he had done this without an argument, without some pretext that either of us could pretend was a reason. He threw me on the bed and raped me.

As my body was under assault, as always, I laid motionless, but my mind was racing: *What did I do? How did this happen?* I came up with nothing—there was no reason for this at all. The thought was shattering. I had usually been able to sense a build-up, to tell when

Kevin was rising toward an attack, but now the rules had changed. Now that it had come like this, without warning, it could happen again. My fear had become a reality, and Kevin was unpredictable now. Without rules, I couldn't protect myself. Now, there was nothing I could count on.

A week later, we went to see the new Julia Roberts movie, *Sleeping with the Enemy.* In it, the protagonist, Laura, fakes her own death to escape her abusive husband. I watched Laura comply with her obsessive and controlling husband's demands, and I was mesmerized by the look on her face as she tried to control what she could to keep him from getting angry. Paralyzed, I sat in the theater, my real-life abuser sitting beside me, staring at the screen as Julia Roberts turned all the soup cans in the cupboard so that the labels faced the front. Kevin sat placidly beside me. He didn't recognize the wife on screen. Nor did he recognize the husband.

That any other person could live my situation had been beyond me. I'd seen abused women on talk shows and in movies. They were to be pitied. But my situation, I told myself, was entirely different. I had a husband who needed my help desperately. I wasn't an abused wife. Abused wives are supposed to leave their husbands. But I was a wife destined to *save* my husband. My mission was clear and I had put so much into making Kevin happy so that the abuse might stop, that I would not fail, not at any cost. So I watched Julia Roberts cover her bruises with makeup. I watched her serve her husband a picture-perfect meal, then get punched and kicked in the middle of their picture-perfect multimillion dollar home. I watched her husband turn on a dime and offer her soothing strokes with the same hands that had just beaten her.

None of this was a wake-up call for me. Not yet. Looking back, the movie did make me profoundly uncomfortable, but I couldn't say why at the time. The discomfort was seeing a version of myself I didn't believe existed—that I didn't *want* to believe existed. How does anyone respond to seeing something like their own ghost? A haunting parallel life that shouldn't exist, that violated everything you believe about yourself: your worth, your safety, your reality? What I did was watch the movie in silence next to my husband. I went home and resumed the life I had come to know as my own. And then, a few nights later, while Kevin was out of town for work, I called my mom.

CHAPTER THREE

I perched on the arm of the sofa with the phone cradled between my ear and shoulder, feeling the solitude of our empty apartment. Kevin wouldn't be back for several days. The sun was down but I hadn't yet turned on any lights. Into the wide windows of our twenty-fifth-floor condo, street lights and shop lights flooded up. I could see people shuffling around inside apartments across the way. I talked to my mom that night like I did most nights, embracing the sound of her voice, her stories, her soft laughter. I don't remember what my mom asked me, but something about the darkness and knowing for sure Kevin was not listening on another extension made me say, "Mom, things aren't good between me and Kevin."

It was the worst thing I had ever dared to say about our relationship in the six years since we'd been married. I had made it my job to make Kevin look good, praising him to my mom and friends, showing off his flowers and gifts.

"What's not good?" she asked.

I could hear the caution in her voice, as if she were talking to a runaway foal who might bolt before she could slip the lead on. I had thought about how to phrase it a million times, over all the nights I'd sat in hotel rooms and in parking lots, dreaming of having the courage to tell someone.

"He just has a bad temper," I said, forcing my voice to sound breezy.

"When I called on Christmas morning, you two were fighting," she recalled.

"Yes," I said.

When she had called to wish us a Merry Christmas, Kevin had been abusing me, and I had been unable to hide my distress. I couldn't muster my normal giddiness about one of my favorite days of the year, and my grief must have seeped through in my voice. Truthfully, I had not wanted to hide it—it was Christmas, and she was my mom. We should have been happy.

Christmas morning in Toronto

"Elaine, is he beating you?"

Her question hung heavy in the air. She hadn't forgotten Fern's story about Kevin's ex-wife. I couldn't answer right away. I certainly didn't gasp in shock and denial. I could not make myself say the words, but my silence had already said yes. My mom was patient; she knew me. She knew I just needed time.

I closed my eyes. I imagined how it would feel to tell the secret I had clutched so tightly for six years, just as I had in those hotel rooms. I held the word in my mouth. I could almost feel its shape.

"Yes," I said.

I felt like I was in one of those falling dreams, the world suddenly ripped away from beneath me.

"Fern was right," my mom said, barely audible. "She tried to warn us."

She lapsed into silence, as if caught up in that long-past moment. I leaped to my familiar defensive poses, but I felt lethargic, clumsy.

"It's not that bad, Mom," I said. "He would never really hurt me. It's only happened a few times. He had a bad childhood; I'm trying to help him."

I sounded like I was reciting from a long-ago memorized script. There was a pause from the other end of the line.

"Elaine, I need some time to process this," my mom said faintly.

"Okay," I said. We were both silent for another moment. "Bye," I added.

"I'll talk to you soon," she said.

I put the phone on the table beside me. It was fully dark now, the lights outside doing little to brighten the room. I felt exhausted, not as if I had worked too hard, but as if something had been taken from me. I didn't want to go to sleep. I just wanted to sit here, in the darkness, and be alone.

And then I was terrified of what I had said. My secret was out. I couldn't unsay those words to my mom, and could hardly believe I had said them at all.

She called back soon after, barely able to push out the words.

"Why didn't you tell me about Kevin before?" she asked.

"Mom," I began. I went on to explain Kevin's past. I was falling back into an old, familiar, comfortable story. I recited the lines I'd told myself for years, downplaying the abuse and focusing on Kevin's pain. She lent a sympathetic ear, but I did my best to minimize the harsh realities of my life with Kevin.

"That's terrible. It must have been awful for him. He told you all that?" she asked.

"Yes. It was really bad. Nothing like how I grew up," I said.

I could feel myself pulling my attention away from the still aching bruises and back into protection mode. This facade of a beautiful life Kevin and I had built, that gleamed off of every corner of our condo, in every beaming photograph of us—I couldn't risk failing to protect it by failing to help my husband.

"So, sometimes he gets upset," I continued. "It's a lot of old stuff. But you know Kevin. Couldn't be more charming and fun." I ensured my voice carried a sense of lightness. I added, "I'm doing everything I can to help him."

"Yes, I understand," my mom assured me. "I know you, Elaine. No one was ever stronger or more stubborn than you." She gave a small laugh. "Whenever you make your mind up about something, there was no stopping you. There was never a challenge you couldn't take on or fix."

I smiled into the phone, filled with relief and sensing myself return to calm.

"Not ever," she continued. "Remember when you changed schools? All by yourself in eighth grade?" She laughed a little at the memory.

"Yes," I said, the same memory slowly returning to me as well. "Yes. I'd had it with Kerry Painter bullying me. She was so mean."

"I barely had time to sign the papers and you'd already enrolled yourself at another school!"

We laughed at my tenacity and marveled at how long ago that had all seemed. How I had stood up for myself after years of Kerry dominating all the girls in my class, charming and punishing them with her beauty, popularity, and star-athlete status. She had been a puppet master, deciding who could do or say what, who could be friends. And she had for some reason selected me to isolate and harass, forbidding any girl to be my friend. She had created an intolerable situation for me at school, and as I wasn't prepared to put up with it any more, I decided to switch schools. I smiled sadly at the thought of that girl.

When we hung up, I felt almost like my old self. The empty apartment felt a little warmer, a little brighter than just a few moments before.

Whenever my mom and I talked from then on, I forced myself to not bring up anything related to Kevin other than how successful he was at work, how church activities were going, and other topics that would keep her from asking questions. Still, I knew my mom and she knew me, and even though I would try to disguise the pain I was in, she could sometimes tell from my tone that something was wrong. "What's happening?" she would sometimes ask in a worried tone. I would tell her about everything good and bright in our lives. If there was a hint of discord between me and Kevin, I added in a story about Kevin's childhood abuse and neglect, always reassuring her that everything was all right. I had this; I was in control. No need to worry.

* * *

A few months later, Kevin was offered a promotion and we would be moving again. Over the past eighteen months, Toronto had become a place of escalating control, perversion, and physical abuse, so I was ready to go. I packed up my office and said goodbye to my team.

"I sure am going to miss you," Craig said, standing in my doorway. "You've done a terrific job for us. You are one of the most talented people I've ever hired."

"Thank you," I said, pleased and glum and hopeful all at once.

"Where are you off to?" he asked.

"Vancouver."

"Beautiful city. You'll do great there."

I nodded.

"Is it for your husband's job?"

"Yes."

Craig stood quietly and then reached for the door handle. His face was kind and a little sad.

"Well, good luck then," he said, and closed the door.

The relocation was a company move, and so everything was done for us; one young man introduced us as the supervisor of the whole project. He was rugged and attractive, and I knew as soon as we met him that Kevin had set his sights on him as someone he wanted me to be with. This was the man through which he wanted to finally live his long-awaited cuckold fantasy of me being with another man. In the weeks leading up to the move, Kevin discarded all subtleties as he made his intentions for me clear: his demands were now blatant and outright. His power over me was growing as I weakened, and he knew it, but my repulsion at Kevin's demands was growing.

We made plans to drive across the country, a 2,700-mile summer road trip before settling into our new home and Kevin's new job, and we were going right alongside the movers. The trip seemed eternal as Kevin grew more serious about wanting to set me up with the rugged supervisor, pestering me as we drove until his constant badgering became our road-trip theme song, playing in my head even when he was not speaking.

When we were nearly there, we stayed one night in the same motel as the movers, including the young supervisor, and Kevin decided this was the best opportunity for me to go to him. I sat on the edge of the motel room bed, immobilized, made ill by a cocktail of emotions. The idea of this hook-up, in this motel, with this man I barely knew repulsed me, and more than that I was sickened by Kevin's constant, endless demand. I was so angry I was paralyzed by it: I worked so hard to live only in the moment, to survive the day and no more, but it was becoming impossible. I knew what the future held, because I was already living through it. I was staring down at my hands in my lap, so I could not see Kevin's face, but I knew what it looked like: twisted and ghastly, burning with fury he seemed to think was righteous. He leaned close to me, his breath hot on my ear.

"If you don't go to his room right now I am going to beat the shit out of you," he hissed, little flecks of spittle hitting my cheek. As soon as the words left his mouth, I felt all the anxiety and stress that had been in my gut for days boil up. I leapt off the bed and ran to the bathroom, barely making it to the toilet before I vomited.

"I'm sick," I gasped when I could speak. "I can't go, I'm too sick."

"Fine! Get into bed," he snapped. He then forced himself on me for what felt like the millionth time, yet this time I experienced a distorted sense of relief. When it ended, he turned over and went to sleep. I closed my eyes and leaned back against the pillow, relieved, at least for the night. *God protected me tonight,* I thought to myself. *He knew I could not do it and I didn't know how to find an escape, so He gave me one.*

Our apartment was on the fifteenth floor of a beautiful high-rise in the middle of a shopping district, and we could look out the windows and see people coming and going all day. The bottom floor of the building was a movie theater, which we frequented in our pajamas. When things were good between me and Kevin, they were very good, and I was able to experience reprieves filled with hope from the dark realities that were my life.

We established ourselves in a new church congregation and began to make friends in the community. One couple, Kara and Jack, were newly married and in their mid-twenties. They too had met in church and were not Vancouver natives, though they had been there longer than we had. We formed a fast friendship, enjoying concerts, church dinners, and movies. I had not yet found work, and we weren't sure how long we would be in Vancouver, so I spent a lot of time with Kara, who managed a housing complex for foreign students and had a lot of free hours during the day. We spent afternoons at both her house and mine, shopped, exchanged recipes, and tried out new home décor ideas and craft projects. It was fun puzzling out the still relatively-new art of homemaking together and I liked her down-to-earth, easygoing personality.

One day after Kevin's abuse had been especially brutal, Kara noticed that I was quiet and asked what was wrong. I thought about Kevin dragging me across the room by my hair, and the rug burns across my shins still stinging every time I took a step. I heard the echoes of his voice, calling me vile names. I felt his spit on my face and his weight on top of me. I hesitated for a long moment, looking at Kara's face, which seemed to radiate kindness. Then I said it.

"Kevin is . . . abusive . . . sometimes."

Maybe it was that Kara hadn't known me for long and I imagined she wouldn't be quite as shocked at the news, or shocked at me. She'd never known the youthful, independent, strongheaded version of me. I felt brave as I heard the words come out. There was no way to take them back. It wasn't the kind of thing I could play off as a joke or pretend she had misheard. I waited, breathless, for her reaction, but her face was neutral. She didn't seem to be reacting at all.

"I'm sorry to hear that," Kara replied, as if I had just told her I'd broken the zipper on my favorite jacket.

We turned the conversation abruptly back to other things, and I watched her placid face remain unchanged. I was filled with confusion and embarrassment.

The next day, Kevin began screaming as soon as he came home from work.

"I hear you had a conversation with Kara."

He bit the inside of his cheek and grabbed me by the throat.

"What did I do?" I asked.

"You told Kara about us," he screamed. "Jack called me. He said, 'Do you know what Elaine says about you?'"

Kevin's hand tightened around my throat. "You c**t!" he hissed, his face hot and distorted, pressing into mine. This time was the same as all the others.

It had been confirmed. My fear that I wouldn't be believed had come true. Still relatively new in our lives, I hadn't yet done with Kara and Jack what I did with all our other friends: building up Kevin and making him look like the perfect husband. Because they hadn't been exposed to my effusive praise or excuses for when he was not at his best, I thought that if anyone might have believed me, it would have been Kara. But she had not. If I couldn't trust her, I couldn't trust anyone. Despite my years of loyal deference and passing every test Kevin had given me, his paranoia had now been validated, and he kept me on a shorter leash than ever before. I was never to be trusted again.

Despite this betrayal, our relationship with Kara and Jack did not change. We still went to concerts, church dinners, and movies. All four of us acted as if nothing had happened. I wanted to talk to Kara, to explain how hurt I was that she had betrayed me, the courage it took for me to tell her and what it meant that she hadn't believed me. I wanted her to know what Kevin had done to me that night because of what she had done. But I said nothing. I never told Kara anything personal again.

Acting as if nothing happened had become my way of being. Putting makeup over bruises, wearing long sleeves, smiling and praising my husband. The lessons were etched in my mind like stone. *Tell no one. Trust no one. Don't test the waters. They're all frigid. No one will believe you anyway.*

Summer was approaching, as was the end of our first year in Vancouver. Kevin and I celebrated our seventh anniversary. People asked us regularly when we were going to start a family. I always quietly demurred and changed the subject. "We've got time," I tried to say brightly. The truth was, I might have been ready to be a mother, despite having little exposure to kids in my life. I might have thought about it more if I hadn't been waiting for Kevin to change first.

Kevin posed the question again to me at dinner one night, and I felt the pressure mounting. "So, when *are* we going to have a baby?"

I knew, at 26, the window for an easy and healthy pregnancy wouldn't stay open forever. I knew that Kevin liked kids and wanted me to get pregnant badly.

"I want to be a father," he said firmly.

"You are," I replied, reminding him of his three kids, who lived with their mom back in Calgary.

"I never got a real chance to be a dad," he said ruefully. "Beth kept them from me. She was a monster."

"I don't know," I said. "I'm not ready yet."

"I'm not having any more kids after I turn forty, so you had better hurry up and decide, or I'm not doing it," he barked.

"I want things to be . . . different first," I stated.

Kevin didn't respond. It was the same talk after every time. *This can't happen anymore, Kevin. I want to have kids, but not when you're like this, not with you hurting me.*

I know, Elaine, I'm sorry. I'll be different, I promise. You'll see.

Not again, Kevin. Not again. How can we ever have kids like this? Again and again this same cycle.

The truth was, I couldn't imagine bringing a child into the world. Though the thought of motherhood filled me with hope, wonder, and a deep sense of joy, having a child seemed deeply irresponsible.

And then, out of nowhere, Craig called one afternoon.

"You haven't forgotten your old boss, have you?" he asked with a laugh.

"No, never," I assured him.

"We need your help, Elaine," he said. His voice was the same, soft and lilting with humor. "We also miss having you around. So how would you like to come back as our sales manager for six weeks?"

I leapt at the chance. Kevin even encouraged me to go once he heard what my salary was going to be, and that I would live with Nicole to save money. Thinking about being back in my old role, living with my best friend, and free for a time from anxiety, pain, and deceit, I could feel myself unclenching. My smiles were offered genuinely and not as a mask.

Shortly after I arrived, the company received a reservation from the actress Anjelica Huston, who was in town on a movie shoot wanting to rent a private yacht and have a romantic picnic for herself and her new husband. Craig wanted to captain the boat himself that day, and he asked me to be his assistant and tend to the celebrities' every need. As it turned out, there was not much tending to be done—the couple kept mostly to themselves, seeming to enjoy the beautiful and bustling Toronto harbor on a hot and humid summer day. Craig and I stayed at the front of the boat and we also had most of the day to relax as the white yacht glided regally across the water. He told me he had recently separated from his wife. I had always known that Craig was in his mid-forties, older than Kevin even, but the age difference didn't seem to matter as I looked at the sunlight warming his tanned shoulders. He had built this cruise line with his brother out of their shared passion for boats and sailing. He loved every minute of it, from booking clients to polishing the siding after a corporate event. I told him about my life in Vancouver and my mom in Calgary. He was a generous listener. I noticed how contained he was within himself, not needing to show off his accomplishments or fit himself into my life. He was just there, right there, with me.

After we dropped our guests off back at the dock, Craig suggested we go to dinner to celebrate a job well done. It seemed indulgent after an entire day of leisurely cruising the harbor, but I couldn't say no. Before the meal was over, he leaned across the table and kissed me. It caught me off guard. I wish I could say it was pure romance, that I was swept off my feet. But I was married, and so, technically, was Craig, so I pushed back. Not only that, I was seven years into trying to get Kevin to be the loving husband I hoped he could be, and I was failing.

"I can't be with you," I said softly. "We're married to other people."

"I know you're married, but it seems like your hearts not there. My heart hasn't been in my marriage for a long time. We're getting a divorce." He was calm and steady. I knew that saying no wouldn't result in a blowup or accusations thrown at me.

"I have too much going on," I said. "There's too much to figure out."

"Then," he said softly, "let's just enjoy the rest of the summer."

Toronto was a festive and energetic city. Its vibrancy represented light, life, and everything I had been missing. Craig and I worked side by side, enjoying each other's company on the yachts and in the office. After work, we often went out to dinner and talked for hours about everything and nothing at all. The world felt steady, predictable. Work was fulfilling, my friendships were real, and there was no double life to hide from anyone, no cover-ups. My need for constant vigilance had dissipated and I could just *be*.

At the end of the summer, Craig said, "Stay. Stay here with me, and we can see where this could go."

I had fantasized about him saying these words and about what would come after. I knew in my heart that Craig was more than a life preserver for me. He was someone I cared for, someone I could fall in love with. And so it seemed unfair that I had spent this carefree summer with him, pretending like things could be as they were forever.

"I don't know," I said. "I have to go home and sort things out. Maybe I'll come back when I'm ready."

"There will be a job waiting for you," he said.

"Thank you," I said, my voice nearly breaking. "I just need to make sure I'm making the right decisions. I made a commitment to my marriage and Kevin really needs my help. He's a mess and I'm the only one who can heal him."

"I think you'll be back," Craig said.

I didn't respond. *I doubt it*, I thought.

I wanted to believe him. I had serious doubts and my commitments were weighing on me. But when I envisioned myself back in Vancouver with Kevin, the picture was hazy and unreal.

Once I returned, the abuse became more frequent. Several times a week I endured Kevin assaulting me, the depth of his remorse dwindling after each incident. Just as before, I waited until he fell asleep, then ran away to a hotel. The bills added up, thousands of dollars in just a few months. The price of staying alive. In those cramped, anonymous rooms, locked safely behind a deadbolt, I let myself make plans for a new life. I dreamed of Toronto, where I would have Nicole and a job, a place for myself in a city I already knew. But even when I was physically away from Kevin, his hold felt as strong as ever. All my plans couldn't translate into my actually leaving. The task felt beyond my power. And despite my fantasies, my imagination wasn't nearly as strong as it seemed. I had been with Kevin since I was eighteen years old. My only experience of being a grown woman was with him. This relationship, this dynamic, this man was all I knew. And I knew him well. His reaction to my leaving would not just be terrifying, it would be dangerous.

One night, less than a month after returning from Toronto, Kevin slammed me into the wall so hard, I lay shaking in the bed beside him hours later.

"Please don't run away tomorrow," he mumbled, half asleep.

This same dance again. The same worn out moves, so devastatingly predictable I felt like I had lost my own will to follow this script. I listened, like always, for the sound of him falling asleep. I thought of Toronto. My way out was more real than ever. I would have a job and a place to stay. I would have a life all my own waiting for me. I would be far away from Kevin, farther than an anonymous hotel or a dark parking lot. I looked at myself in Toronto, confident and free, a thousand pounds lighter without having to wear my fear.

The next morning, I watched Kevin get ready for work, my angry silence filling the room like it always did the morning after. I knew he would leave for work and wish me a good day. I knew he would call throughout the day and wear my anger away until he could come home and act like everything was fine. I watched him leave the apartment, then his car emerge onto the street below from the vantage of our large front window. When he was out of sight, I grabbed a suitcase.

I shoved everything I could into the biggest bag we owned and called a taxi to take me to the airport. As I prepared to go, terrified thoughts scurried through my mind. Packing to leave was always the most dangerous time. *What if he forgot something and comes back?* I thought. *What if he comes back to check on me? He must know I'll leave again.* I kept one eye on the door. He had to know I would be gone by the time he got home. Yet that day he never returned; maybe he just didn't bother, so cemented in his own confidence, so assured that he would get me back as he had every time before. *Not this time*, I thought. I wouldn't let him read the next line in our usual script, and I wouldn't read mine either.

When I got to the airport, I walked straight to the ticket counter.

"One ticket to Toronto on your next flight out," I said firmly. "What time will that be?" I added quickly, calculating how quickly he could get to the airport from our apartment.

"It's at 1:00 p.m.," said the agent. "When would you like to book the return?"

"No return," I said.

I barely pushed the words out. My mouth was dry and my heart was racing. Those two words meant I was not coming back. I picked up my bag and my one-way ticket, then walked toward the gate. I called Nicole from a pay phone before I boarded.

"I'm leaving Kevin," I said.

"What?" she gasped. "Elaine, what's going on?"

I hesitated. Once I told her, there would be no going back. I looked down at the ticket in my hand: The decision had already been made. "Nicole, he's been abusing me."

I heard a stifled sound over the line, something I couldn't make out. "Hold on a second," Nicole said, her voice tight. "I had to close my office door. Elaine, tell me you're leaving him." I could hear that she was crying.

"I am. I wanted to ask you—"

"Come stay with me," she said fiercely. "Come for as long as you want."

"I'm at the airport now," I said.

"Okay. Call me when you get here."

"Okay. Thank you so much, Nicole. I'll see you soon," I said.

"I'm going to kill him!" she burst out before composing herself. "I love you. See you soon."

After we hung up, I called my mom.

"I'm leaving Kevin," I told her. "I'm at the airport now. I'm going to stay with Nicole for a while." There was a brief silence; I could imagine her, swallowing the news.

"Good," she said. "You're doing the right thing. How do you think Kevin will react?" she added, her voice low, as if we might be overheard.

"I don't know," I said. "I'll call you from Toronto."

I waited anxiously to board the plane while images of Kevin chasing me down flashed in my mind. Kevin talking his way past security to get to me. Or buying a ticket just so he could stalk through every terminal and find me. *Calm down,* I told myself, staring fixedly at the departures screen for my flight to appear. *He doesn't know where I am.*

At last, we boarded. Kevin had not come. On the plane, I stared out the window with a feeling of unreality. I had finally done it. The secret was out. The vow was broken. I was leaving Kevin. I felt light and heavy. Relief and despair.

Nicole picked me up at the Toronto airport. I called my mom as soon as I got to her apartment. Her relief was audible.

"You're all right?" she asked.

"I'm fine; I'm at Nicole's apartment in Toronto," I said. After a heavy silence, I asked, "What's wrong?"

"Kevin called me," my mom said. "He was looking for you. He said he was on his way to the airport."

I closed my eyes, shocked into silence. I hadn't been crazy to feel afraid. He had come *this* close to catching me.

"Well, he missed me," I finally said.

Kevin always seemed to be one step ahead of my thoughts: outsmarting him had become a course of higher education I had never wished to pursue. But I had made it out. I had graduated.

The next morning, I went to Craig's office. I saw the team gathered in the boardroom as I made my way to the door. When I knocked and entered, Craig jumped out of his chair, his eyes shining. He didn't even try to hide his excitement. Everyone else got up to welcome me back. Craig stood off to the side, smiling. After the meeting ended, the room emptied and I could turn to him alone and say, "I'm back for good."

"I knew you would be," he beamed.

True to his word, Craig gave me my job back and even called a friend to arrange a car for me. I was overwhelmed, not only by the sudden, massive change, but by how quickly and unhesitatingly Craig and Nicole showed up for me. The experience of telling Kara had shaped how I thought everyone would react. When I imagined leaving Kevin, I could only think of how impossibly hard it would be to tell the people I loved. I anticipated having to endlessly defend myself against accusations, from interrogations and other people's judgment. I had never imagined that the people who loved me would not only believe me, but would help me so willingly.

While Craig and I enjoyed each other over dinners, night sailing trips on the lake, and even romantic cottage getaways, Kevin called every day. He called the main office and my desk extension. He sent flowers and letters relentlessly. Packages arrived at my door all through the week. He called Nicole's apartment. He called my mom, who was on an eighteen-month church mission trip in Guatemala, racking up nearly $10,000 in international charges for the hours he spent telling her how much he had changed and how much he loved me. Kevin knew how close I was to my mom, and the kind of influence she had on me. He knew he had to get her on his side. He even had his sister, Jenny, call and write to me. *We love you,* one letter said. *We hope you will give him another chance.*

And then he played a new card. He went to see a therapist who specialized in anger management, sexual dysfunction, and domestic violence. He continued to leave me and my mom messages about how well his therapy was going, what amazing progress he was making, and how different things would be when we finally got back together.

Years of trying to convince my mom that Kevin's abuse wasn't that bad, combined with Kevin's charm offensive, had begun to persuade her as well. Her mind struggled to reconcile my experiences with the fabricated persona that Kevin had painstakingly constructed over the years.

"Do you think you should give him another chance, Elaine?" my mom said on the phone. "He's in therapy; maybe he *has* really changed," she added.

"I'm not confident that he has," I said quietly.

I had told her I was moving on, and that Craig was helping me. She was concerned that I was moving on to someone new too quickly.

"Maybe I can go somewhere else. I can stay with Grandma for a while and get my head straight," I said hopefully.

"I don't think that's a good idea," she said. "It might be stressful for her to be in the middle of everything. She's getting older."

That evening, Craig and I were at his place watching a movie. It was late and I was drifting in and out of sleep on the sofa. I could feel Craig beside me. The weight of his presence was nothing but kindness, patience, and generosity. What was I doing to this good man? Leading him on when I knew I wasn't available, not truly, to be with him? All this time he'd been radiating love and support, and I'd been too busy trying to sort out my nightmare of a life to be fully present with him. Was this any way to treat someone I loved? I did love Craig, but I'd never been able to tell him. I hoped desperately that he knew despite my lack of words.

Then I felt him shift closer to me. I closed my eyes and held still, too afraid of what might burst out of me if I looked at his face at that moment. I quieted my mind and body and let him think that I had fallen asleep. Craig lingered over me for a long moment. Then he whispered, "I love you." I let the words hang in the air. I tried to breathe them in and make them a part of my body. How many times had he done that while I was actually sleeping?

Six months after I'd left Vancouver, Kevin was still calling daily and sending flowers, balloons, cards, and gifts. They were bright and celebratory, what you would give to someone who would be happy to hear from you. One day at work, I could hear the receptionist trying to push Kevin off the line.

"No, I'm sorry," she said. "She's not available. No, I told you, she's not. What kind of emergency?"

I felt my skin crawl. Kevin wouldn't be above faking some emergency to get me on the phone. But then the receptionist waved at me. When I didn't get up, she came to my desk.

"I know," she said, before I could tell her she was being scammed. "Look, I'm the one who has been fielding his calls. I think this one is for real. Something's actually happened."

Reluctantly, I took the phone. Kevin's voice came over the line, broken, small, and pleading. "My dad died, he had a heart attack," he said. "I don't know how I'm going to make it. Please, will you come?"

After the way he told me his father had treated him, I never understood the way Kevin revered him. But I didn't doubt that his grief was real.

"I'm not staying," I said. "But I'll come for the funeral."

I flew to Salt Lake City the next day. Because of Kevin's father's high place in the church, his funeral was a massive affair, the church equivalent of a state funeral. Everyone knew that Kevin and I were separated and I could feel their eyes on me. I braced myself for displays of kindness meant to entice me back, or for outright pressure for me to return.

I sat beside Kevin during the service. His eyes looked moist. He'd never cried as long as I had known him—not for joy on our wedding day, not when he was begging me not to leave him. He'd never shed a tear over any part of our life, good or bad. I watched him out of the corner of my eye as they eulogized his father and prepared to entomb his body. If I thought I'd ever see him cry, it would be at this moment. He didn't. Not throughout the entire day and not after.

After the funeral, we talked at the hotel. Kevin told me about his psychologist, and for the first time in many months he made his pleas to me directly.

"Come meet Robert," he said. "He's helped me change. Please, please, let me show you. I promise I'm different. Please come back. Especially with my dad gone, Elaine, I need you. Please, will you come back?"

"I'll speak with Robert," I conceded. "I'll see for myself if you have really changed."

I flew back to Toronto to pick up more of my things, and to tell Craig and Nicole I was heading back to Vancouver. Nicole helped me pack for my flight.

"How can you be sure he's changed, Elaine?" she pressed.

"He sounds different. He seems different," I replied.

"Okay," she said, handing me a folded shirt to place into my suitcase. "Okay. I'm not convinced. But I love you. You can come back here anytime."

"Thanks," I said softly.

The morning of my flight, Craig offered to drive me to the airport. He was in tears.

"I knew it," he mumbled as he steered the car along the freeway. "I was afraid this would happen. You went back and saw him and he's somehow convinced you."

I stayed silent, looking at the blur of the landscape as we sped past, somewhat surprised by the depth of his grief.

"I love you," he said. "Don't go back to him. You can't."

"I have to go back and see for myself," I said, trying not to let my voice waver. "I've invested so much in trying to help him. If he really has changed, I should see it through."

"No, you shouldn't. He is not a quality guy. You don't owe him anything. You really think he can change? After all that you've told me? He has no character."

"You're probably right, but I still need to figure it out," I pushed back.

"I get it—you need to go and deal with this. I understand, but please come back."

"I just have to make sure I make the right decision," I said. "I've sacrificed a lot. I don't want it to have been for nothing."

"I love you," he repeated, firmly this time. A statement and a question. "We can make a good life together here. You're so happy when you're here, when you're with me. I can see it in you." I didn't reply so he pressed on. "So, will you be back?"

I said the only thing I could, the only truth I could offer him. "I don't know."

* * *

Back in Vancouver, I unpacked my things in our guest room. I went to see Kevin's therapist, Robert, hoping he would explain to me why he was so sure that Kevin had changed. Robert wore a white dress shirt with the sleeves rolled up and greeted me at his office door with a firm handshake. He was a tall man with a large frame and receding brown hair that was turning to gray. He had an air of confidence about him, and he began by listing his credentials to me.

"Most of my work has been with men in prisons," he said. "Or men going to prison or just coming out—men with anger issues, who have been violent and abusive to the women in their lives." He leaned back in his chair, looking at me appraisingly. "You see, Elaine," he said, "my work in rehabilitating abusive men has been immensely successful. The techniques that I use will, by the time Kevin has finished his treatment, completely rid him of the desire to behave violently. Even the thought of being abusive will be repulsive to him."

Robert's office was polished and professionally designed. His degrees hung framed behind his desk, and he had a bright panoramic view of the city from his window. His confidence was unmistakable, and it gave me confidence in his ability to change Kevin. He knew for certain that his work would succeed.

"I don't understand how," I said. "What has changed?"

"I have given Kevin tools to control his anger. By the time our work is done, he will literally be incapable of committing an act of violence against you." Robert glanced at his watch. "Let's meet again and have Kevin join us."

In the week between that first meeting and when we were set to see Robert again, Kevin did seem different. Kevin could now just walk away from little things that would normally have caused an explosion. When we disagreed over whether I would cook dinner or order take out, he didn't react. He didn't berate me. He was conciliatory and said, "Okay, I'm fine with whatever you want to do." There was a calm I had never seen before. He was kinder in bed. He had even thrown out the bag he kept under the bed while we were apart.

"I didn't just change mentally," Kevin told me one night. "Everything is different spiritually, too. I talked to the bishop."

I couldn't believe what Kevin was telling me. He had gone to our bishop and other senior ecclesiastical leaders to confess his sins and cleanse himself spiritually. He told me he had repented before them and before God. It felt like a huge step toward real change. And I had to admit that I was noticing the changes. Kevin was reading scriptures and praying daily. There was no more violence in bed, no more talk of coercing me into sexually deviant behavior.

I wasn't sure I was a person who fully believed in miracles back then, but my mom did. She believes God can change a person inside and out. I was also starting to believe it was a possibility, but very slowly and very cautiously.

After Kevin and I saw Robert for the second time together, I decided to tell him about Craig. I couldn't keep it from him, not if I was going to give things a fair chance. There couldn't be that kind of secret between us.

"We were never intimate," I assured him. "But we went out together, kissed, and had started considering long-term plans."

Kevin listened, half-nodding with a distant look on his face, taking it all in.

"I thought I should tell you," I said softly.

He got up and headed to the bedroom. As he passed the sofa, almost in slow motion, all six feet and two hundred pounds of him fell like a cut tree. He collapsed and didn't try to catch himself. He hit the tile face first, with a dull thud.

"Kevin!"

I ran to him. His arms lay tucked beneath his body. I turned him over and saw his eyes wide open.

"Elaine," he whispered. "I can't live without you." He closed his eyes and tightened his jaw. "I can't believe you had feelings for someone else. I can't be without you."

"It's okay," I whispered, checking his face for cuts and bruises. "It's okay, I won't leave you, I promise. Sit up. Let me see that you're okay."

There was something deeply vulnerable about him, lying there in shock at what I'd said. For all his past talk of wanting me to sleep with other men, the actual idea of it had made him faint. Maybe it was his work with Robert or the work of God. Either way, the change was stark. I waited until we were getting ready for bed that night to bring up a question I needed to ask.

"I need to talk to you," I began. "You have to help me understand why I should fully trust that you've been able to change? Why is Robert so sure that you won't be abusive?"

"He has given me tools to deal with my anger," Kevin said. "I have also aligned myself with God," he replied. "He is helping me through this." Then he lowered his voice. "I have to tell you something I've never told anyone before. I made a promise to Satan many years ago."

"What? What do you mean, you made a promise to Satan?"

"It was a little while after we got married, about two months. I was just so amazed that you had married me—I couldn't believe I was so lucky. You were so beautiful, so incredible, and I wanted to keep you happy but I was so afraid I couldn't. One night, I went into our living room. I got down on my knees and prayed to Satan, saying, 'I will worship you, as long as you will give me everything I need to keep Elaine happy.'"

"You made a deal with the devil?"

I was incredulous, trying to process what he had just told me.

"Yes," he said flatly.

I stared at him, unsure of what more to say. Kevin had always been more deeply informed than I about our religion. I came to our church as a convert, but he had been raised within it by his high-ranking parents. He'd described having doctrine crammed down his throat since infancy, making him not only a true believer, but a resentful one. I had never challenged him on matters of faith, both because I believed he knew more than I did and because I was wary of triggering childhood memories. "My parents loved the church more than they loved me," he told me more than once.

In trying to heal Kevin, I had never dared to put the church before him, leaving him to be the spiritual expert. And this meant that now, as I listened to him describe his pact with Satan, I didn't feel like I was in any position to challenge what he said. Maybe all those years and all that pain had been caused by an evil force. Who was I to say otherwise? Maybe my scars were proof enough that the devil had been at work all along. So perhaps it was possible that now the pact was broken. Kevin had returned at last to God and we would become the family I had always hoped for.

Slowly, we began to repair our relationship, and began to consider resuming our life in Vancouver. Kevin was not abusive, and I wanted to believe the changes he made would be permanent, that God would indeed be at his side now. He continued to see Robert and we attended church regularly, giving me both faith and hope that our future was bright. I wanted God to be at work in our marriage and inside Kevin. In some of the darkest moments of pain and fear, I had asked myself where God was. I desperately wanted to believe that He had not abandoned me but was pushing for me to be better, perhaps so that Kevin could be better. I attended church with renewed focus on seeking assurances that we were on the right track with helping Kevin, and that I was doing the right thing by being there with him.

But I missed Craig. I didn't realize how much until I was cleaning out the cabinet beneath the bathroom sink and came across my travel bag, which I had last used in Toronto. Inside was a small bottle of the lotion Craig used on his skin every day. I didn't know how it had gotten into my bag, if I had taken it or he had placed it there. I twisted off the top and inhaled his scent, feeling my heart break there on the bathroom floor. The depth of the love I felt for him flooded me. I knew what I was giving up, what I was leaving behind in Craig. He was a good man. He cared about me. I couldn't bear the thought of him holding out hope for something that could never be. While Kevin was at work one afternoon, I called Craig.

"I'm so sorry," I told him. "I've made my decision. I'm not returning to Toronto."

"Are you sure about this?" he asked, his voice heavy and deliberate. "He's not a good guy, Elaine. I don't think you should do this."

"I'm sorry," I repeated. "I have to be here. I can't give up on Kevin."

He said he understood. "I love you," he whispered.

"I love you, too," I replied just before hanging up.

One Sunday, a few months after I'd returned to Vancouver, I stood alone after our church meetings, waiting for Kevin to finish talking to some members of our Sunday School class. An older woman approached and touched my arm. I didn't know her name, but she seemed to know who I was.

"I want you to know," she began gravely. "I don't know what it is about your husband, but I have an uneasy feeling that there are things I don't know. So when I heard you had left him I was happy."

I looked over at where Kevin stood talking, then back at this stranger, who felt strongly enough to tell me that it was good that I'd left him. I wanted to ask who she was, who she *thought she was.* And I wanted to ask how she knew what she knew. Was this some sort of spiritual message I was supposed to hear? Before I could, she disappeared into the crowd and Kevin was back at my side.

* * *

In late spring, three months after Kevin's dad died, Kevin was offered a new position—an even better one—back in Calgary. We would move back to my hometown. My mom returned from Guatemala just as we arrived, and we lived with her while we looked for our own place and I looked for work. I wondered how Kevin would do without Robert's help, but he seemed to be at ease and there were no abusive incidents, even through the stress of the move. He was good to my mom, though he'd never spoken fondly of his own mother. I think he blamed her for standing by while his father abused him physically and scarred him emotionally. He usually referred to both his parents by their first names, a strangely detached act that seemed disrespectful yet necessarily assertive.

We found our dream home, a builder's showpiece. At 2,500 square feet, and already exquisitely decorated, it was beautiful beyond words. Kevin's career success seemed to grow with every transfer. I was proud of how well he was doing at work and I wrote him a card saying so, addressing it to Kevin at our new address so it would be his first piece of mail there.

Coming back to Calgary meant we could pick up with our old friends. Most were like us, married but without kids yet. We invited groups of friends over to show off the space and warmth of our new home. Kevin played the charming host once again, lighting up everyone he talked with, making them feel like they were the most important person in the room. We talked late into the night about how the party went as we straightened the house back up. I began to feel stable and grounded. I even planted a garden with my favorite flower—tulips—along with big pots of geraniums and petunias. I discovered my knack for decorating and turning our home into a warm, well-designed haven. I started cooking more complicated meals. The calm lasted for longer than it ever had before. I looked around at our beautiful space, our home, and the idea of having a baby suddenly filled me with warmth instead of dread. Motherhood felt possible, even welcome. With a baby, Kevin would be tender, I said to myself. He would be the kind of man I always knew he could be. I threw out my pack of birth control, but I still tracked my cycle closely. I could envision the possibility of getting pregnant, but couldn't fully commit to trying just yet.

Then one Saturday about five months later, as we were tinkering with appliances and making small repairs and decorative touches, I came into the bathroom to find Kevin on a stool changing a lightbulb.

"I could tell you one of those lightbulb jokes right now if you want?" I teased.

He leapt from the stool and onto me like a panther, grabbing me by the neck. He threw me into the wall and choked me, cursing into my face, his features twisted and red with rage. The switch inside him, which had somehow been off in Vancouver and since we'd moved back to Calgary, had flipped. I couldn't help but wonder if it was because the threat of me leaving was gone now. If the new house meant that I was here for good and he didn't need to work to keep me anymore. I was devastated. All we had gone through in the last year to get us to this good place—all his work with Robert, my saying goodbye to Craig, our move to Calgary, our families and friends cheering for our reunification and Kevin's transformation—it had all been for nothing. My mind raced toward a solution, but to a different problem now. How could I get myself out of this? Without Kevin knowing, I met with a divorce lawyer, someone my bishop knew. But then, my period was late.

* * *

I took a home pregnancy test alone in our bathroom and saw the big pink plus sign. It was January and I had been off birth control for a year, holding open the possibility of a baby while remaining cautious about Kevin's behavior by avoiding intercourse during ovulation. Kevin was out of town and wouldn't be home for three more days. I sat there, stunned, the plastic stick in my hand, at what was actually happening, and what was about to happen.

Our family physician, Dr. Heide, squeezed me in for an appointment the next day.

"What brings you in?" she asked cheerfully as I sat with my legs dangling over the exam table.

"I took a home pregnancy test," I said. She raised her eyebrows at me as if to say, *And?* "And it said I'm pregnant," I concluded.

"Those things are pretty accurate, you know," she smiled. "But we'll give you a blood test just to be sure. And congratulations!"

"Thanks," I said.

She looked at me. "You are happy about this?"

"Yeah," I answered.

I was afraid. A baby would be a blessing, a miracle even. Yet there would no longer just be myself to protect, and I was already so exhausted from all the pretending and enduring Kevin's abuse alone. Having a child would now tie us together forever. As I considered all the ways becoming a parent would change me, I also felt a glimmer of hope that it might change Kevin, too.

I bought a book of baby names and a roll of shiny blue wrapping paper. I wrote out a card and made a reservation at our favorite Italian restaurant for the night Kevin returned from his trip. In the days I sat alone with this news, not even sharing it yet with my mom, something else began to grow in me. It was all the joy and hope, beginning to crowd out the fear. It was my new life as a mother. It was the miracle I was being trusted to carry. Just as I had never fantasized as a girl about my wedding, neither did I ever imagine myself as a mother. It all seemed so abstract, so unfamiliar. I was still swimming in questions and uncertainties. But what I knew for sure was that I was more excited than I was afraid.

At the restaurant, I waited until our drinks arrived, then pulled out the gift and slid it across the table without a word. Kevin skipped the card and tore into the wrapping. He stared at the baby book and then looked up at me. I smiled at him, nodding my head in answer to the question I knew he was asking. Out of his speechless daze, his half smile finally widened into a full grin.

"Are you saying we're having a baby?" he asked.

"Yes, we are," I said.

He kept grinning like he didn't know how to stop. "When?"

"End of August," I replied.

It was a beautiful moment in a sea of so many ugly moments over the course of our years together. I was happy and he was happy, for a rare and worthwhile reason. We were overjoyed.

The next eight months gave me hope for our family's future. The abuse stopped completely. "Fatherhood will change me," Kevin promised. "I'll never hurt you again."

"That's good," I said.

My pregnancy was uncomplicated, easy even. I felt the healthiest I ever had in my life. My mom described feeling this same way when she was pregnant with me. I glowed the way I had always heard women did. My old planning self came to life with a vengeance and I bought every book, took every class, and swallowed every vitamin to make sure that this pregnancy and my baby would be perfect. I picked the name West for the boy I was going to have. It was strong, masculine, and memorable, all the things I knew my son would be.

Just after dinner on the third of September, five days after my due date had passed, my amniotic fluid began leaking, but I still wasn't having any contractions so my doctor brought me into the hospital for an induction. When my labor started to intensify, I had no qualms about asking for the epidural; I didn't need to prove to anyone that I could withstand pain. Kevin sat on the couch a few feet away from my bed, his mind elsewhere. When he came to stand by the bed I grabbed his hand and squeezed it through two contractions. He twisted away from me.

"You're hurting my hand," he complained. Then he went back to the couch.

Just as they were about to administer the epidural,my doctor came in. He frowned at the fetal heart monitor.

"This doesn't seem to be working," the nurse said to him, as she moved it to different positions on my round belly. "Switch monitors," he said firmly.

Technicians swept in and switched out the monitor, but the heartbeat still didn't appear. Trying to breathe through the pain of the contractions, I looked up at my doctor, who was standing over my bed assessing the situation.

"Let's do it now. An emergency C-section," he said. His voice was calm but swift with intention.

Before I could react, I was wheeled down the hall and then I was under. I woke up groggy, with no idea how much time had passed. My room was empty. I wondered for a minute if I had dreamt it all. Then, a nurse appeared.

"Congratulations! You delivered a healthy baby boy," she exclaimed.

Relief washed through me. My beautiful son was here. I was a mother. And at ten pounds, eight ounces and over two feet tall, he was a sight to behold. I still wonder if I could have ever managed to deliver a baby that big, and if the fetal heart monitor's failure wasn't an intervention from God sparing my body that ordeal.

As we waited to be discharged, I looked over at Kevin, holding West with all the confidence in the world. He bathed him, changed his diapers, and walked him around the room until he stopped fussing. He looked like an old pro and he looked delirious with joy. My body flooded with hope. Our families and friends had already filled the hospital room with flowers, balloons, and more stuffed animals than a child could ever need. At home, there were more gifts and cards and dozens of meals waiting for us. How could I be anything but happy with this much love surrounding us?

When West was a week old, we invited fifty people to our house for a post-baby blessing celebration to welcome him into the church community. It was a wonderful day with our friends, family, and lots of incredible food, most of which my mom had prepared. I chuckled when she brought out a surprise: the top layer of our wedding cake, which she had been saving in her freezer for just this occasion. This was apparently an old English tradition. Throughout the party I periodically glanced over and wasn't surprised to see that no one was eating the neatly sliced ten-year-old cake.

My own new love for West was more intense than I could have imagined. A few days after we came home from the hospital, I gazed at him napping on our king-sized bed, his little body slumbering peacefully in his fuzzy sleeper, and it hit me: what every mother talks about but can never fully describe because it must be experienced to be understood. My maternal love and our mother-son bond came crashing into me as I looked down at him in all his perfection. My life was no longer about me.

Me and West

* * *

At six months old, West went through a sleep regression, and kept us awake through the night for a straight week. My mom was visiting for a few days to help around the house and with taking care of West. On the way home from an outing, West finally fell asleep to the rhythmic movement and hum of Kevin's driving. Relieved, we all lovingly admired the baby's once red and distressed little face as it eased into a calm, sleeping countenance. Before returning home, Kevin pulled over so I could slip into the store for a few dinner items while everyone waited in the car. When I returned with a bagful of groceries, West was wailing at the top of his lungs, big fat tears rolling down his cheeks.

"What happened?" I asked.

No one answered for a minute.

"Oh, he just woke up." Kevin finally replied. "That's all," he added.

My mom remained silent as I reached back to comfort West and get him to quiet down. A few weeks later, with West now back to sleeping well through the night, I handed him to Kevin as my mom and I headed out to do some baby shopping. Just as we got into the car, my mom stopped and said, "Are you sure you want to leave the baby with Kevin?"

"Of course. Why do you ask?"

She hesitated and then lowered her voice.

"Back in the car, the other day," she whispered, "you remember you came out of the store and West was screaming?"

"Yes," I said.

"Well, it's because Kevin grabbed West's car seat and shook it hard. To wake West up."

"What?" I gasped. "Are you sure? Maybe Kevin noticed he was choking or something," I offered.

"Kevin woke West up on purpose," my mom said, her shock still evident. "When I asked him what he was doing, he told me right there.

He was mad that he'd lost so much sleep the night before. Kevin said that West kept him awake all night and that he was *paying him back*."

I was stunned into silence. We finished our shopping but I was in a dense fog the whole time, unsure of what to do. I believed my mom. But I also believed, because I had seen with my own eyes, that Kevin was a good father. He wasn't just attentive, he was doting. And he hadn't hurt me once since before West was born. My shock quickly turned to anger, but I feared bringing it up. Would it break the beautiful spell of peace we had enjoyed for over a year and make things worse? I decided to say nothing to Kevin, and with trepidation hoped nothing like that would happen again. I wondered if he would even remember it.

Me with West

A peaceful year went by without incident, and when West was just over a year old, Kevin and I were ready to try for another baby.

I wanted a girl this time and I read everything I could about how to time intercourse to increase my chances of conceiving a daughter. Creating her was unlike anything we had ever done before. It wasn't me tentatively, hesitatingly stepping into motherhood. I wanted this baby, Kevin wanted this baby, and we would make our wish come true together. Turns out, our timing worked perfectly, and I got pregnant with a girl.

At eight months pregnant, my body was worn out from chasing West around all day and from the size of my swollen belly. I was drifting off to sleep in our bed one night, relieved to be off my feet at last, when I felt Kevin towering over me.

"Take off your clothes," he said.

"Kevin," I said, opening my eyes. "Not tonight. It's really difficult right now and it hurts."

He grimaced, his face turning purple in an instant and his eyes turning glassy. His hands closed into fists and I thought he might grab me or pin me down. But he drove his fists into the mattress on either side of my arms, hovering over me with his face looming.

"What are you doing?" I gasped.

I shut my eyes and wrapped my arms around my stomach. I turned my face away from his, bracing myself for what would come—a fistful of my hair in his hand or my entire throat in his grip. But instead, all I heard was a deep, roiling growl coming straight from Kevin's chest. It was a guttural, animal noise, followed by deep gasping breaths. When I opened my eyes, he was already over on his side of the bed. He flung himself down beside me, yanked the quilt over his body, and snapped off the light. I lay still and silent, in disbelief that this had happened, and at what had *not* happened. Kevin had, for the first time ever, reined himself in, right back from the very edge. I knew then that change was possible, that if he really wanted to, if it mattered enough—as our daughter most certainly did—he could get better. It had taken thirteen long years, but here we were. Something was working.

Navy was born five days after her brother's second birthday. She was gorgeous, intense, and determined from the very beginning, and the most soft-hearted creature I had ever beheld. Like West, she had the striking Hartrick blue eyes, so her name suited her perfectly. With her and West, I was in motherhood bliss. I threw every ounce of my energy into being the best mom and giving them the best life. In truth, it was glorious and I was completely in my element, filled up like I had never been before. My mission was clear and I was obsessed with carrying it out: make my kids' life perfect.

Me with Navy

Navy and West

Looking back, I see that raising kids is about letting them take risks, get hurt, brush themselves off, and try again. It's about helping them tolerate disappointment and loss, and remembering to care for yourself in the meantime. I know all that now, and I believe I knew it back then, too. But my life with Kevin had put everything in black and white. Either we were blissfully happy or he was abusing me. There was no normal; no baseline of regular, everyday life. It was either wonderful or terrifying. And that's the lens through which I saw my children's happiness. If things weren't amazing, what would that mean? All I knew was terror as an alternative. And there was no way on earth I would let my kids experience the kind of terror I had known from their father.

In my babies, I had found a pure channel for all of my passion, my planning, my creativity, and boundless love. In them, I could create the kind of life I had always wanted after I married Kevin—one filled with beauty, joy, and goodness. One that was perfect. Because my children were all those things. In them lived everything that was good about Kevin and me, our best selves walking around in these two little humans we had created. I could keep them safe in ways I had never felt before. I could make them happy in ways I had never been. But no matter how perfect I made their lives; it couldn't change what I had been living with all these years. Still, I put my heart and soul into their happiness at the expense of my own. I thought this was what a good mother should do.

After three years of relative calm, when Navy was just three months old, I was standing in the kitchen putting away the dishes. Beth had come up in conversation, and feeling more confident than ever in Kevin's ability to control his temper, I pushed back at his criticism of her. After a short argument, he suddenly darted across the room. He clenched his hands around my throat in a grim and all too familiar stranglehold and slammed me up against the cupboards. The abuse had started again. I hid it from the kids until I couldn't anymore.

"Mommy? Owie?" One afternoon, two-year-old Navy pointed to a fresh bruise on my forearm, already deepening into a midnight oval. The look of concern on her sweet face broke my heart. I'd pushed up the sleeves of my sweater to do the dishes and had forgotten to pull them back down when I heard her come into the kitchen. Kevin had lost his temper the night before.

"Oh sweetie, don't worry!" I chirped brightly, eager to see the lines on her forehead disappear. "I was reaching for a big bag of sugar and it fell on me! Isn't Mommy silly?" I laughed.

When she saw me laugh, a radiant smile bloomed on her face and replaced her concern.

"Sugar? Cookies? Yay!" she squealed.

"Yes," I said, though I didn't really have the time. "I'm making cookies!"

I flew into high alert and I scolded myself for not being more careful. I knew how to check my body for bruises and check my clothes for the right coverage, but the exhaustion of motherhood was catching up to me.

Fierce love will drive us to shield our children with our own bodies, which is what I did. I hid my bruises. I never fought with Kevin in front of them. I made sure never to set him off so they would never see his true nature. I wanted them to love their father. I couldn't bear for them to fear him or wonder when he might explode, as I did. I made excuses or lied for Kevin. *Daddy's tired and stressed out from work. He just needs a little rest.* They shrugged their little shoulders and scampered back into their imaginary worlds. I swept them off to the park or to the grocery store when I thought Kevin might be in one of his moods. Every week, they spent a day and a night at my mom's house, where she would stuff them full of delicious food and all her famous pies, and I got a few hours of respite from the emotional toll of buffering them from Kevin. I shouldered all of the childcare and all of the housework, wary of letting anything taxing set Kevin off.

This was the needle I had to thread every second of every day. Protect them from their father and, more importantly, keep them from knowing the truth about their father. Endure Kevin's abuse while hiding it from the kids and pretending our family was perfect. Create a false life for them to believe in because the truth felt too ugly for their innocent hearts to bear. Leaving Kevin became an even more distant option. No longer just for my own sense of failure, but for the kids' sense of having an intact family. I wondered what it would mean for them to see only this filtered version of him? I was creating conditions that would ensure I might never be believed, even by my own children. The world already thought Kevin was a doting husband and father, and now I was working so that his children would think the same. My life began to feel like a shop window for me to curate carefully each day with only model-perfect scenes. My kids became delicate figurines whom I needed to keep from being marred in any way.

My best efforts didn't work perfectly. One night, when West was five and Navy was three, I left Kevin to put both kids to bed while I attended a women's event at the church. The next morning, West emerged from his room with a distinct shadow under his right eye. Kevin had already left for work. The night before, he'd told me everything had gone fine. "I can handle them, Elaine," he'd spat. I looked closer at West's eye, still heavy with sleep. The shade of purple was unmistakable. So was the swelling.

"West, what happened to you? Let mommy see your handsome face," I said gently as I pulled him towards me. I bit my lip to keep from bursting into tears. He curled into my chest.

"Um, well, me and Navy had a fight. Then Daddy put me to bed," he said haltingly.

I gave him a kiss and hugged him tightly. "Sweetie, I love you so much. It's okay. You're not in trouble." I looked into his eyes. "What else happened?"

"Daddy grabbed me out of the tub really hard. He was mad I kicked Navy. I tried to say

I was sorry."

"And then what?"

West paused for a long moment. "Then he hit my eye."

"How?" I asked.

"Daddy put me down hard in bed."

"What do you mean? Like how?"

"He threw me."

West's face brimmed with sadness. I saw it clearly in my mind, how Kevin had done to our son what he had done to me. Kevin would grab me by the shoulders and slam me into bed so hard that he would leave dark bruises wherever his fist connected. I remembered how his hands could hurt me in more than one place at the same time.

"You're not in trouble," I assured West. "Everything is going to be okay."

I grabbed a bag of frozen peas and laid it gently against the entire side of his face, then

set him down to watch television.

"Kevin," I said, trying to hold my voice steady on the phone. "What happened last night?"

"I'm at work. Can't this wait?" he asked impatiently.

"No. Tell me what happened to West."

"Oh, that," he said. "That was nothing. The kids were goofing around in the tub, that's all."

"I don't believe you. How did West get a black eye?"

"I bumped him when I was putting him into bed."

He was utterly unconvincing. He wasn't even trying to lie or make an excuse. I could no longer control my shaking.

"Do not ever touch him again, Kevin. Ever!"

"It was an accident, Elaine."

His response was easy. Either he was masking his remorse or he felt none. Either way, it terrified me. It didn't matter anymore that Kevin abused me. I'd handled it for almost fifteen years. But I decided the only way to protect them was for me to never again leave them alone with Kevin. I didn't know how or if that would even be possible, but I believed that I was the only one who could protect them. Maybe someday things would be different. Perhaps I would discover the right words or the secret formula to change what was deep inside Kevin. For now, the one thing I could do was try and shield my children.

CHAPTER FOUR

Nestled in Redwood Meadows, a lush, wooded landscape just west of Calgary, the community hall seemed like the perfect place for a piano concert. It was September 9, a beautiful fall evening. It was, in fact, Navy's eighth birthday and just a month before my fortieth birthday. Kevin parked the car and we looked around for Navy and West's piano teacher, Rudy, who had invited us to the event. Opening the door to the hall, it took me a moment to register the smell of food and the familiar faces inside. A few months before, my mom and Kevin had asked me what I wanted for my milestone birthday. "I don't want any gifts," I replied. "I'd just love a big get-together where all my favorite people are in one place. If it could be a surprise that would be even better!" I said, getting excited. Unbeknownst to me, my mom and friends had done just that. They had spent months organizing this party for me.

As we made our way through the doors, a crowd of voices boomed, "Surprise!" and then started singing "Happy Birthday." I was so stunned I kept touching my face to make sure it was all real. I took in the eighty-plus people I loved best in the world, all wearing name tags that described how they knew me, along with the beautiful, rustic hall crafted in stone and wood, decorated with red roses and black and silver balloons. My close friend Traci, who had a young family, had traveled fourteen hours to be there, and my friend Toni had spent several days organizing group party games, which are one of my favorite activities. An abundant buffet, prepared by my mother and her friends, stretched from one end of the room to the other, complete with a chocolate fountain and a cake adorned with a picture of me as a baby. My friend Stacey placed a sparkling crown on my head and helped me into a pair of silver fairy wings, which I wore throughout the entire night. I smiled brightly at Stacey and my wonderful friends and family, who had made the effort to be there with me.

Kevin was at the mic throughout the night, thanking everyone for coming, announcing when it was time for games or toasts. He described how he and my mom and friends had formed a committee and met several times over the past few months to put this all together, even though Stacey told me later that Kevin had little to do with the organizing. He toasted me with words glowing and sweet. I fingered the scrapbook of pictures and tributes that Nicole, who couldn't be there in person, had put together, and noticed how much Kevin was enjoying the spotlight. The evening was wonderful and exactly how I wanted to celebrate my birthday.

Arriving at the party

As I imbibed the love and thrill of the party, I whispered to myself that things were better than they had been in a long time. After a long struggle with pregnancy weight gain, I had hit my goal of finally shedding the baby weight just before my birthday. I felt strong and fit, like my old athletic high school self. In fact, I was back to my high school weight and probably in even better shape than before. And my marriage was in as good a place as seemed possible. The kids were throwing themselves into sports and music lessons and needing us to drive them to practices and competitions, which we absolutely loved. They participated in Kids of Steel triathlons, and the times we spent cheering for Navy and West were when Kevin and I felt most connected. We were on the same team, marveling at the beautiful, fast, and strong creatures we had created together.

For the past several years, Kevin's physical attacks were happening less frequently. However, any relief in this respite was dampened by the constant verbal abuse, which always held the threat of turning into something more. During his angry outbursts, usually on Fridays, Kevin no longer threw me against walls or the floor, but he still screamed violently in my face, spitting on me as he cursed. Yet, I counted it as progress that I was no longer being choked during most of our fights. At the time, I told myself that I was succeeding, that Kevin was making progress. But my nights were uneasy and tense. In the dark, behind our closed bedroom door, Kevin seemed to feel free to release all his fury, usually when he perceived that I had failed to meet his every perverted sexual demand. At work or in front of Navy and West, Kevin mostly exerted control over his temper. Perhaps he too was invested in the performance of a happy family, saving his darkest parts for when he and I were alone at night. This is when he could unleash the screams and curses, demeaning me and blaming me for anything he could think of, while I used the hum of the kids' room fans to block out the sounds of his real self.

This is what routine abuse does to distort your sense of *good* and *bad*. While I wasn't being beaten regularly anymore, it amazes me now that I could have thought at the time of my fortieth birthday that things were better than they had ever been. Looking back, I can see that what I was doing was barely holding my head above water while telling myself that I was swimming.

* * *

As a fortieth birthday gift to each other, Nicole and I organized a road trip. My mom planned to stay with Kevin and the kids, and I was ready to hand her detailed notes about their schedules and routines (along with perhaps a few charts and diagrams). In typical fashion, I had matching T-shirts made for our carefully planned ten-day adventure between Toronto and the Hershey Chocolate Spa in Hershey, PA. The trip was a dream. Nicole and I drove stretches of highway with the wind in our hair, laughing like teenagers, free from our grown-up lives for a blink of time, and just as deeply connected as always. The days were a whirlwind—a tour of the Welch's vineyard and juice plants, a concert in Pittsburgh, and a ride through Lancaster in an Amish buggy, just to name a few of the places we stopped. After a glorious week, I embraced Nicole at the airport and boarded my flight from Toronto back to Calgary.

Eyeing the numbers above the rows, I noticed him before I even reached my seat. He noticed me too and our eyes connected as I continued making my way down the narrow aisle. He was strikingly handsome, with a raw, earthy ruggedness. The kind of man who looked like he barely made an effort to look good, but looked good anyway. When I found my row and realized he would be occupying the middle seat beside me, I felt the energy in my body change. As I stood before him, he gave me a giant smile and enthusiastically unbuckled his seat belt, like he couldn't believe his luck. "I think this is my spot," I said with a smile, wondering if he could somehow see the butterflies in my stomach.

He and the aisle passenger stood up to let me in. Sliding past him, my body felt electrified. Before my seat belt was even fastened, he leaned in.

"Hi, my name is Joshua Collins," he said with a confident softness. "Josh."

"Hi, I'm Elaine," I said, feeling his shoulder next to mine in the confined space. He was a musician from Ontario on his way to visit his brother in a small town just south of where I lived. He wasn't taking his eyes off me.

"You're absolutely beautiful," he exclaimed.

I flushed and smiled. "Thank you." What might he say next?

I learned that Josh had been a semiprofessional hockey player and was twenty-eight years old. Could he tell that I was older? As an adult, I have often been told that I look younger than my age, so maybe he had no idea I had just turned forty. I wasn't wearing my wedding ring. I hadn't worn my ring for years. When I had gained weight, it no longer fit, and when I lost the weight, putting it back on somehow seemed like declaring an enduring love I didn't have for Kevin any longer.

The meal came, the lights dimmed, and Josh and I continued talking throughout the flight. "Do you want to watch a movie with me?" he asked after a while.

We selected one on his screen and settled in. He shifted slightly and leaned his left shoulder on mine. The magazines I had bought to read, the pillow I had brought for a nap, and the snacks I had packed to get me through the flight—they all stayed securely under the seat in front of me as a magnetic field seemed to surround me and Josh. A few minutes into the movie I felt his hand lay gently and suddenly over the top of mine. I held still with every ounce of my strength, fighting off the instinct to flinch or pull away from this unfamiliar touch. Instead, I let myself feel its warmth and its weight. As we were watching the movie, I realized I was only seeing the shapes on the screen, with no idea what the plot was or even the names of the characters.

The voices in my head began as whispers and then they became shouts. *I want to have this last forever. I never want to land.* My thoughts were becoming dreams, dreaming of a different movie, one with Joshua and I. One where, like a magic carpet ride, our airplane just kept flying and we would land in a far-off place where we could be together forever.

I don't know if I had ever felt anything close to this with Kevin, even in the beginning. Why hadn't I noticed the absence of these flutters and flashes, the emptiness instead of euphoria? Our marriage was, at this moment, the best it had ever been. But what did *best* mean in a marriage like ours? On a stormy sea there can be many sunny days, but the darkness still looms and always threatens. I knew that my life was mine; it was the one I had chosen, the one I had fought for these past twenty years. My marriage was a truth that I had settled into, that I had come to terms with. It was devoid of any feelings like the ones coursing through me as I sat shoulder to shoulder with this stranger on the plane.

"I never asked you," Josh said softly as the movie ended. "You're not in a relationship or anything, are you?"

The truth was there, heavy as an anchor. Just as real were the excitement and passion waking up in me. Could I feel this strongly for a person I'd just met? Regardless of my feelings or hopes of a magic carpet fairy tale, I knew that at the end of the flight my life would be waiting for me. I knew more than anything else that I had West and Navy to protect. But as long as we were in the air, in these seats, I wouldn't have to give up this feeling. Yes, I was married, I was a mother, and there would be no future with Josh, but for a few short hours, I could be swept away like I'd suddenly been transported into the greatest romance novel ever written about chance meetings.

"It's complicated," I replied vaguely, and gave no more details.

The pilot announced that we were about to start our descent into Calgary. We both looked out my window observing the twinkling lights of the big city down below in the dark. I suddenly felt his face draw close to mine, and a small, delicate kiss on my cheek, just at the corner of where my lips began and my cheek ended. I looked at him then, staring straight into his dazzling eyes.

"I wanted to do that," he smiled. "Just in case I never get another chance."

He pulled out the napkin that we'd gotten for the in-flight peanuts. He wrote his number on it. "I hope maybe I do get another chance, though. Will you call me?"

I tucked his number into my purse. The plane landed and the lights flashed on. People unfastened their seat belts and reached for their bags. Josh and I walked off the plane together and into the terminal, where each of our lives stood waiting for us. There was Kevin, ready to take me home. A few feet away stood Josh's brother. My heart dropped. My whole body sank with the reality that I would never see Josh again. That I would never feel this intensely alive again. I let Kevin hug me, but backed away quickly, my body tensing at his embrace.

I went through the motions in the airport, waiting for my suitcase, making small talk with Kevin, pretending to be interested in what he was saying. Josh and I looked at each other across the terminal, not taking our eyes off each other while I tried to not let Kevin notice. I was quiet on the drive home, fighting off tears as I stared out the window. I spent the next several days lost in my thoughts, fantasies, regrets, and fears. I felt more trapped than ever before. I wanted to get back to that flight and rediscover the feeling of freedom and possibility. It wasn't that Josh was the one who got away, or even someone I knew I wanted to be with. Josh simply ignited something in me I didn't believe existed anymore. I wanted to get back on that plane and back to the version of myself that had begun to take shape.

Almost as soon as I landed back in Calgary, I called Nicole and told her the whole story of Josh. She listened carefully. She asked for details.

"That was the best story ever!" she squealed.

Nicole, a voracious reader of romantic novels, also seemed to forget for a minute that I was married and had a life at home that didn't make it possible. "Wow," she sighed. Then after a pause she asked, "So, how are things with Kevin?" Her voice was steady and gentle. "Fine," I replied.

"Really?" she pressed.

Since her visit the year before, she had been different about Kevin. It had been her year to visit me in Calgary and I had put her downstairs in the guest room for the week. While she was with us, I spent much of the visit frantically trying to keep Kevin calm and maintain a semblance of peace by keeping the kids on their best behavior too. Since Nicole's last visit, the kids had grown and it was more challenging for me to run interference between them and Kevin. The pressure and the stress of keeping everything peaceful and "perfect" were pushing me to a breaking point.

One morning, while Nicole and I were out looking at model homes and gathering decorating ideas, Kevin called, angry and frustrated. He had lost his key card for work. I talked him through every place in the house he may have left it, but he grew more agitated with each passing minute. Nicole waited patiently while I tried to help Kevin. Finally, I gave in to his insistence that I come home and find his card for him.

"He's a grown man, Elaine," Nicole said. "Can't he just find it himself?"

I told her that I was sorry to cut our home tour short and cancel our lunch, but I had to help Kevin. I knew she didn't fully understand my anxiety. How could she? I know to her, it looked like I was bending over backwards about something my husband should have been able to do for himself. I know she looked at me wondering where her confident, no-nonsense friend had gone. But all I knew was that I couldn't risk Kevin blowing up, especially in front of Nicole. If I helped him find his card, he could go to work, Nicole and I could get on with the fun plans we'd had for the day, and maybe he wouldn't humiliate me in front of her.

But later that night, my secret broke through. We finished dinner, Nicole helped me clean up and we all watched a movie and said goodnight. She and I were going to get up early and drive to the mountains for the day after I got West and Navy off to school. Kevin and I went upstairs to our room and when he closed the door, he launched into a rage. It was about a pile of clothes, which he screamed was blocking the door to the laundry room. I felt that Kevin was upset because my attention was focused on hosting Nicole and making sure she was happy, rather than him. Even with two floors between us, Nicole heard him screaming and cursing at me. She approached me about it the next morning, while I was sitting in our den.

"What happened last night?" she asked, after emerging from the basement, carefully opening the door to check that Kevin had left for work. Before I could ask her what she meant, she said, "I heard everything."

"I'm sorry," I offered softly.

"Don't apologize! You haven't been yourself this whole trip. You've been stressed and on edge. You haven't been able to relax for a minute. It's like you're not even here with me because you're all wrapped up in catering to Kevin. What is going on?"

"He just needed some help finding his card."

"You acted like if you didn't find his swipe card, it would be the end of the world."

I couldn't tell Nicole that it might have been the end of the world. That I was afraid of Kevin grabbing me in front of her. "What *did* you hear last night?" I asked fearfully.

"I heard everything!" she replied. "I heard him screaming at you, the most vile and disgusting things. A hundred times worse than anything I've ever heard anyone say to a person. I heard you telling him to calm down but he just kept screaming. I called Doug, I was so scared. I couldn't stop crying. All I could do was get on my knees and pray but what I wanted to do was come up here and get you away from him. I still do."

I saw the steely determination in her eyes, and all of her love and concern for me. But I did what I had always done in the face of anyone's concern that I was anything less than expertly handling things. I put up my armor.

"No, you don't need to worry. It was nothing. We had a fight. It happens."

I steadied my voice as best I could to convince her that I was fine, that what she had heard was a normal marital spat. I couldn't bear the thought of Nicole finding out that Kevin's abuse had never stopped.

"It was not just a fight. It was awful. I was going to call 911. Please, Elaine, let's just go." I could see her jumping into protection mode. She had been this way since we were young, when she had wanted to hit Tod Beretta's head with a book on my behalf. Nicole went on, "Kevin's at work now. We can get out of here. Pack your things. I'll help you. I'll do whatever you need to keep you safe. Just get out."

"I can't leave," I replied. "I have to be here. I'm supposed to be here. It's up to me to repair Kevin. And I need to protect West and Navy."

I knew Nicole trusted me as her friend and as someone who had always been honest with her before. We talked for a while and I convinced Nicole that I was fine, that I had everything under control. I tried to assuage her worries and vowed that we would enjoy the remaining days of her trip. She tried to press me to leave again.

"I love our visits each year," I told her. "I live for this time with you. I need this time to get away from everything. When we're together, I get to be myself. I'm happy and unafraid. I don't want our time together to be anything less than the escape I need it to be."

Nicole nodded. She had understood. Throughout our friendship, she did serve as my respite and my reprieve. She welcomed me to her home and came enthusiastically to mine, bringing me the joy and diversion I so needed.

"I can't convince you to leave? Are you sure, Elaine?"

"Yes, I'm sure."

"I just hate that I will have to fake being nice around him from now on," she said bitterly. "But I will do whatever I can to make sure you're okay and happy."

After telling Nicole about Josh on the plane, it had opened the door for her to ask how things had been between Kevin and me since she had last been at my house. Once again, as always, I told her that things were fine. I needed the story to be true. I needed to believe that I was fine. And if I successfully convinced her that I was fine, then hopefully she would stop asking me about it. And I wouldn't have to face the reality that I really wasn't fine.

* * *

Not long after I returned from my birthday road trip, I took my mom to the airport. The ride was quiet and I was still grappling with the fact that she was leaving for eighteen months. When she told me of her plans to spend the next year and a half in Ecuador on another church mission trip, I was in disbelief at first. She was such a constant, supportive, and warm presence for me and the kids, and I leaned on her heavily. She regularly joined us for swim meets and triathlons, piano and singing recitals, shopping trips, and vacations. Every Sunday, she arrived at our house with a large-handled wicker basket crammed full of casseroles, fresh vegetables, pies, and always her legendary homemade buns and my great-grandma's apple salad—a full-on banquet just for the five of us. West and Navy adored her, and surprisingly, so did Kevin. I sometimes wondered if Kevin was even capable of love, but he seemed to love my mom even more than his own. Still, none of her kindness ever stopped him from criticizing my mom when she wasn't around, just as he did everyone.

I'd also come to depend on my mom to take the kids for their weekly sleepover, and to let me bring the kids to her house when Kevin felt particularly explosive. She was my safety net below the tightrope of the life I was living and I felt like someone was about to cut the lines that kept the net in place.

In Ecuador, her task would be to serve as a mission nurse for hundreds of young missionaries, most of them between nineteen and twenty-one years old, assigned to teach in Quito and the surrounding area. She would look after their health and well-being while they were living away from their families.

"I wish you wouldn't go," I'd told her when she first broke the news of her leaving. "I'll miss you."

"I'll miss you too," she replied. "I'm not really excited about going either, truth be told. But it's for you and West and Navy."

"How is it for us?" I asked, already knowing the answer.

"You and I both know that Kevin needs to change and I pray every morning and night for that. This trip is a huge sacrifice of time and money to go and serve as a missionary away from you and the kids, but I know Heavenly Father will repay that sacrifice by answering my prayers," she replied.

"I know why you're doing it and I'm grateful, but it's still hard for me to feel excited about it," I said.

"Sacrifice brings forth the blessings of Heaven," she said, quoting from my favorite hymn at church. "God is a God of miracles and I know he can help Kevin."

I realized that my mom was about to undertake eighteen months in a foreign country to help me and my marriage. While she didn't know the worst of it, not even to the extent that Nicole did, she knew things still weren't good. Kevin was difficult and mercurial. She knew that he needed some kind of intervention in order to really change. She was doing what she could, what was within her power, to get him to change.

At the airport, I embraced her and said goodbye. The kids were eight and ten years old now. They were independent and interested in many things, and we would write to her and talk on the phone as often as we could to keep her up to date on our life. I was scared as I watched her walk through the gate to board her flight. Driving away from the terminal, the words that kept going through my mind were, "I hope we survive until she gets back."

Looking back, the time around my mom's departure was calm and, for the most part, predictable. But, as always, just under the surface of all that outward stability, there was a rippling undercurrent of uncertainty. There was an ever-present fear that this stretch of calm could not possibly last. A foreboding that if I didn't do things exactly right, if I didn't keep it all organized, if I didn't balance these spinning plates of children, activities, work, and marriage perfectly, they would all come crashing down around me. And my mom, the rock I clung to through every storm, was thousands of miles away.

Despite the diminished frequency of physical attacks, Kevin continued to scream, belittle, and make threats and I never truly felt safe or at ease. One afternoon as Kevin was driving home from work, we argued on the phone. The kids were at swim practice and I knew they would be home shortly after him. The threat in his words, his volume, and his tone all told me that it wouldn't be safe for me to be in the house when he arrived. His burning anger all but scalded me through the receiver. Knowing he was only a few blocks away, I hung up, terrified. With nowhere to go, I ran out the door in my stocking feet and hid behind a fence in the alley. The phone, still in my hand, began to light up with Kevin's name. Again and again he called but I didn't pick up. I heard him pull into the driveway and go into the house. A few minutes later, I heard him get back in his car and drive away. *He must be looking for me*, I thought with dread. What would he have done if he'd found me crouching out there, too afraid to be in my own house? After he'd driven away, I went back inside and tried to calm down before the kids' car pool dropped them off. A text flashed across my phone. *I'm sorry. Where are you? I'm not mad anymore.* I knew that the worst of this storm had passed and that by the time the kids got home, he would be calm enough to control himself. But things could have gone very differently, if Kevin had found me in the alley or if the kids had come home early. The nearness of those possibilities sank deep into the pit of my stomach.

As busy as things were with the kids in school and multiple activities, Kevin was becoming more reclusive. Every night after work, he retreated into our bedroom. When I didn't find him in bed, I would often find him in the family room looking at pornography on the computer. Kevin had been obsessed with porn as long as I'd known him, but now he was looking at videos and pictures during the day, and I worried that the kids might see him. He began to avoid us more, the kids included, unless there was a swim meet or big event to attend. On Saturdays he enjoyed practicing their triathlon training with them on their bikes and on runs, and the kids loved it. I made the kids' dinner, checked their homework, made sure they brushed their teeth and cleaned their rooms. I chauffeured them to and from school, swim practice, piano lessons, church activities, play dates, and singing lessons. And all the while I cheerfully made excuses for their dad's isolation. He's exhausted from work, I would say, smoothing over their confusion. He's coming up on a quarterly deadline, he's just back from a big trip. Anything to explain or dismiss his behavior and keep them believing in him as a good dad, a loving dad. The dad they deserved.

Slowly, almost too slowly to register any alarm, the frequency of the physical abuse began to escalate again. Looking back, there was no obvious explanation for this escalation. In fact, we had seemed to be making progress with the diminishing attacks. All I knew at the time was that Kevin was set off by any number of things, including the kids, the house, and my choices, but the quickness with which his anger appeared intensified. So did his need to control me and the kids. He bought the kids cell phones and insisted we wear them at all times, wanting to arrange for each of us to have a way to carry them on the belt of our pants. If I ever missed his call, he would leave screaming messages and call again and again until I picked up. He texted throughout the day from work, sometimes hourly. It was always a small question, or to tell me about something that had happened at work, or a suggestion about the kids' sports.

One afternoon, the kids and I were shopping for school clothes and I had forgotten my phone in the kitchen. I realized what I had done when we got to the mall, but the kids needed several things and I wasn't going to turn around and go home at that point. We finished our shopping and returned home. When I checked my phone, there were over forty missed calls from Kevin. There were twelve voicemails, each of them more enraged than the previous one. "You f**king c**t. Where the hell are you? Answer my calls!"

I knew he would be in a state when he got home from work. As if I were assigning battle stations, I raced to get West and Navy busy with an activity and then set myself to cleaning, doing laundry, emptying their backpacks, making a grocery list—any activity that ensured I wasn't sitting down when I heard the garage door rolling up. Only he didn't come storming in. He seemed calm and happy to be home, keeping his frustrations at bay until the kids went to bed. And then he attacked me in our bedroom.

Like an old muscle memory, I went into survival mode. *Fix it*, I could feel my body telling me. *Fix it and this will all go away.*

After my mom left for Ecuador, his attacks, with the same choking, spitting, and throwing me to the ground, were happening at an accelerated pace and he was more cavalier and aggressive in ways I hadn't seen before. He now seemed less concerned about me leaving, or about the kids and neighbors overhearing.

So much had changed since Kevin and I had married twenty years ago. I didn't revert to my high-functioning abilities to manage Kevin's moods, the kids' behavior, my behavior. I had become too exhausted to keep Kevin's environment perfect so that he wouldn't have any need to blow up. I didn't feel as strong as I used to. Maybe it wasn't possible anymore with growing kids who had their own burgeoning and independent personalities, whose behavior I could no longer monitor or manage all the time.

As the kids grew older, I couldn't run interference between them and their father as much anymore. As babies, I could scoop them up and out of the room when they fussed. I could make sure Kevin had them only when they were in a buoyant mood. I could take on all of the difficult parts of parenting by myself, to keep Kevin from ever raging at them. But now, they were ten and eight years old, with deep feelings and needs, and the human condition of making mistakes as they grew up. They didn't always listen, or clean up after themselves, or keep their milk from spilling. They were normal and wonderful kids who were flawed like the rest of us, and it was getting harder to manage them or control Kevin in front of them.

I remembered that when West was six years old and Navy four, Kevin's sister Jenny enrolled the entire extended family in the 10K "Bolder Boulder" race, just outside of Denver, Colorado, where she lived. Thinking it would be a fun thing to try together, we traveled to Boulder and prepared for the run with nearly twenty of Kevin's relatives. We agreed that West would probably walk most of the way, but we would encourage his love of racing and make it a fun event. Navy and I planned to meet West and Kevin at the finish line. The night before the race, West woke up in the middle of the night, wracked with the flu. His little body was aching, feverish, and shivering violently.

"Oh no," I whispered as I kissed West's clammy forehead. "Looks like you're sick, sweetie." I told Kevin I would stay back at the hotel with him and Navy and meet everyone at the finish line tomorrow. "Have fun," I said, trying to be upbeat and encouraging.

West and Navy peered over their covers at us, tucked into the big queen bed in our hotel room as Kevin and I stood over them.

"Not happening," Kevin snapped. "He's not skipping the race. We came all this g*ddamn way. My whole family is here. He is going to run that race."

"Are you out of your mind?" I raised my voice. "Look at him! He's too sick to even get out of bed. He can't run a 10K. He's only six years old. It could be dangerous!"

"Daddy," West's little voice barely squeaked over the covers drawn near his face as he sat up. "I don't feel so good."

"He's not running, Kevin," I said.

I saw the movement in a flash. Kevin's mouth twitched and he made that same motion of biting down on the inside of his cheek. I didn't have time to take a breath before he grabbed West by the collar of his pajama shirt and shoved him hard back down in his bed, closed his fist and pressed it into West's chin and cheek. I yelled, and just as suddenly, Kevin let go of West, snapped his head around and put his hands around my throat, slamming my entire body down on the other bed.

"I'm taking him," he spat in my face as he squeezed his hands tight and cut off my breath.

"No!" I rasped as loudly as I could, trying to push him away. The kids remained motionless in their beds. As quickly as Kevin had lunged at me, his hands released and he stood up. He straightened his clothes and looked at all of us.

"I'm sorry. Look, I'm very sorry. I know I'm a bad guy."

He sat down on the bed and cast his eyes down at his shoes.

"I know I shouldn't have gotten angry but this race is important to me. We came all this way." He looked at the kids, who were staring at him, almost too afraid to breathe. "I didn't mean to be rough. I just want us to do what we came here to do, what we promised that we would do. My whole family is expecting us to run the race. How's it going to look if we back out now? Can you try a little harder, maybe? Can you run the race and do what you promised?"

West nodded his head and Kevin stood up. "Good. We're a family that keeps our promises. We're not going to be a family that backs out of things we commit to. Always and forever, right?"

Kevin had deployed this phrase a thousand times. It made its way into every grand conversation he would have with me or our kids about our family or the future, as if he were willing it to be true that our family would be everlasting. Once, when I had presented him with a surprise Rolex, he had eagerly flipped it over to look for an inscription, only to express disappointment that I hadn't thought to engrave *Always and Forever* into his gift. But they were his words, not mine. I never said them back to him.

Card included in a bouquet of post-abuse flowers

Kevin left the hotel room and went to the lobby for a snack, and I tucked the kids back into bed. "It was a long drive," I said, pulling up their covers. "Daddy is tired and he isn't feeling like himself. I'll talk to him," I promised.

I could see the hope and the trust in their eyes. West and Navy adored their father. They loved triathlon training with him. They wanted to please him and make him proud. And they wanted to believe that I, their mom, would do anything for them. I had made these same reassurances for years to my mom, to Nicole. *I've got this*, I always said. *I can handle it.* My kids had always seen me as the leader of our family, the one that looked after them, but also looked after their dad. I could take care of myself and everything else too. My kids needed me to be strong and to take care of them. They nodded and obediently went to sleep.

The next morning, Kevin got West up to run the race, even though I could tell he hadn't shaken his flu yet. His face was pale, brave, and sweet. I waited anxiously at the finish line watching each person cross beneath the banner. There he was, my strong, courageous little boy who had made it and was still standing. I held back the mountain of tears that had built while I was waiting and worrying.

I knew from experience that when Kevin had an agenda, nothing was going to get in the way of executing it, no matter the cost. In this case, his reputation mattered more than our kids' safety. Kevin was especially conscious of appearing perfect in front of his family. Those relationships always felt fraught, especially with his mother. Whenever we were around them, Kevin was on high alert to maintain our appearance and behavior. He talked endlessly about his successes at work or about a recent vacation we'd taken. He seemed to need to impress his mother and siblings more than anyone else on earth. He would speak endlessly about West and Navy's achievements; about the gifts and extravagant things he would buy them and how he "will never say 'no' to anything they want." He would exaggerate the facade of our perfect life far more in front of his family than with anyone else.

Kevin was at his worst with me during Sykes gatherings. He told me how much he hated his family, never wanting to travel to spend time with them, yet always putting on his best performances when they were around. The strain of this counterfeit behavior would be unleashed on me once they were out of sight or we were behind closed doors. Some of his worst abuses were during or after time spent with his family. When I married Kevin I had been very excited to be part of a big family, something I had never experienced as an only child. Once we had children I was especially excited to have West and Navy get to know their cousins, aunts, and uncles. But it became impossible. I feared every reunion or invitation to meet and run a race together, conflicted by wanting to be part of the Sykes family, but knowing it would come at a cost.

* * *

My kids were learning how to handle Kevin. I had shielded them from the majority of his outbursts but I was also teaching them how to placate and diffuse him when they saw him getting angry. They had watched me do it all their lives, and now they were taking on the task for themselves. Once, as I combed Navy's tangled and matted hair after her shower, Kevin snatched her comb from me and began running it roughly through her long brown locks. He was always obsessed over our appearances, wanting each of us to look picture-perfect, reminding me that our clothes and hair reflected on him. I could see Navy wincing as Kevin attacked her knotted hair.

"What a mess," he muttered, yanking Navy's head back with each pull.

"I'll finish her up, Kevin," I offered.

"No, I'll do it," he said angrily. After a few moments, his frustration boiled over. "How did you even let her hair get like this?" he barked.

I held Navy tightly in my arms while he continued to yank the comb through her hair.

I turned her face toward me and put my finger to my lips. She stifled a cry and mouthed 'help me.' I told her silently that it was okay, it would be over soon. She nodded and understood, holding still and quiet until Kevin had untangled her hair and left the room, following up with his standard apology for getting angry. I had protected her the best I could at the time by coaching her through the moment, but stood frozen the next day when he came through the door with a large bouquet of flowers for her as an atonement for losing his temper.

West was the one especially attuned to deescalating Kevin, and often inhabited the role of peacemaker in the family. Naturally easygoing, West loves when everyone is getting along and does his best to create harmony wherever he goes. He, too, had learned how to placate Kevin when he could see him getting angry. After he and a friend accidentally broke the bathroom doorknob, I sat in the hallway trying to figure out how to get it to unlock from the outside. When Kevin came home and headed for our bedroom as usual, he saw me and grabbed the screwdriver out of my hand.

"I can handle this, Kevin," I protested.

I knew better than to let him attempt to fix anything in the house. It usually ended badly, as Kevin was not very handy and easily frustrated by his own clumsy attempts to fix things. "Don't worry about it," I said.

"I can fix a damn doorknob, Elaine," he snapped. "How long have you been at it? How did this even happen?"

"I did it, Daddy," West admitted without hesitation.

"Why did you do this?" he shouted, his anger escalating.

Kevin tried unsuccessfully to release the lock, but it wouldn't budge. As his frustration mounted, I heard West's voice grow steady and very calm.

"I'm sorry, Daddy. It was totally my fault. You shouldn't have to come home from work and deal with this. You want me to get you anything?"

"Get a coat hanger. Now!" Kevin demanded, but there was less of a charge in his voice.

West retrieved the coat hanger and Kevin bent it into a hook to try and unlatch the door.

"That's a great idea, Dad. I wish I had thought of that."

Eventually, Kevin forced the door open, threw down the tools, and stormed into our bedroom. I cleaned up the debris and marveled at how West had used his voice and demeanor to keep his dad from getting angrier. I had never consciously taught him to do that, and this time wouldn't be the last. I realized at that moment that it had been me who had shown him how hundreds of times. I wanted, more than anything, to teach my kids the values that mattered most, the ones my own mom had taught me: kindness, honesty, helping others. I not only wanted them to be good human beings—polite and respectful of others—but generous and compassionate. Now that they were getting older, it wasn't just Kevin's angry outbursts I needed to shield them from, but his character. Could I raise them to be selfless and loving when their father cared only about himself?

A few nights after the doorknob incident, Kevin and I were getting ready for bed. I took a breath and said flatly, "You can do whatever you want to me. I'm choosing to be here. But you can't bring our kids into this. You will not treat them like you treat me."

The image of West and Navy mirroring my behavior flashed in my mind. I admired their maturity and intuition, but I mourned for their innocence. I thought about Navy singing to herself in bed late into most nights. When I asked her about it one morning, she confessed, "I try to stay awake for you."

"Why?"

"I want to stay up so that I can clean up the house after you go to sleep. There's so much for you to do and you work so hard. I really just wanted to help you, Mommy."

Her sweetness and caring nearly made me cry, though it wasn't unusual. She was always tenderhearted, and I had more than one schoolteacher tell me Navy was one of the kindest and most sensitive children they'd ever taught. "In all my years of teaching, I've never met a purer heart," her fifth-grade teacher said one day. Another reported that Navy, always the athletic team captain, made it a point to choose the least athletic, most shy girls for her team first. She was always the first to advocate for the underdog. All children are born without guile, but I frequently worried that Navy wasn't meant for this harsh and cruel world: her heart too soft, her goodness too unspoiled, her thoughts too virtuous. Her unfettered trust in everyone else's goodness, I feared, would make life infinitely harder for her than most. She was a little caretaker, deeply nurturing, and a born problem-solver. I dreaded the possibility of seeing that love betrayed or that spirit crushed.

What I wanted most in the world for my kids was to be carefree, not needing an education about how to dance around their father's rages. They were starting to be more aware with these few incidents and I could see signs of things to come. I wanted to go back to the way it was when they were babies, when they were blissfully unaware. I was more than willing to take all the abuse onto myself if it would spare them. I wished for them to be tiny again, and so much easier to protect.

Once they're grown, I can leave. The thought both startled me and settled somewhere deep inside. Maybe this marriage would not be always and forever. I could live for my children until they were out of the house, taking care of themselves. I could put myself between them and their father until then. The possibility of failing to repair Kevin didn't frighten me nearly as much as him physically harming one of the kids. They would be out of the house in just a few years. What if I could hang on for just a little while longer?

Until then, I could be an outward example of strength, confidence, and determination for them. I was the president of their swim club, the head of our church's youth events, the organizer of all their play-dates, practices, and school activities. I was an enthusiastic leader in the community and in our family and wanted to stay the capable and spirited mom they knew, taking care of them and making sure they wanted for nothing. What they didn't see was that their father placed all this responsibility on me because he couldn't be bothered with it. He handled his own work and his own needs, but no one else's. I was in charge of the house and the kids' lives because without me no one else would do it.

It was another one of Kevin's traps, making me shoulder every decision and every task to exploit my strengths and my love. For a long time, I believed that while Kevin controlled me with his violence, I in turn controlled everything else. But it was always me frantically trying to ensure our lives would run smoothly so that no ripple would ever set Kevin off.

Kevin lay down on the bed without looking at me. I waited for him to respond to my demand that he never again lose his temper around the kids. It was, after all, meant to keep up his image of a good and loving father. We both wanted the kids to adore Kevin and never be privy to the darkest sides of him, to what he was truly capable of. And yet, I could see that image was in danger of slipping away if Kevin couldn't handle a broken doorknob or some tangled hair. "You can't speak to the kids like you do to me," I pressed. "Or lose your temper with them."

"Like I've told you for years, if you ever try to divorce me, I will take the kids," he replied calmly. The steel in his voice chilled me. "They are *my* kids. I guarantee you that I will win. I will take them, Elaine."

Without another word, he snapped off his light.

I sat in the darkness and held the weight of his threat, trying to imagine a reality without my kids. The thought of it stopped my breath. I believed every word he said. I'd seen Kevin's ire at his colleagues or family members. I'd seen how long he could hold a grudge and exude resentment. I already knew what he was capable of doing to me. I tried not to imagine what more he would be capable of.

For as long as Kevin and I had been married, changing him had been my goal. I could never have imagined failing at that purpose. Even with hardly a spark of affection between us, let alone any deep love or partnership of a marriage, I still couldn't leave. I also knew down to my core that no one would believe my reasons for leaving Kevin. Not only had I spent two decades building up his reputation as the perfect husband and father with the perfect family, anyone who knew me saw me as a bold, self-assured, and independent woman. I would never be believed to be battered because no one like me would stand for that.

And Kevin could convince anyone of *anything*. The people closest to me—my mom, Nicole, even my own children—all believed my charade. How could the rest of the world believe the opposite? Whether at the kids' school or in our church, at swimming, family reunions, or with my closest friends, I presented as happy and carefree. I took charge of committees and organized events, solving problems for everyone while my own secrets lay in wait behind my bedroom door.

Lying next to Kevin in the dark, I couldn't imagine leaving him nor continuing as we were. I was trapped between a life I had designed to look perfect and the life that was destroying my self-worth. All I could do at that moment was promise to take upon myself all of Kevin's temper and his demands, all of his outbursts and foul, dehumanizing vitriol. I would step in as a buffer; I would absorb the blows for my kids.

* * *

The cognitive dissonance grew overwhelming. Too many things were clashing and too much was slipping out of my control. For two decades, my identity had been wrapped up in my ability to manage Kevin. I had done everything I could to help him, enduring pain and diminishment and denigration so that I could do what I believed was my job: to save Kevin. And then the exhaustion of motherhood, which was intensified by Kevin's lack of help and the anxiety of the kids getting older and starting to see sides of their father I had vowed to shield them from. Living with Kevin was depleting enough, but compounded with all the juggling, arranging, placating, and facade-building, I was threadbare. My soul was parched. I was less and less able to over function and throw myself into my home and my kids and started looking for ways to simply numb the pain.

I didn't smoke or even drink alcohol, but I soon learned I wasn't immune to addictive behavior when I was feeling this helpless and alone. My drug of choice became food. Food was how my mother cared for me, and how I cared for my own children. It's as natural as anything for a mother to nourish. But during this time, especially with my own mom away in Ecuador, food was my substitute for the affection I was so desperately missing. I wanted to feel good when everything felt bad. Even if it was fleeting, the pleasure of something tasting good was a momentary reprieve from the pain. When the meal was over, I wanted to feel good again, just for a minute, and so I would eat again. Sometimes I would be in pain from overeating, feeling sick and bloated. It was a disordered, maladaptive way of wanting to feel a different pain than the one I was used to feeling. And what did it matter? I was long past caring whether I was attractive to Kevin, and, I would say to myself, I had bigger things to worry about than whether I fit into a size six.

The nights were the worst because I dreaded going to bed with Kevin. The thought of going upstairs to our room, where he might become unhinged and brutalize me for anything or force me into intimacy that served only his pleasure, became utterly unbearable. I stayed up later and later, often sweeping the fridge clear of the leftovers I had just put away from our dinner. During the day, I exercised zero portion control and took in sugar and carbs and decadent takeout. I ate when I wasn't hungry because I was constantly starved of safety. I wanted to feel cared for and this seemed the only way to do it.

All the work I had put into getting myself into shape was vanishing. I regained every pound of baby weight I had lost and put on fifty more pounds on top of that. Over the next four years, I would gain 125 pounds, steadily pouring into my body what my heart was missing. Only I could never, ever feel full because I wasn't feeding the right part of me. I was wearing my exhaustion, my fear, and my loneliness on my body. My body bore the evidence for how out of control I felt, how incapable of self-care I had become. My energy plummeted. I couldn't keep up as well with running after the kids and taking care of the house. Going up and down the stairs grew laborious and left me gasping for breath. I couldn't fit into any of my clothes, and bought more and more in bigger and bigger sizes, trying to shop my way out of sadness. At the kids' swim practice, volunteer pool officials wore white pants and a blue shirt, which I dreaded so much I almost quit.

It was Kevin who made being attractive tied to my value as a wife. But appearances had always mattered to me. I had been told I was a beautiful girl since I was born, that I should be a model, even. Strangers would sometimes stop me in the stores or at the mall. Our neighbor Karen, whose house I had been at for dinner when I took Kevin's call for the first time, told me from the time I was young that I looked just like Snow White with my dark hair, blue eyes, and porcelain skin. How I looked was part of my identity and self-esteem, and I took care of my appearance. I also loved experimenting with good clothes and makeup, although my mom had always taught me to maintain a healthy, natural look, not overdone. Beauty and style had mattered to me. Now that whole part of myself was gone. I felt light-years from the attractive person I once was. The Elaine who had made an exhilarating contact with a stranger on a plane felt like a distant memory of a person I was no longer sure had ever really existed.

Kevin observed the weight gain and took every opportunity to drive it into me like a knife. He would show West and Navy old pictures of me when I was slim. "Look, this is when Mommy was beautiful, before she got fat," he would say. Where before they loved me as I was, they soon became embarrassed when I was around their friends and would ask me if I was going to lose weight. But my eating was out of control and I couldn't stop.

At one particularly low point, I had broken my ankle slipping on a patch of ice after a swim club dinner party. After arriving home from the hospital I could barely get myself in and out of bed. I knew Kevin well enough to know that he wouldn't help me, but I didn't imagine that he would be capable of completely ignoring me when I fell hard on the floor on my way back from the bathroom the same night. Lying there, just feet from our bed, I was exhausted and emotional from the ordeal and in so much pain I couldn't even manage to crawl the rest of the way. Our little dachshund, Swizzle, that I had gotten for the kids, was frantic. She whined and ran in circles around me, feeling my distress.

When Kevin finally came into the room, he walked past me as if I weren't even there. He got himself ready for bed and then slipped under the covers. But not before saying, "I guess you're just too fat to get up now."

I remained motionless on the hard floor, quietly sobbing at his casual cruelty and the fact that the only creature who cared about me at all was Swizzle.

Looking back, it feels like I was being honest for the first time. I ate because of everything I was feeling. I ate out of loneliness, fear, regret, dread, shame, and hopelessness. My life was out of control, so why pretend anymore that I could control anything else? I couldn't control Kevin; I couldn't shield my kids; I couldn't protect myself from his abuse. Control was the furthest thing from my grasp. My body was screaming at me to be honest about it at long last.

Over the next two years, as my body grew in proportion to how hard I tried to medicate my sadness, a depression slowly crept up on me, as did my own sense of failure. It was my slow recognition that I wasn't actually fixing Kevin. I wasn't changing him. I wasn't helping him. Or, if I'd done so at all, it certainly wasn't lasting. I believe our bodies and minds try to shield us from the worst fears or traumas. Mine kept me from fully seeing the end of my marriage for a very long time, from seeing that there was a core to Kevin that was never going to change, either because he was incapable or simply uninterested.

Besides food, my other coping mechanism was continuing to throw my whole being into my children. Everyone knew me as the "extra" mom who went above and beyond, but it had now become the only place where I could still feel like I was good at something. Of course I made sure their clothes matched perfectly, their meals were nutritious and fun, their every need was met. But then there were the elaborate themed birthday parties I planned and the designer cakes I decorated myself, often staying up the entire night to complete them. I hosted sleepovers, delivered school snacks, planned extravagant holiday trips complete with scavenger hunts around every new city. Giving my kids special days was part of how I loved them well, and it filled me with pleasure to do so. But as Kevin's abuse escalated, the kids' care became another form of numbing. I obsessed about every detail in their lives, striving for perfection, all so I could distract myself from the truth that everything was so very far from perfect.

At the time, I lived in darkness, too numb or dissociated to stop being constantly on the move. I had made it my life's purpose to help Kevin, and he had been all too willing to make it my problem and responsibility. So when he abused me, it was my failure. It was my lack of effort. Early in our marriage, I imagined the future we would have once Kevin was fixed. I couldn't conjure anything specific, but only a distant feeling of peace, a calm at long last. Maybe I had known all along that it would never be possible. Later in the marriage, I sometimes imagined what it would be like to have a husband who was kind to me. And there was my trap. A kind husband wasn't Kevin. If Kevin were no longer my husband, it would mean that I had failed at achieving what I set out to do. The only way to get the kind of husband I needed and deserved was for this marriage to fail. I had twisted myself into an impossible position, with the weight of everything squarely on my shoulders.

The contradictions swirled and became too much to bear. In order to survive, I tunneled into the present with vengeance. I didn't look far beyond how I would survive the moment at hand. This was what survival mode meant for me, breathing and breaking down my day into the smallest increments: make breakfast, get dressed, get the kids to school. I set my sights on getting through every task as if my life depended on it. But doing that has its price.

While focused intently on the present, there's not much room to look toward the future. I no longer knew how to look beyond the next minute. What would the kids' future look like? I had always known they would grow up, go to college, fall in love, and fulfill their dreams. They were too bright and too full of life to do anything short of living to the fullest. But that vision had grown hazy, as had thinking about my own future. What would my life be when I turned forty-five, when I turned fifty? I couldn't even imagine it. For years, I would dream at night of what it would be like to be with a man who was kind, gentle, thoughtful, careful. I could only imagine it because I had read about it and seen it in movies. And my grandfather had been that to me. I had dreamt about it for so many years, it was hard to believe it would happen now.

Meanwhile, Kevin talked of nothing but the future. He made grand plans for big trips and vacations, graduations, and holidays. I began to recognize the gaslighting in his talk of our perfect family. While he used to be able to sweep me away with his words, I was no longer able to fall under their spell. I didn't believe our family was perfect. I had once believed that if I worked hard enough, I could make it so. That it was within my power. Somewhere along the way, that shifted to making our family appear perfect to others, while I grappled with the storms within. Now, even that idea was slipping away, no longer possible as reality became harder and harder to conceal or explain away. Most days, I didn't recognize my life at all.

CHAPTER FIVE

Karla began writing Kevin letters from rehab. Kevin had few friends at work, so it was surprising to me that this woman who worked within his sales department, and I'd heard very little about, was reaching out to him while she was in treatment. She had worked from his remote office in Edmonton, which sits about three hours north of Calgary. Kevin never showed me her letters, but told me that Karla needed to get clean for herself and for her family. She had checked herself into an in-patient facility to get treatment for her addiction to alcohol and cocaine. Kevin told me Karla was married with a set of twins a few years younger than Navy, and a grown daughter whom she'd given up for adoption at birth, but kept in contact with. She was maybe in her late twenties and of Lebanese background. I had a vague memory of Kevin mentioning her before, telling me she was a major flirt with all the guys in the office, even rumored to be sleeping with one of the married bosses. I had no idea then of the role Karla would end up playing in the lives of me and my children.

Kevin began communicating with Karla regularly, almost like a sponsor or mentor. He encouraged her to get clean, then stay clean, and go back to work as soon as she was ready. I was touched by his concern. He updated me regularly on her progress and I rooted for her. Later that same year, after Karla completed her recovery program, Kevin continued to check in and he encouraged her to join him in triathlon training. It was a different side of him, and I encouraged him to help her. She sounded like someone who needed help and I was always willing to help rescue someone in need. Her family life sounded messy. She had been abandoned by her mother and raised by a father who brought various women into her life. Sometime after she left home, she dropped out of eighth grade, and at age fourteen had become a prostitute for a while.

By the time we came to know Karla, Kevin was not only bringing our kids to triathlons, but he was training for several himself. Karla also began training for a competition, which is how we first met.

We were bursting with pride that Navy was ranked the number-one female triathlete in Canada that year for her age, and West earned the title of Male Youth Triathlete of Alberta. It was the height of triathlon season and we had traveled to Kelowna, British Columbia, for the youth national championships. After we settled into our hotel room, we decided to stretch our legs on a stroll around the Okanagan lakeshore. Kevin noticed Karla first, walking with her kids Matt and Maya, around the hotel. "Hey, that's my coworker who I told you about. The one who was in rehab."

She was a short, attractive woman with platinum bleached hair and an athletic build.

"Should we say hi?" Kevin asked.

"Sure," I agreed.

"Funny meeting you here," Kevin called out.

Karla waved enthusiastically and walked over to meet us. She shook my hand and told me she had heard a lot about me, Navy, and West.

West competing in triathlon

"It's very nice to meet you," I greeted her. Then I noticed her training clothes. "You're competing this week?" I asked.

"Yes," she replied. "It's my first triathlon and I'm pretty nervous. Luckily, Kevin's been helping me train. He's the one who thought I was ready for this, so here I am. I kind of can't believe I signed up."

It had not been just a chance meeting, despite Kevin's apparent surprise at running into her.

"Oh, nice," I said.

The activities surrounding the event took up every moment, and I didn't have time to dwell on the inconsistencies between Kevin and Karla's stories. Over the next few months, she became a steady presence at every triathlon event across British Columbia and Alberta.

There were other women besides Karla. I learned much later that Kevin had pursued my friends relentlessly and indiscriminately. It didn't matter if they were single or in a relationship, but most were married. It didn't matter how close they were to me, or how his behavior might ruin my friendships. He pressed me for information about any woman in my circle of friends or acquaintances, always wanting to know details about their relationships, especially if they were having troubles. At first, he just seemed to be taking an interest in my friends, and therefore me. But looking back, he was mining me for information he could use.

My friend Traci cut off all contact with him after he repeatedly pursued her and then forced a kiss on her during a family trip we all took together. She was so shaken by what he had done she was in tears. One Sunday morning, Kevin kissed my friend Stacey in front of everyone after attending a birthday brunch hosted by her and her husband Tom. I knew Stacey from West and Navy's preschool, and after brunch was over and we were all saying our goodbyes in the parking lot, Kevin walked over to her and gave her a long kiss right on the lips. He didn't seem to care that his wife, her husband, and all our kids watched the whole thing. Later, Stacey would make excuses when declining my invitations to spend time with us as couples again.

Barb, from the kids' swim club, joked regularly and uncomfortably about Kevin's flirtations with her, although she'd told him clearly that she was married. Krista's husband, Rob, told her explicitly to stay away from Kevin after witnessing his excessive flirting via text. Sharon declined Kevin's invitation to become his running partner and go out for long stretches alone together. These are just a handful of the women I know about, who have told me themselves about Kevin's inappropriate words or actions and how he ignored or overrode their discomfort. I can't even calculate all the friends I've lost because of him, or how many more I don't even know about, either because they were too embarrassed or too polite to say anything.

But Karla stayed in our lives. She was the one who ended up responding to Kevin's advances. In the beginning, I saw Karla as a project, another person to save. But soon I found myself letting her in as a friend. She came into our lives quickly and found openings to invite herself to join our family. She ingratiated herself eagerly under Kevin's pursuit, while she likewise pursued us all. She folded herself into our family until there was no getting rid of her.

She was warm and polite, easy to talk to, self-deprecating in her humor, and a generally pleasant person to be around. In the beginning, she was just as welcoming in return. Our families visited each other several times that year. It all felt normal and we enjoyed each other's company. When Kevin and I drove to Edmonton to see Beyoncé in concert, Karla offered to host our whole family and watch the kids while Kevin and I attended the concert. Her home was beautiful and well-appointed. Her husband, Allan, owned a chain of auto body shops and they seemed to be doing very well for themselves. Her kids got along well with ours. A month or so later, Karla brought her kids to Calgary and our families spent the day at an amusement park. She bought all the kids matching pajamas and even trinkets for me and Kevin.

A few weeks later we made another trip, this time to the famous West Edmonton Mall. While I shopped, Kevin took West and Navy to the large indoor water park. Karla had offered to pack lunch for Kevin and the kids. When I met up with them around noon, he had just opened up the lunch Karla had sent. It was extravagant: homemade hummus, gourmet sandwiches, fresh veggies, homemade desserts, specialty drinks.

Like many of her gifts, her praise, and her gratitude, it was all a little too much. Everything looked crafted to impress someone special. It instantly struck me differently from her previous gestures. I wondered if I was missing something. I also just had a sense that *something* was off. This was too much, too showy; inappropriate somehow. But at the time, I brushed away any suspicions of impropriety. I knew Kevin would never cheat on me. His excommunication from our church years earlier, for the inappropriate relationship he and Beth had when they were serving as missionaries, left a scar he talked about frequently. I knew he would never want to feel that pain again.

By December of that year, I had learned that Karla was estranged from several members of her family because of her childhood, filled with abandonment, instability, and loneliness. "It must be so nice," she commented, "to have such a lovely family that cares about you."

"Tell me about your family," I said.

"Allan is abusive," Karla confessed. I was taken aback by her openness with something I could relate to but couldn't tell anyone. "Kevin has helped me so much."

"Oh?" I asked. The kinship I initially felt toward her was suddenly muted by the overwhelming irony that Kevin was trying to rescue someone in an abusive relationship.

"He helped me a lot during rehab, and he's helping me now with getting away from Allan."

It wasn't like Kevin to put himself out there for another person. Acts of charity by Kevin usually only occurred when they could be acknowledged and admired, or served some other ulterior motive.

"Come for Christmas," I said excitedly, wanting to encourage this compassionate side of Kevin I'd rarely seen. Karla smiled at me delightedly.

My mom had finally returned from Ecuador, and was hosting Christmas at her house for the first time since before she'd left. I was so happy to finally have her home, but I thought back to the eighteen months that she was away and how much had changed while she was gone. I had worried about my own survival, and I suppose I *had* survived. But Kevin's violence had escalated, I had gained seventy-five pounds, and the healthy, strong, and hopeful me that my mother had left on my fortieth birthday was no longer there. She made the sacrifice of going away as a missionary expressly so that God would help me, and help Kevin, but instead things had gotten even worse. I was struggling to understand why, but I did wonder, for a moment, if the situation getting worse was, in fact, an answer in disguise.

On Christmas, Karla arrived at my mom's house and joined our family party with my mom's siblings, many of my first cousins, and their families. Karla was a friendly and gracious guest, insisting on bringing a dish to contribute to the meal. "Please don't let me arrive emptyhanded," she begged. We sat chatting at my mom's oversized dining table for a long while. She talked with me most of the evening. She talked to me even more than she talked to Kevin.

It might seem naïve that I didn't suspect Kevin and Karla were having an affair. She came into *our* lives, not just his. Along with thoughtful gifts and gestures, she would send me emails and texts, plus handwritten notes and letters telling me how grateful she was for our closeness. I enjoyed her company, and she seemed like she really cared about having a friendship with me. She was kind to my kids. Strangely, Karla's involvement in our lives coincided with Kevin's escalating cruelty.

* * *

In April, Kevin won another President's Club trip, this time to Spain. It was an all-expenses-paid reward for those who'd had an exceptional year of performance at work. He was, despite his inability to control his behavior at home, still a top salesman at his company, regularly exceeding his goals and outperforming his colleagues. Kevin still had the power to charm, cajole, and woo people into becoming his next sale—just as he did to me every time I threatened to leave him. Whatever stress he felt at work, he brought it home to me at the end of the day, while keeping up appearances there. These President's Club trips were a regular occurrence for us. The year before we had gone to Dubai. That trip had been punctuated by several of Kevin's rages, one of which ended with him smashing a hotel clock after I had bought a decorative area rug for our house that he didn't want.

This year, we spent a week in Barcelona with his team and their spouses, guided to breathtaking sites and dining in posh, contemporary restaurants. The city was full of life and excitement and Kevin and his colleagues were in a celebratory mood. I was usually excited about his President's Club trips but had grown so large that I was dreading trying to find something to wear for the gala events or the fun activities that were planned for us each day. I was embarrassed but hoped that I didn't look as awful as I believed I did. As a treat for ourselves, Kevin and I extended our stay one more night. His boss and coworkers flew home, and then it was just the two of us with twenty-four hours to ourselves in this historic city.

But, as often happened when we traveled, there were signs of a storm coming. The tension and anger in Kevin would build and on our final day in Spain I could sense an impending eruption. The feeling was the same as it had always been. A darkness brooding, a heaviness in the air. The tension was palpable, and I resorted to trying to placate him and prevent an explosion. I was particularly frightened that day. All of Kevin's colleagues were gone, the organizers had left and I was in a foreign country far from home, unable to speak the language, with no safe place to go. I was feeling exceptionally vulnerable and deeply regretting the choice to extend our trip. "I just need to keep Kevin calm until we get on our flight," I kept telling myself.

We spent our final day looking for something for my mom to thank her for watching the kids. In one store, Kevin picked out a bright red apron with the word 'Olé' on it. When he grabbed a second apron, I said, "I don't need that," playfully brushing it away. "You like to order in anyway," I teased.

"It's not for you," he replied. "It's for Karla."

I tried to tell myself it was sweet and thoughtful. That maybe I should pick something out for her or her kids as well.

Getting ready for our last day in Barcelona

Later, in the middle of a large food court, Kevin began an especially cruel verbal assault unlike anything he'd unleashed recently. He couldn't yell because of the crowd, but his growling voice was like a dagger. It came out of nowhere. There was no fight, not even a disagreement about anything. He simply turned on me.

"I don't know why I ever married you," he taunted. "You're a fat and disgusting c**t. You make me f**king sick."

I stiffened and kept walking, determined to hold it together until we could catch our flight the next day.

Evening came and we found a quiet Spanish bistro for dinner. We were seated outside, waiting for our dinner to arrive, and the single candle on the table threw low shadows across us both. We had been together all week so we struggled to find something to talk about. Without warning, Kevin looked up at me.

"Elaine, I'm ashamed to have you as the mother of my children. Anyone else would have been better. They should be embarrassed to call you their mom," he said.

Opinions only matter when you value the person that voices them, and I certainly had given up valuing Kevin's thoughts of me long ago. Kevin's insults and unprovoked verbal assaults had been pervasive throughout our entire marriage, but over time I had learned to not let them penetrate me anymore. He said cruel things and then he also said "I love you" every single day of our lives together. I don't recall exactly when I stopped saying "I love you, too," but it had been a very long time. Falling out of love had been like a slow death, which happened alongside my growing love for the kids. They were the center of my universe and every ounce of energy I put into their care was rewarded with their goodness, kindness, and decency. All the while, the effort I put into Kevin seemed to go nowhere. I wasn't helping him get better. I was just trying not to let everything fall apart.

I knew who I was, and above all else, I absolutely knew who I was as a mother. Though I knew his words weren't true, that night at the bistro, they somehow gained traction on the Teflon armor I had shielded myself with through years of constant criticism. I did everything for my kids, almost entirely on my own, plus I spent every waking moment trying to shield them from their dad's violent and true personality. The kids were the one place where I still had an immense amount of pride, the only place where I still took joy, and I was making the ultimate sacrifice—my own happiness, health, and safety—to make sure they were unharmed. The words appeared in my head without me actually thinking them. *He is a monster.* As I sat there processing what he had uttered, I became so angry I couldn't speak. We said very little, and returned to our hotel. I wanted to scream but I couldn't. I needed to get on the airplane, back to Canada.

Back at the hotel, I came out of the bathroom to find Kevin on his back, naked on the bed in the lamp-lit room, complaining that there was nothing on TV in English. The sight of his body disgusted me. As I walked past the end of the bed, I felt a sudden chill run the entire length of my body. But it was more than a passing cold. It was deeper than that, and more frigid. It was a kind of darkness passing over me, then passing right through me. In fact, the whole room felt engulfed with darkness, like there was an evil presence in the room that was palpable but not visible.

As a person of faith, I can say that I have felt the opposite. I have felt light and lightness, the presence of God through His Spirit, multiple times in my life. I have felt a spiritual connection to God, and I'm familiar with recognizing and being in tune to that connection. I know, that is, when God feels near. But in this moment, alone with Kevin, with no one in this country whom I could call, no one who even knew my name, I felt completely alone. I became terrified. The air felt like lead and God was nowhere.

Even after all the years of abuse, if someone had asked me if I ever felt afraid that Kevin would kill me, my answer would have been, no—at least, not intentionally. Until that night. For the first time in the twenty-three years I had been married to Kevin, I felt fear for my life. Looking back, I often wondered if what I had felt was real, or if my imagination had gotten the best of me. Was this the night that Kevin truly contemplated it?

I returned to the bathroom and prayed. I prayed so hard that I would be okay and I would be able to get on that flight and return to Canada. I wanted to get back home, where someone would notice if I went missing. My mind raced. I wanted to be back with my kids and my mom. I prayed that Kevin would fall asleep, that this night would end, and that God would just let me get back to Calgary.

Final night in Spain

I left the bathroom and got into bed. I was grateful that he decided to masturbate instead of demanding sex; however, he insisted I lie next to him and talk out some lurid fantasies until he was satisfied. This was typical at home, and it was often a time when he would become violent. I was very careful to do what I was told and hoped it would be over soon so he would fall asleep. When he finally did, I stayed awake until I could see the sunlight beginning to appear, until I could begin packing for our very early flight back home. We boarded our flight a few short hours later. I closed my eyes and leaned against the window of the airplane after a long sleepless night and I quietly thanked God for keeping me alive.

* * *

Besides food, I sought comfort in homemaking. I surrounded myself with beautiful, contemporary furnishings and had tried from early on in our marriage to make our homes warm and inviting so that I would have someplace safe and welcoming amid all the chaos and fear. I knew when I first toured the house that it would be perfect. I had been looking for a new home for us for a couple of months now and when we returned from Barcelona I happened upon this absolute stunner I couldn't pass up a viewing. Upon entering, the first thing you saw was the spacious and open living room that flowed straight into the kitchen. The ceilings were twenty feet high, with windows stretching toward the roofline, flooding the spaces with western light and a view of the Canadian Rockies as far as the eye could see. Navy and West would have their own bathrooms and between their bedrooms was a sitting room all their own. I envisioned kids sprawled across beanbag chairs watching movies, grabbing snacks from the little kitchenette minifridge I would put there. Navy would have the room with the balcony, fit for a princess. Their friends would fill the house with teenage laughter and sweet awkwardness.

It didn't make sense to buy a new house when our family was on the verge of falling apart. It seemed impossible to endure the unbearable levels of abuse Kevin was inflicting on me, but perhaps it was his plan all along to break me down so that I didn't have the strength to fight back anymore. The harder it was for me to stand up to him, the more control he had over me. All I knew was that I was desperate for something, anything, that could make our life feel normal again. I held onto the hope that I could make it until West and Navy were grown, driven by the powerful love of a mother for her children, willing to endure my own pain to protect them. That kind of devotion is what kept me in a dangerous situation, even as I struggled to maintain an impossible and humiliating facade. That deep love and desperate need to protect were my only remaining sources of strength and motivation.

When I took Kevin to see the house, I knew he would like it. It was impressive and would fit with the persona we had cultivated over the years. The complete wardrobes he used to buy me in our first years of marriage had evolved into Porsches, Mercedes, BMWs, expensive Italian business suits, massive designer wardrobes for the kids, and every toy and latest electronic gadget that was new and available. A five-thousand-square foot-house with a driveway that could fit all those cars and more fit right in line with all that.

Earlier, we had abandoned the plan of building our own house, due to permitting delays and a problematic land developer. We sold our undeveloped plot of land for a nice profit, but still, this dream house would cost significantly more than we had ever planned to pay to build our own. Kevin made a good living but the money only came in when he closed a deal and earned a commission, or when he was given a bonus. Between those times, we put everything on credit cards. He was generous with gifts and spending, but he had no idea what we could afford since he paid no attention to our finances. I had always been solely in charge of managing the house and paying the bills, but I wasn't keeping us to a budget. He sometimes spent lavishly to apologize for abusing me. I spent to make our home beautiful, host elaborate dinner parties, take us on luxury vacations, keep our children looking picture perfect, and—as I did with food—numb the pain. We both lived above our means and didn't think about saving. We ended up buying the house, my mom helping with the down payment.

The reality of moving in was far from smooth. When Kevin asked me, for what seemed like the hundredth time, "Why are we still living out of boxes?" I had no answer. Or rather, the answer was simply that I had no good reason for not having unpacked yet. We had the bare essentials to get by—our beds, a couch, a dining table. But other than that, we had been living in a sea of boxes for weeks. I hadn't even unpacked the kitchen. It's hard to recall how I fed the kids. Our new house was almost five times as big as the tiny rental we'd been staying in, and it felt cavernous with our spare belongings.

What was holding me back? The unwillingness to create one more facade, the inability to choose the perfect art or rugs or throw pillows. The inability to curate anymore. To create a space I knew would be lived in by Kevin and inhabited by my fear. My depression had become debilitating. And my weight was continuing to climb. Everything was harder. All the things I could do easily for so many years, my mind, my emotions, and my body were now immobilizing me. I couldn't move, I couldn't work, I couldn't do the most basic functions, let alone handle moving into a new house, the work and responsibility of which would be mine alone.

It was here, in this empty and unpacked new house, that a realization finally settled on me. I couldn't make it in this marriage from now until West and Navy were grown. The years that remained would be unbearable. I had already given up on curing Kevin. I had given up on our marriage, but I had clung to the idea that I could keep our little family together until my kids were strong enough to be on their own. And now that belief was dying too.

I was paralyzed, barely functioning. Something was ending. I must have realized it, even if it wasn't completely conscious. I was heavier than I had ever been. I didn't recognize myself or my life. I was completely exhausted. I had needed to be strong for so long that my muscles were atrophying as I continued to try and carry the weight of keeping up the pretense. More importantly, it was getting harder and harder to keep up the illusion for West and Navy. It was getting harder to protect their innocent, perfect world from the dark secret that had been lurking behind the curtain of their entire life. Kevin was turning the temperature up at a time when I couldn't summon the capacity to even get the socks folded for the week. My world was crumbling. Had it already crumbled? Was I just opening my eyes to the rubble I had once convinced myself was a fairy-tale castle?

Things didn't seem like they could sink any lower, but then another crack in the facade of our life appeared. I didn't know how much longer it could possibly all hold together. Just before we moved into the new house, Kevin and I had a massive argument. My suspicions about Karla had grown. After willing myself to believe that theirs was an innocent friendship based on helping someone desperately in need, I could no longer ignore the muffled calls Kevin took from outside or in the garage. I had seen Karla grow comfortable—too comfortable—with trying to parent my kids. The woman I considered a friend to our entire family was moving in on my life.

On a triathlon day I braided Navy's hair in preparation for her race and sent her off ahead with Kevin, only to arrive shortly after to find Navy's braid taken out and styled differently by Karla. She texted West that she was so proud of him and told him how handsome he looked after winning a big race one Saturday. Another day, I arrived at my kid's summer camp only to discover Karla had arranged to become a volunteer. She even took West to get his learner's permit to drive. I couldn't conceal how shocked and enraged I was as West walked into the house bursting with pride, and I upset him with my reaction. Karla knitted herself in as though I wasn't married to their father, as if they were one family, with herself and Kevin at the center. I had never caught them, nor had there ever been definitive proof, but I was no longer convinced that Kevin would never cheat on me, even under threat of another excommunication. There was no longer anything I believed he was incapable of.

Our fight about Karla happened in the middle of the day. Kevin had come into the laundry room, where I was putting clothes into the washing machine, and told me he was tired of my suspicions and my insistence that she was too involved in our life. I didn't respond, so he began screaming obscenities at me, grabbed me, and backed me into the corner of the small laundry room, his face so close to me that his nose was pressed against mine. He threatened me with his fist and when I tried to get away into the hallway, he grabbed me by the throat and threw me face-first into the wall. Both kids were home, upstairs in their rooms, but this time Kevin's rage and lies blinded him, making him forget that this was a side of himself he was never to show when the kids were around.

This was an all-too familiar scene, except for one thing. For the first time in our marriage, I fought back. I'm not sure what stirred inside me that day, or why instead of trying like always to calm Kevin down and simply protect myself, I fought back. I screamed and shouted for him to stop. I tried to push him off me; I pummeled his back. For several seconds he didn't react, letting me pound at him with the sides of my fists, he then looked at me and grinned. He then lunged at me harder than I had experienced in a very long time, and I was no match for him in physical strength. We wrestled into the hallway, neither of us realizing that Navy had come racing down the stairs. From her room, she had heard the commotion and had stopped at the top of the stairs to listen. I'm not sure what she heard or how much she saw, but I will never forget the pitch of her young voice when she screamed, "Shut up!"

Kevin let me go in a flash and walked into the kitchen. Navy, ever the problem-solver, asked us both to sit down on the couch in the living room. Facing us, she sat very straight and looked solemn.

"Why are you fighting?" Navy demanded.

It was painful for me to watch my daughter try to defuse the situation, touched by her concern but devastated by the reality of what had just happened. I didn't have the strength to tell Navy that we could handle things without her intervention, which would have been an obvious falsehood anyway, so I allowed her to mediate as a way to distract her from the awful things she had just overheard. I wanted to tell her not to worry, that we were grown-ups and could take care of ourselves and her and her brother. But Kevin was quick to jump in with an answer.

"It's because I want to move away from Calgary, but Mommy doesn't want us to."

Somehow, it sounded like he was blaming me with his cover-up. Navy looked thoughtful for a moment, her eight-year-old brain searching hard for an answer to a problem so much bigger than her. I felt my arms still throbbing from where Kevin had grabbed me.

"Why don't we just stay here for a little while longer?" she finally said. "Then we can move. That way, everyone will be happy."

Kevin and I thanked her for her concern, then Kevin fled upstairs to the bedroom. I was left to comfort Navy and assure her that everything was all right. I realized that in her mind the match had been equal, that we had been "fighting." She had no idea that Kevin had been attacking me, the same way he had done all her life while I broke myself trying to maintain her innocence. I stroked her hair and told her I was fine, that nothing was wrong. My words felt hollow. I don't know if she believed me like she once did.

She was older now, growing wise while remaining as compassionate as ever. I could tell she wanted to help us, that she felt the need to make right whatever was wrong. This was the girl who cared for the lonely girls at school, whose heart was unfailingly tender. And I hated that her heart now had to bear this burden of her father and me fighting and that she felt responsible to make everything okay. I was terrified she had seen something that I had worked her whole life to shield her from. I realized then that I no longer had the energy to fix or pretend anymore. I felt depleted, like an empty and abandoned shell on the shore. I no longer knew how to make this reality anything but what it actually was.

CHAPTER SIX

Kevin didn't travel with us to Ottawa, Canada's capital, to celebrate Canada Day on July 1. Instead, my mom and I flew there with the kids, with plans for us to stay for a week and celebrate. After that, I would be off with the kids to visit Nicole and her family in Toronto for a week and my mom would head home. Kevin had work meetings in British Columbia come up at the last minute.

"I have too much to do this week," he said. Go ahead with your mom and the kids," he insisted. "I'll be able to join you in Toronto next week."

I was secretly relieved. My mom would help with the kids and we would be free from Kevin's intensity and impossible-to-please attitude about everything. We planned an amazing week of fireworks, and I bought the kids red curly wigs, shirts, and face stickers emblazoned with the Canadian flag. But on the night of Canada Day, just after we had arrived in Ottawa, Navy became very sick. She was lethargic and feverish. It was right at the time that H1N1, the swine flu epidemic, was infecting thousands in Canada and spreading like wildfire. I was worried that she had contracted it, so on the night of Canada Day, we watched the fireworks from the tall windows of our hotel room overlooking Parliament Hill.

My mom and the kids on Canada Day

The kids fell asleep after the fireworks and my mom and I stood at the window watching the crowds of people celebrating into the night from our spectacular vantage point. Our dark room glowed with the lights from the concert and revelers below. It was in this quiet that I turned to my mom and said, "I think it's time for me to finally leave Kevin."

"Oh?" she asked gently, inviting me to say more.

"It's over," I replied. "I can't do it anymore. I'm barely functioning."

"What's happening?"

"It's not getting any better with Kevin. I don't think he will ever change. I think I'm done."

"Okay," she said. She waited.

"I can't keep it all together anymore. I thought I could fix him. Then, when that didn't seem like it was ever going to happen, I thought I could stay until the kids were grown. But I can't do that either. I can't wait that long. I don't think I'm doing West and Navy any favors anymore."

"It's been terrible. And I know you don't even tell me most of it," she said.

"I don't recognize myself. Nothing about who I know I am is in alignment with how I'm living. What's important to me—my values, my goals, every plan I had for myself—they've all sat lifeless while I dedicated my entire being to helping Kevin. Nothing that I envisioned for myself has come true. I really believed there wasn't anything I wasn't capable of, including healing Kevin, but I have nothing left to give."

She was patient, as she had always been. We had had similar conversations in the past, but I hadn't been ready to give up hope at those times. She'd been supportive of my plans, and when I didn't follow through because I was too afraid of leaving my kids without being able to control Kevin's behavior around them, she was also afraid for them. But this time was different. This time I needed to save my own life too.

I started to formulate a plan in my mind. I thought about a lawyer. I thought about how I would compose the note to tell him I was leaving.

My mom asked, "What's your plan?"

"I need to stay with you when we get back from Toronto," I said. "I just need some time to get everything arranged."

"You can stay with me as long as you want," she said.

"I'm going to hire a lawyer and a therapist."

"That sounds wise," she assured me. "They can help you put together a plan. An exit plan."

"I'm pretty sure he's having an affair with Karla," I said. It was the first time I'd acknowledged this out loud, let alone to another soul. My mom was quiet for a moment, the way she was when thinking of the right words.

"This may be exactly what you want," she said.

Her words landed heavily. She wasn't wrong. I didn't want to be with Kevin, but I was unclear how his relationship with Karla was going to play out. Maybe, though, his having an affair would be an easier way out than packing up the kids in the night and escaping. Maybe *he* would actually leave.

"You're right," I replied. "Maybe this is a gift."

I looked over at Navy and West, sleeping angelically and still looking innocent and so young. I thought about what Kevin might teach our son about being a man and how to treat women without me supervising every conversation. West had woken up happy and smiling nearly every day of his life and has always displayed a gentle nature that nothing seemed to shake. At every opportunity, he used to stroke my hair or hold my hand, especially when we sat together in church. He loved being around people and was rarely happier than when surrounded by friends carousing in the backyard. It was with relief that I looked at his face and basked in his utter sweetness. *What will happen now? Will he be okay?* I asked myself.

At the same moment, I worried about what Navy was learning from me about how to behave around men, and what kind of behavior she should tolerate from men. She saw me as the strong, capable, even-tempered one, the one who came up with all the solutions for her, West, and also her dad. But was she also learning to be accommodating, at the sacrifice of her own will and happiness? Had she always been a natural fixer like me, or was this something she had learned from watching me try to fix everything? I wanted her to love her father, but I shuddered at the thought of her marrying someone like Kevin. I needed to show her something different.

I sighed as we watched the crowds disperse and the lights outside go dim.

Despite my anxieties about the kids, I was flooded with resolve that this was finally it. That this was necessary: for me and for West and Navy. Knowing I could lean on my mom through this gave me added courage. I was grateful for her love and I knew that she would be there for me through it, as she had been for anything I had ever needed her for.

"I love you," she said.

"I love you, too."

By morning, Navy was getting sicker, so I found the nearest hospital and rushed her in. Just before the automatic sliding doors opened to let us in, I read a sign taped at eye level: "If you think you have H1N1, put on a face mask." The doctor who examined Navy said she might have H1N1, but she also might just have the flu. He told me to monitor her and bring her back if she became worse. We had planned our four-hour drive from Ottawa that day and on the way, projectile vomited all over the back of my seat in the rental car.

We made it slowly, haltingly, to Toronto and hunkered down at Nicole's. My mom flew back to Calgary and I tended to Navy day and night. Nicole was the perfect host and kept West occupied with her boys. When Navy's breathing began to grow ever more labored, I took her to the doctor again. This doctor in Toronto said she had pneumonia, which I learned later was a common misdiagnosis for H1N1 at the time. Kevin finally arrived from British Columbia. I prepared to assume my role of tending to Kevin in addition to nursing Navy and tending to West, but it was like Kevin wasn't there at all. He was distracted, on the phone for work constantly, barely registering that our daughter was gasping for breath. I learned later that she actually could have died from the seriousness of her condition, and was lucky to have survived.

As I had since we'd arrived, I stayed up all night listening for Navy's breath. Kevin and I slept in Nicole's boys' twin beds, with Navy curled on an air mattress between us. Every few minutes, she would sit up and gulp for air, coughing violently, almost unable to catch her breath. On his first night in Toronto, Kevin slept through it all. When I opened my eyes to the first rays of the sun the next morning, I realized I must have drifted off for a few minutes. Navy had finally fallen into a deep sleep, her breath somewhat regular. I looked at her and then at Kevin. I had come through one of the scariest nights of my life completely alone, even though my husband had been right there next to me.

The next day, Kevin was on the phone yet again. I waited for him to finish but he carried the phone into the bedroom and sat on one of the beds, continuing to talk while I helped Navy sip some clear broth.

"Things are fine," he said. "We haven't really been doing much. How was your day yesterday?"

I snapped my head around. This wasn't a work call.

"Did you do your long run?" he continued. "You'll need to get your miles in this week or you won't be ready for our race in Kelowna at the end of the month." It sank in then that he was talking to Karla—in front of me and in front of Navy, who was soaked with sweat and still unable to get out of bed.

"What are you doing?" I asked sharply.

He covered the end of his phone with his hand. "I'm talking to Karla. I'm not hanging up."

He said it matter-of-factly, without hesitation or any hint of shame. He looked right at me as he continued to chat with Karla, listening to the details of her day, laughing, asking questions, and saying he missed her. He was openly having an affair right in front of me. With our critically ill child in the room.

From the time Karla had packed that fancy lunch, I'd harbored suspicions about her relationship with Kevin. But now he was flaunting it. My friend Traci had told me only a few months earlier that Kevin had said to her that he could do anything to me and I would never leave him. Here was more evidence that Kevin thought he reigned over me with absolute, unfettered authority—to manipulate me, hurt me, and now flagrantly cheat on me, entirely in the open. Watching how disengaged he was, I was filled with both blinding anger and devastating relief. He was occupied, perhaps obsessed, with Karla. What else but obsession would make him stop sneaking around to have an affair and bring this other woman into the same room as his sick daughter? It was beyond disrespectful, thoughtless, and arrogant. He was so sure of his control over me. He was so sure that I would put up with it all. Until that moment, I would have said that Kevin was right. But now I was becoming sure of something else entirely: that a life without Kevin's cruelty could exist for me.

* * *

Navy recuperated and we returned home from Toronto, the gravity of my decision beginning to take hold. I had left Kevin numerous times, but this was different. This was a decision twenty-three years in the making. This wasn't me leaving crying, bruised, and shoeless in the middle of the night. This was my decision to not spend another day trying to fix Kevin. This was no longer wanting to hope that West and Navy were now old enough to call for help if Kevin hurt them. This was realizing that I now was a skeleton of my former supermom self, and that I couldn't be the mother West and Navy needed, not while we lived with Kevin. This was realizing that physically, mentally, emotionally, and even spiritually, I had nothing left in me to give. This was giving up the idea that I could solve every problem ever presented to me. I finally realized that the only person who could fix Kevin was Kevin.

But first, I had an emotional reckoning to face. For the entire last week of July, I sent West and Navy to a sleep-away summer camp. I had seven days to do what I needed to do. I put the kids on the bus to camp, then headed home to my computer and typed Kevin a long and raw letter. In it, I stood up, fought back, named his sins, claimed my own failures, and told him I was leaving and that I was never going to change my mind.

I wasn't yet afraid for my safety, knowing that Kevin would never believe that I would *actually* leave him. But I didn't really write the letter for him. I knew that he would dismiss my words, just as he had all these years. I wrote the letter for myself. I knew that if I put it down on paper, and then told the kids this was happening, that I would follow through this time. I wouldn't be talked back into a life of fear and pain. I wouldn't be guilted or manipulated into not believing my own eyes, ears, or bruises again.

But I also knew Kevin, and when he saw that this time was different, I wasn't going to be able to just pack my bags and leave. His words resounded in my head: "If you ever try to leave me, I will take our kids." I believed him to my core even if I didn't know what, exactly, he would do. The nightmare scenarios haunted me—would he lash out and hurt them? Would he take them and run and keep them from me? I knew from experience how cruel and vile Kevin could be when he was angry, and I couldn't risk my kids being on the receiving end of it, not after the years I'd spent absorbing it for them. I was terrified they would be scarred for life.

I taped the letter to the wide timber front door of the house we still hadn't unpacked and fully moved into. Then I packed a bag and left for my mom's. For seven days, while the kids were away, I cried and grieved on her couch. Each day, I confronted a different loss: the good parts of the life we had built, the happy life I dreamed for so long of having and now knew we would never have, the kids' chance at a two-parent home, the financial freedom I had enjoyed, the stigma of a divorce, my once unshakable optimism. I worried over what was about to be uncharted; this decision was about to alter everything we had all known for so long.

For seven days, I also slowly wrapped my mind around letting this immense secret out into the world. Leaving Kevin would mean that I would take off the twenty-three-year-old disguise I had dressed myself in everyday in front of all our friends, neighbors, teachers, coaches, family, and even my kids. I would be seen as a battered wife. People would wonder why I stayed for so long. They would judge and even criticize me. More than that, I was convinced no one would actually believe me. I had good reason to be afraid of not being believed, especially after what happened when I told my friend Kara.

But I had finally realized that it didn't matter what anyone believed. I knew I couldn't do this any longer. The world had never seen my bruises or heard my screams, but it was okay. After so many years of trying to heal Kevin, it was time to heal me. But there were still so many unknowns. I had no idea what this would mean for me and my kids. I wondered who I would tell first? What words would I choose? And who would stand by me?

It was agonizing and cathartic. In the space of my mom's serene home, where I always felt safe, everything could come to the surface. As it came, I prayed for God to help me through it. So much of the grief was decades old. The emotions came in waves—rage, fear, regret, shame, hate, and even love for much of what our family had shared in the good times. All the while, I was saying goodbye to my marriage and the life I knew. More than anything, I had given up believing that somehow, some way, it could have worked out. I couldn't remember a time when I had wept this openly. I talked to my mom a little bit, but it was something I had to go through alone. Each day would end and then I would do it all over again the next day, grieving the loss of each piece of the life I was saying goodbye to.

On my third day at my mom's, Kevin called.

"I got your letter," he said.

"I want you out of the house before West and Navy get back on Saturday," I demanded.

"I'm not leaving, Elaine."

"I'll see you at the end of the week, Kevin. We can tell the kids together and we'll figure out next steps."

For the rest of the week, I read everything I could on how to help kids cope with divorce. I studied recommendations on how to tell them, how to keep them healthy, how to make them feel safe, whole, and loved. Knowing his history, I was unsure whether Kevin would give West and Navy's emotional well-being the same consideration, so I emailed him extensive notes from one of the books, hoping that he would at least read through them and understand how important it would be for Navy and West's mental health that we handle the transition with care.

I never dreaded anything more in my life than I dreaded telling my kids about the divorce. I was supposed to protect them, but my words were about to break their hearts. I was about to shatter their world and pull back the curtain for a first glimpse into what had been lurking behind it their entire lives. I knew that they would need time to adjust to the change, so I decided to take it slowly. I would ask Kevin to move into the basement to let the kids transition into our separation with more ease. I could tell that despite my plan for us to tell West and Navy, he still wasn't taking me seriously.

The week came to an end and the kids came home from camp. As I gathered my things, I realized I felt hollowed out but lighter somehow. I was finished grieving. I felt ready to move on with my life. I also made two appointments, one with a therapist and one with a divorce lawyer. I was about to start sharing with other people the secret I had hidden for so long. I knew that telling other people would help me to not lose my nerve and go back on my plan. Kevin and I had agreed on a time to meet at the house to give the kids the news. He told me on the phone how pleased he was about the divorce; however, he was insistent that I be the one to tell them. I told them to go into our room and sit on our bed for a talk.

I know a small part of me was hoping for a miracle right at that moment, so I wouldn't have to tell them. Yet I knew that no miracle would occur: I had been waiting for one for almost a quarter of a lifetime. As I prepared the words, it felt as though my most prized possessions were about to be dropped off the side of a mountain. The minefield I had precariously carried them through had ended at a ledge, with no path left to keep them safe. Kevin sat by and let me explain everything to the kids. Their faces were straining to understand the news.

"Mommy and Daddy are getting a divorce, but we will live in the same house while we figure things out. Daddy will be downstairs, Mommy upstairs." I took both their hands. "This doesn't have anything to do with you or how much we love you. Neither of you did anything wrong. We still have a few things to figure out, but it will all be okay."

I talked to them for a few minutes longer, giving them both hugs and telling them they could talk about it more whenever they were ready. Kevin, without saying a word, left the room. West did what he always did, which was to exude calm, but was the first to ask a question: "Will we still be able to have family dinners with Grandma on Sundays?"

"Absolutely, we will," I said.

"Okay." He turned and went quietly to his room. But Navy had gone ashen. She looked wounded. She didn't cry but it was obvious she was distressed. Later that day, in an effort to distract and comfort her, I offered a trip to Build-a-Bear, where she picked out a special stuffy that I suggested could help when she was feeling especially sad or lonely.

Kevin moved his things down into the basement without incident. It was a first step, and a first victory for me. I pictured the conversation between Kevin and Karla and thought about how happy Karla would be that Kevin and I were now sleeping separately.

Kevin didn't try to charm his way back upstairs. He didn't apologize. We never, in fact, talked about divorce explicitly. It was as if our lives would just continue with us in separate corners. All this meant that I needed to make a plan to leave him, to get myself and my kids safely out. I knew I couldn't predict what Kevin would do when he finally realized that this marriage was over, and that it wasn't going to be the same as every other time, when he was able to convince me to return.

* * *

A few days later when I took the recycling out to the garage, I was surprised to see Kevin's car parked in the dark. He must have come home without me realizing. Then I heard his voice, raised and agitated. His tone was harsh and angry. I heard him clearly through the car door.

"G*ddammit, Karla, he put his f**king tongue down your throat!" Kevin hissed. "If you don't want to be with me, then say so. Why are you doing this?"

He sounded hysterical and enraged. He was jealous that she was involved with someone else, I realized. He was hurt. It was almost too incredible to believe. I heard him tell her that he loved her, that he adored everything about her, and that he wanted to be with her. I listened for a moment and stepped quietly back into the house.

A few minutes later, I heard the car door slam and Kevin stomped into the house.

"You were talking to Karla," I said.

"No, I wasn't," Kevin replied, his voice steady and assured. A simple statement. A fact.

"I heard you just now."

"I wasn't talking to Karla," he replied, his voice calm. The outrage I had overheard vanished like smoke.

"Please don't," I sighed, my eyes rolling. "I heard you with my own ears. Just be honest for once."

Kevin's face was placid and unwavering. "I was talking to my admin assistant, Elaine. You must have heard wrong. Her name is Clara, remember?"

"You were talking to Karla," I insisted. "I heard you. You know, I know you flew to meet her in BC instead of coming with us all to Ottawa," I added, feeling bolder than ever. "Carolyn Neish was your flight attendant. She told me that you said you had been to see Karla at her summer home."

Kevin didn't acknowledge my accusation. It was typical for him to ignore what I said so I would end up questioning my own sanity.

"My admin assistant is having a bad fight with her boyfriend. I was trying to help her out. That's all."

I wouldn't let him get away with it this time. Though I was firmly committed to seeing the divorce through, I decided that I wanted to hear the truth. Not for any kind of reconciliation or forgiveness, but for its own sake. "You sounded mad that she's cheating on you. Must feel terrible."

"Clara and her boyfriend fight all the time," he continued, as if he hadn't heard a word I said, as if his words were all that mattered and he didn't even owe me the courtesy of acknowledging what I'd heard.

"Stop," I said, questioning why there was still a charade about his involvement with Karla at this point.

"Stop what? I'm telling you the truth. Why would I lie?"

I stared at him in disbelief.

"Come on, Elaine." His voice softened. "I wouldn't lie to you, not about something like this. Clara and her boyfriend are having problems. I have been there for her before with her personal issues and she's feeling so down right now. What could I say?"

"You could say no," I snapped.

"You're right, I should," he sighed. "I shouldn't have gotten involved. I'll stop. I promise." He smiled at me. "I'll keep my distance."

And there I was, caught up in Kevin's story. It was like I had helped him see the light and draw better boundaries, like I was helping him be better at his job. He stepped toward me.

"No, Kevin," I stepped back. "I heard what I heard. Just tell the truth."

"I'm telling you the truth. You think you could have heard correctly through the rolled-up windows?"

"Yes," I insisted.

"You didn't hear half the conversation I had with Clara while I was driving. All the drama and what an asshole her boyfriend is and how miserable he makes her. She is a mess. Now he wants to work it out but she doesn't."

"It really sounded like you were talking to Karla," I said.

"I wasn't," he replied, his eyes locked on mine. It went on like this for a while, my energy waning and my defenses wearing down. By the end of the night, I found my head spinning.

Kevin had talked, as he always had, until I couldn't think straight anymore. His insistence that he had been talking with Clara, his placid surety with not so much as a waver in his voice or a missed step, made my own sense of reality lose footing. We went to bed, Kevin in the basement and me upstairs.

Alone in the bedroom, I couldn't help but marvel at Kevin's persistence and skill. I couldn't believe that he had taken me all the way from what I had heard with my own ears to his twisted fabrication. And yet, I felt unsure about what I had heard only a few hours earlier. I hadn't just caught a few scraps of their conversation. I had heard Kevin's voice clearly. I knew what I heard. But it felt like trying to hold onto water with my bare hands. I realized, in a way that I hadn't before, how utterly convincing his lies were. He could make me believe almost anything. He had done so our entire marriage, maybe because I had wanted him to. Suddenly, I doubted everything he had ever said to me. Every story about his ex-wife, Beth, his neglectful and cruel parents, or the sexual abuse he suffered at the hands of his brother-in-law—I wondered what, if any of it, had ever been true.

CHAPTER SEVEN

Soon after Kevin moved to the basement, I secretly attended my appointments with both the divorce attorney and therapist. A lawyer in my congregation recommended Claire Wolf's legal services and gave me her number. I arrived at her downtown high-rise office and was taken to a large, empty boardroom and seated at the end of a very long conference table. I noticed Claire's spiky red hair and modern glasses as soon as she walked in the room. Her demeanor was tough. She looked confident, bold, like she wasn't afraid of anything.

I heard myself say the words, "I need to start the process of divorcing my husband." They hung in the air, sounding very real and very final.

Claire handed me a stack of paperwork. She walked me through each of the pages. On one of them I needed to select the reason for seeking divorce. My only choices were irreconcilable differences, infidelity, or abuse. Before I had an opportunity to make my selection she offered, "A lot of people put down abuse, but it's not a very common thing in reality. Fighting doesn't constitute abuse. You can mark irreconcilable differences."

"It *is* abuse," I replied. My voice was steady. "He's physically violent with me."

"Oh," she said, looking startled for a moment. "Then that's what we'll file."

She asked for a photo of Kevin that they would use to serve him the papers.

"I'm not ready to do that yet. I'm getting a plan in place to leave. I need to make sure I can get me and my kids out safely. I'll have to call you once that happens, and then we can serve him."

"We can do that. You can fill out the papers now, we'll get everything in place, and then we'll serve him as soon as you give us the go-ahead."

I went to my appointment with Dr. Comm next. I had never sought therapy before so I wasn't sure what to expect. He was tall and slim, soft-spoken, and very kind. As it turned out, we belonged to the same church. I was grateful we shared similar faith beliefs because he understood almost immediately that I seemed to want a spiritual sounding board as much as therapy. Dr. Comm also understood that I needed a clear escape plan.

"You need to get yourself out of this situation," he said firmly but gently.

I hadn't even told him everything yet. I'd barely begun to unpack the years of abuse. We made October 8 my exit date. I was to have everything in place by then and be ready to leave. Until then, Dr. Comm and I would meet weekly.

At one appointment, he advised me that if there was another incident, I should call the Sheriff King Home, a shelter for women in abusive relationships and in danger of violence.

"I'm not calling them," I replied.

"Why not? They will house you and your kids. You'll be safe there."

"I can't," I said. "I can't be that person."

"The kind of person who goes to a shelter?"

"I hate thinking about myself that way. I don't want to identify as someone who needs to escape to a shelter. I have resources that those women do not."

Dr. Comm was patient and kind. He didn't insist that I had to go to a shelter. But he did make me promise him one thing.

"If he's violent with you again, you have to call the police."

"That's really hard for me," I said.

"Why?"

"Calling the police means inviting the world into my problems, letting everyone see what's going on."

"Have you ever called the police for help before?"

"Once."

"And how did that go?"

"Nothing happened, really. My kids were asleep at the time, so they told Kevin to leave and cool off. Kevin came back a few days later and slept in the guest room for a while. I do recall that the abuse stopped for longer than usual afterward."

"Yes," he said. "The statistics are very clear. When you call the police and report the abuse, it makes the abuser less likely to repeat the behavior."

I believed him, and agreed that I would do what he was asking. It was hard to make myself believe that promise.

From the time Kevin first became abusive, he would never admit to it. He would minimize the pain he caused me and compare our relationship to a well-known movie at the time called *The Burning Bed*. In it, Farrah Fawcett played an abused wife who eventually took her revenge on her alcoholic husband. Based on a true story, the movie depicted gruesome violence and a protagonist who lived in poverty and isolation. Kevin used this movie as a contrast with my life—a beautiful home, friends, children, security. He reminded me that I wasn't in the hospital with black eyes and broken bones. The message was clear and I bought it: I am nothing like that character; therefore, I am not abused.

I believed him for a long time. I'm not exactly sure when things changed. In time I realized that bruised arms were the same as black eyes, and pain from an attack was still painful, whether I suffered in the hospital or at home. But I did know that abused women go to shelters and I still couldn't see myself as one of those women. I refused to let that be me. There were many sessions when Dr. Comm and I didn't talk about my plans to leave. We talked a lot about God instead. The truth is, I went into every session planning to talk about Kevin, but each time, something pulled me elsewhere. Perhaps part of it was that I wasn't ready to completely talk through my plans. Though Dr. Comm never judged me, I was also embarrassed to delve into just how long the abuse had gone on.

I grappled for years with the fact that I chose again and again to stay with Kevin after all that he had done to me. Would people understand if they knew? Would they understand that it was because saving others was a compulsion so woven into my identity that I didn't know how to put myself above that obligation? Because of my shame, I had shrouded my circumstances in secrecy for so long. Trying to rewrite the narrative was difficult. But ultimately there was something else I needed to work out before I could take this step.

"Where has God been in my life?" I said one day. "I did everything right. I saved myself for marriage; I did everything I could possibly do to make this work, to try and help Kevin. I have sacrificed everything, especially my own physical, emotional, and mental health, to protect my kids. I stayed committed to a marriage I should have ended two decades ago. I prayed for Kevin to change; I prayed for a way out of this marriage that would keep my kids whole, so I wouldn't have to worry about their safety or their emotional well-being. I even prayed for some kind of accident so we could be free and the kids would never find out who their dad was. I prayed for a miracle but none ever came. None of it mattered."

"To God?" he said.

"God certainly didn't seem to care about all my efforts," I said. "I was filled with faith that if I did everything I could, He would look after the rest. My mom even made sacrifices, going to Ecuador for a year and a half. That didn't matter either."

Dr. Comm continued to listen.

"God knows how terrified I am of any psychological damage to my kids. I have wanted to protect their emotional health since before they were even born. That has mattered to me probably more than anything else. I can't shield them anymore and I need God to protect *them*, at least."

"They have their own paths to take, and your sacrifice hasn't been in vain," Dr. Comm replied. "You protected them through the most important and formative years of their life. They will be okay. Thanks to you, they have the foundation they need."

This went on for weeks. We talked about how God works in our lives. I never thought about divorcing Kevin as part of God's plan for my life. I thought He would make it right. But I was now starting to sit with the belief that maybe everything was unfolding exactly as it should. Understanding who I had become as a result of my experiences was making everything I had gone through more palatable. On bad days I expressed my grief and disappointment, my lament that God had abandoned me. On good days we talked about other things. Dr. Comm listened. Outside of work, he was serving as a bishop of his congregation, but he felt like my bishop and my therapist. He was exactly what I needed. I worked through the parallel ways I tried to live with both God and Kevin. The common denominator was my belief that if I just did my part, I would get the results I wanted. If I were obedient, faithful, sacrificial, and prayerful, God would bless me. They were two sides of the same coin. And I believed every ounce of responsibility was on me, and me alone. I only now realized I might have been wrong.

* * *

At the beginning of October, with my exit date one week away, I was coming to terms with not being able to control other people's behavior, or being able to control God, deeply frustrated that it had taken me this long to fully grasp that idea. I was also getting used to the idea of actually leaving Kevin. I was preparing for where we would live and how different life would be. I was excited, but also having a hard time picturing this reality after so many years of it appearing unreachable.

I still didn't have a complete plan, however. There were too many moving parts and I felt overwhelmed. How could I get myself and the kids away without Kevin coming after us? I didn't want to pull them out of school or disrupt their lives. Sometimes I thought the only way out was for us three to disappear, but it hardly seemed fair that they would have to give up their normal days filled with piano, swimming, singing, and friends. I had given Dr. Comm permission to contact the Sheriff King Home and the women's shelter on my behalf, letting them know of my plan. I had absolutely no hope that Kevin would take our departure well and the reality of exposing the kids to his worst side was still filling me with dread. He couldn't be trusted to put their emotional well-being first, to make compromises and custody arrangements. He would never make this easy for me or for them. I knew I needed to line up a place for us to stay long-term, make sure my mom was ready to stand up to whatever tactics Kevin would deploy, and plan out what we would do in the weeks and months after we left. But I was paralyzed with fear over my kids, and clinging tightly to the idea of finding a way to pull this all off without them having to pay the price.

At one of our meetings, my lawyer, Claire, told me I would need to get a job. I had done some event planning on the side, but for thirteen years my primary focus had been on my children and the thought of making career plans was both thrilling and terrifying. Slowly, I let myself embrace the idea of completing my education and finding a job in hospitality or event planning, of taking care of Navy and West on my own, independent of Kevin's paycheck. But there was still no concrete plan in place.

It was October 1, and we were still surrounded by unpacked boxes. My depression, along with my intent to sell the house once I left Kevin, was continuing to keep me from the task of unpacking the house, especially the den, where I sat checking my email that night. It was after midnight, and not unusual for me to stay up late, as it had become my habit over the years to delay going to bed with Kevin.

When Kevin walked in and saw my screen, he flew into an instant rage. The open email was from my friend Traci, who lived in Wyoming. She was one of the women Kevin had pursued behind my back after she had helped to organize my fortieth birthday party. Uncomfortable with his advances, she cut him off entirely. Kevin asked me to cut off all communication with Traci. I didn't know the details, only that her excuses to not spend time together any longer coincided with Kevin commanding that I cut her out of my life. I had no intention of losing my friend, so I maintained quiet contact with her.

Traci's email was about buying and shipping swimsuits for the kids. But all Kevin saw was Traci's name on my screen. "Why did you choose her over me?" he screamed. He had a water bottle in his hand, and towering above me, slammed it repeatedly against the chair I was sitting in. Screaming at me, only an inch from my face, he then threw the bottle, cocked his arm back and let his fist fly directly at me. It landed on my arm with a sharp, radiating pain. The next thing I knew, Kevin had grabbed me by the jaw and pulled me up out of the chair. He threw me across the room and onto a pile of boxes, where the cardboard cut my face as I landed. I picked myself up off the floor and heard Kevin opening the front door to the house.

I reached for the phone, ready to make good on my promise to Dr. Comm. I dialed 911, but before I could know if the call had gone through, Kevin raced back into the room. He lunged at me, grabbing the phone and throwing me with it across the room, back into the boxes. The jagged cardboard shredded my skin, but before I had time to cry out, Kevin was above me again. He grabbed my hair and yanked me up as I screamed from the pain. He dragged me out of the den to the front entryway of the house, and threw me down the cement steps, outside onto our driveway.

I'm outside, I thought. *I'm out.* I couldn't believe he had been reckless enough to actually breach the walls of the house. I looked around me, surrounded by the vast night sky, and I was filled with a sense of freedom. The crisp air and my throbbing body seemed to hover and stretch out that moment. Still digesting my good fortune, I raced next door and furiously rang their doorbell. She came to the door faster than I expected given that it was now after 1:00 a.m. Kevin was standing in his underwear on the threshold of our front door. "No, Elaine, don't do this," he pleaded. "Don't do this," he repeated. He was soft and contrite, his tone having changed at warp speed from the rabid animal he'd been only moments ago.

My new neighbor, whom I had only met once, asked who it was through the door. "Elaine," I said. She opened the door to let me in, and I asked her to call 911. Just as she did, I heard the phone ringing in my house. My call to 911 had connected. I could hear Kevin telling them that everything was fine now.

At my neighbor's, all the lights were off except for some recessed countertop lights glowing dimly in her kitchen that cast shadows into her living room, where I waited. My neighbor got off the phone and told me the police had been dispatched in response to the 911 call I had made from my house.

Soon, two police officers arrived at my neighbor's house. One was male, about forty-five, the other was a young female, tall and slim, who appeared new on the job. I looked around for a light switch but didn't know where any of them were. Would they be able to see the cuts on my face and the bruises forming on my wrists? They entered the living room and stood above me where I sat on my neighbor's sofa.

"Tell me what happened," the male officer demanded.

I told them the entire story of Kevin's rage, how he had punched me, thrown me, dragged me by my hair, and threw me outside like a bag of garbage.

When I finished, the male officer sighed and said, "We'll go over and talk to him now."

My stomach turned to lead with fear. Kevin would tell them anything they wanted to hear in order to make this all go away. My neighbor and I didn't say a word and she never turned on the lights. We waited in the chilly blackness for the officers to return.

"His story," the male officer said when they returned, "is very different from yours." I looked over at his younger female counterpart. She had been silent this whole time. The male officer stood above me and shone a light into my face. I felt like some perpetrator being interrogated. "You're not bleeding," he said.

"I have been enduring this for the past twenty-three years," I said through the burning pain in my jaw. "And now that I've finally called you, you don't even believe me?" I added with disgust.

I couldn't believe what was happening. Had Kevin managed to convince them too?

"What do you want from us?"

"I want him out of the house. I want him to leave. I want to go check on my kids and I need him not to be there."

"Why?"

"Look at what he did to me!" I cried. "Why would you think I want him to stay in the house with me after this?"

"Do you believe your children are unsafe?"

"No," I began.

"Then why do you need your husband to leave?"

"Not because of them, but because of *me*. Why can't you make him leave because of what he did to me?"

"You're telling me that your husband has been beating you for twenty-three years? With your kids in the house? But you don't think they're unsafe?"

"I've been protecting my kids! I've been standing between them and their father their entire lives. They're safe *because of me*."

"So you do believe your children are safe?"

"Just get him out of the house," I shouted. I could feel my panic rising. What if they didn't arrest him or make him leave? What if I had to walk back into that house after calling the police? Then what? "He was violent with me. Why isn't that enough to arrest him?"

"But you don't believe he's a danger to the children?"

"Yes!" I screamed. "Yes, he's a danger to them. Now will you make him leave?"

Something broke as soon as I uttered those words. I felt a tear running through the fabric of my life, of my very being. It was as if, all at once, a foundation gave way under a weight it could no longer bear. In the moment, it didn't fully hit me. My body was coursing with adrenaline and I was deep in survival mode. But what shattered then was my own self-imposed narrative and my very identity as a mom, and the commandment I had kept never to tell anyone about what Kevin had done to me.

As soon as my children were born, I swore an oath to protect them, even from their own father. I made it my life's goal to fill them up with love and joy and shield them from the rest, often by taking Kevin's abuse. It was the only way I had ever known to keep them safe. It was the only thing that mattered. It was my one job as their mother. And now, I was telling this stranger that my babies were not safe. He had the power behind his uniform and his badge to determine how this night would end for me. This officer could send me back into my house where my husband had just attacked me so viciously. I said the words, *my kids are not safe,* in order to save myself and them. I felt like I had failed, even though this was exactly what I needed to do to protect them. I couldn't keep them safe by myself, not anymore. It should have never been my job in the first place, but I hadn't known any other way.

"If you think your kids are unsafe, then I'll have no choice but to get other people involved. You're not going to like it."

I had been gaslighted for over two decades and I decided that it would end here. I wasn't going to be bullied or threatened out of believing my own story anymore. "Go ahead," I glowered at him and his silent, useless partner.

I was irate. At Dr. Comm's insistence, I had finally mustered the courage to call for help when I had only relied on myself for so many years. And as with Kara so many years earlier, I hadn't been believed. I now knew with certainty that there wasn't anything Kevin couldn't make someone believe. His ability to lie and persuade was beginning to feel superhuman.

"Okay, then he'll leave." Without another word, the male officer turned on his heel and headed toward my house.

The female officer stayed back, waiting for her partner to return. We sat in silence for several minutes when, for the first time all night, she spoke. "I'm sorry about my partner."

I looked at her, still angry, but surprised she was apologizing for him. "We can get really jaded doing this job." Then, she handed me a pamphlet on domestic violence. I nodded slightly, acknowledging what she had said, feeling in a strange way like she was connecting with me as a woman.

The male officer returned. "He's leaving, but he's allowed to come back in the morning."

Kevin wouldn't be arrested. He was simply told to spend the night somewhere else, that he could return in the morning when things had settled down. They treated it like a minor domestic tiff instead of the full-on brutal attack it was.

Kevin did comply with their request to leave. As soon as he was gone, I immediately got on the phone to my mom. It was 3:00 a.m. When she arrived, she took pictures of my injuries with my cell phone and we then devised a plan for how we would all be gone by the time Kevin returned to the house the next morning.

My escape had come one week early. Not knowing what time Kevin would be back, I knew we needed to be gone early. I was still trying to figure out how I would finally tell the kids about their dad in language they could understand. We would stay with my mom until we could figure out what to do next. I packed a few things for me and the kids while she headed home, waiting for our arrival in a few hours. It was Friday morning now. I went into West's and Navy's rooms well before their alarm went off.

"Time to get up, sweetie." I sat on West's bed beside him, giving him a kiss on the top of his head and rubbing his back. He was now thirteen years old.

"We're having a special day today. We're going to take the day off of school and go see Grandma!" I said cheerily.

I hadn't slept yet and my mind was hazy with how I was going to tell them something I had rehearsed a thousand times since they were born, hoping I would never have to.

"For a special treat we're going to stop at McDonald's for breakfast and I'm going to tell you a story."

"What kind of story? What are we doing? What about swim practice?" West asked, looking confused as he sat up, rather than intrigued or excited. He knew it was strange for us to be up so early and he never missed school. He got dressed while I went to wake Navy, now eleven, to tell her the same thing.

"We'll talk more about it in the car," I said.

We piled in the car, the kids in the back seat quietly looking out the window as we made our way to the McDonald's nearest my mom's house. West and Navy, always full of life, were somber and gray. There was no mistaking the palpable dark cloud that hovered over our drive that morning. Somehow without any words they knew nothing would ever be the same again. We pulled into the drive-thru, got our hash browns and breakfast sandwiches, and parked in the shopping center lot adjacent to the restaurant. I unbuckled my seat belt and twisted around to talk to them.

"Can you tell us the story now?" West asked. Navy was quiet.

I took a deep breath. I closed my eyes and said a silent prayer that I could find exactly the right words.

"First of all, I love you more than anything and you've done absolutely nothing wrong; you're perfect," I started. "Daddy also loves you. You know how Daddy has a fun side, the side that you get to see? The side that takes you on bike rides, helps you with your triathlons, and makes you laugh."

They nodded.

"Daddy also has a mad side. That is the side of Daddy that I get to see."

I pointed to my cuts on my face. I then showed them my arms. There was no way to explain it otherwise. I couldn't find the words. Everything I had kept hidden from them for so long was revealed.

What their dad did to me—what he had been doing to me all of their lives.

"Daddy did these things to me and it's not okay for him to do that. Just like I've taught you, and you're taught at school, it's not okay to hurt someone else, right?" They both nodded their heads slowly. "Well, it's not okay for adults to do that either. Daddy and I can't live in the same house anymore because of it," I said.

I let the information sink in. That their dad was abusing their mom. They looked at the purple marks and angry red scratches. They were silent. And they were deeply confused. Yet, I could see they understood. West and Navy had never wanted for the knowledge of what was right or wrong. They were so good. They were everything I could have ever dreamed of as a mom.

We talked for a while there in the early morning. The kids were slowly coming to terms with the situation, but I knew it would take many more talks before they would have a real grasp of it. For now, it would have to be enough that they knew the truth, that they were safe, and that they were hearing it from me.

"I don't know exactly how things will be in the future. But I promise that you will be safe and loved. And that you didn't do anything wrong."

I watched West for a moment, his face revealing how hard his young mind was working to understand what was happening. I waited for him to speak.

"Can I ask you something Mommy?"

"Of course, sweetie. What is it?"

"Do I have Daddy's mad side, too?" he asked finally.

My heart cracked. At that moment, I knew leaving was the right decision and the only decision. I couldn't let my kids, my beautiful and perfect kids, think for one minute that anything was wrong with them. Kevin had done enough. *His damage stops here*, I vowed.

I took a moment to gather myself. Then I looked West straight in the eye and said in my clearest, surest voice, "No. Absolutely not. There is no part of your dad's mad side in you."

His shoulders loosened and the color returned to his face. He seemed to want confirmation of what we both knew: that his natural sweetness and gentleness would never be tarnished by his father's personality.

I turned to look at Navy. "What questions do you have for me? Can I tell you anything more?"

She didn't answer, only half-shook her head and kept staring out the window. I twisted back around, put the car in drive and headed to my mom's. I knew that at her house, they would feel more settled, safe in a place they had known all their lives as full of warmth and love and care.

* * *

I got us to my mom's as fast as I could. I made sure we locked the door behind us and then let my mom help the kids get a snack and turn on a TV show while I called Claire.

"I'm out of the house," I told her. "It's earlier than I had planned, but he attacked me last night and I took the kids and left. I'm at my mom's."

"Good. Okay." She sounded flustered, distracted. "You need to file for an Emergency Protection Order. An EPO."

"What is that? I asked.

"It's like a restraining order, but it has more legal clout. If you can get one in place it will keep Kevin completely away from you and the kids."

"Can you do that for me?" I said.

"I would," she said, her voice rushed and low. But right now, I'm in the middle of another emergency situation and I can't get away.

You will have to file it for yourself, Elaine. You can do it today, as soon as we get off the phone. Let me walk you through the steps."

I was about to navigate a system I knew nothing about and I was going to do it on my own, but my life had been full of hard things and, like this, I had done them mostly on my own. I listened to Claire, took notes, then told my mom I needed to go down to the courthouse.

"Do not, for any reason, let Kevin in the house," I said. "Don't answer his calls. Just stay here. I'll be back as soon as I can."

I hated leaving them, knowing that my mom's house would be one of the first places that Kevin would come looking for me. But I had no choice.

I sat in the Calgary Court Center for what felt like hours, seeing other people arrive, and watching them get assigned a legal aid attorney to plead their case. They were being processed through the system—a system that I was now part of. *I don't want to be here,* I thought. *I hate this, all of it. I hate Kevin. Why is this happening to me?*

Over the thunder of my own thoughts, I could hear the conversation at the counter with a man standing in line in front of me. "I need an EPO," he said. I snapped my head up, then looked back down so he wouldn't notice me listening. "My wife is abusing me," he explained.

He was thin, with a slight frame and a soft voice. He was being abused by his wife and he was asking for help, just like I was. His head was low and his face somber. The way the lines were formed around his mouth, it seemed like he had been sad for a very long time. I felt compelled to say something to him or ask him if I could give him a hug. For a few moments of reprieve, I forgot about myself. Seeing this man in front of me, I felt a shift in everything that had happened this morning, last night, throughout my whole marriage. He was in my very situation, except with the added shame and humiliation of being an abused husband in our society. If he could do this, so could I.

When I finally got called in to speak with my court-assigned lawyer, she began hurriedly taking me through the paperwork as though I was some sort of battle-scarred veteran misusing a system put in place to protect people.

Great, another jaded person who is supposed to help me, but instead doesn't believe me, I thought to myself, exasperated. She made little eye contact with me, filling out forms while asking me a series of unfamiliar questions. The air was filled with her impatience with me, and my frustration with her condescension and contempt.

In the middle of yet another exchange in which I asked her to explain the EPO process and she proceeded to repeat herself at a patronizingly slow pace, my phone rang. It was Kevin. My phone rang again, and again. He then texted me asking where I was and where the children were, saying that he was going to call the police. I asked her what to do and she told me to ignore it. My phone rang again and it was my mom, but I silenced it and tried to stay focused on the meeting. My phone rang again: it was West's number, followed up by my mom's number again. Finally, I picked up.

"What's happening?" I asked.

My mom's voice was so loud that my lawyer across the desk could hear her clearly. "Elaine, Kevin is here. He's trying to get in!" In the background, I could hear Kevin pounding on the door. And I could hear Navy screaming.

"Mom, slow down. What's going on?"

"I don't know what to do. I can't hold onto her!"

"Who?" I yelled.

"Navy! She's trying to open the front door and let Kevin in. She's too big for me to hold onto!" "And the phone won't stop ringing. He keeps calling over and over again."

I tried to keep my voice level despite my rising panic. "I'll be home as soon as I can. Just stay in the house. Don't open the door!"

Navy's hysterical voice came through the chaos of the doorbell ringing, the pounding on the door, and my upset mom. I could hear her clearly, her young voice distressed. "Daddy won't hurt me," she cried. "Let me talk to Daddy! I'll be fine! He'll listen to me."

The lawyer leaned over the table and said, "Tell her to call the police, now."

I told my mom to call the police and hung up. I glared at my lawyer, my eyes burning with the accusation, *do you believe me now?*

She sat up straight in her office chair. "This is exactly why EPOs were created—for people like you, in this situation." She then leapt out of her chair and braced her hands on her desk.

"Are you ready to stand up and talk about this in front of a judge? Let's get this done."

We entered a courtroom and stood before a judge. In the viewing seats, a handful of people sat waiting for their case to be heard. I thought I might be able to testify to my need for an EPO standing next to my lawyer, but instead I was asked to take the witness stand.

My lawyer spoke on my behalf, describing the events that had taken place. She talked about Kevin's height and strength, indicating that he was much stronger than me and that I was unable to physically defend myself.

"He's a triathlete competitor, sir," she explained. "His size and strength make him especially dangerous to my client."

The judge looked at my arms and my face. "Are those cuts and bruises from your husband?"

"Yes," I replied.

The judge granted my request. I was given an Emergency Protection Order against my husband.

I checked in with my mom as I headed out of the courtroom. Eventually, Kevin had stopped banging on the door and screaming. West texted me that his dad had left. They didn't know where he had gone, but he was no longer outside the door. I told her to take the kids bowling and to a movie to get their minds off what was happening. I had been gone most of the day, but finally left the courthouse with my EPO in hand and instructions to go to the police station next. The order forbade Kevin from coming within 1,600 feet of me, my kids, or my mom.

When I arrived at the District 2 police station I was assigned an officer who was refreshingly kind, and at that point the nicest person I had met since this had all started. She took me in a separate room, listened to my story, reviewed the order, and explained how it would be served to Kevin. I asked her about charging him and she suggested that now that I had the EPO, I wouldn't gain anything by charging Kevin.

"Sometimes it's better to not poke the bear," she said.

She commented on the police report from the night before. Each of the officers had recorded an entirely different story about the incident.

By the time I was on my way back to my mom's house, it was almost dinner time. I had spent the entire day away from my kids, but it had been to put structures in place to protect them, and myself.

Less than half a block away from my mom's house, I pulled over on a quiet residential street to use my cell phone. In my rearview mirror I saw a flash of headlights from a car pulling up behind me. It was Kevin's car. Terrified, I hit the gas and sped away with him close behind me. I called 911 as I tried to maneuver away from Kevin.

"We're trying to locate Mr. Sykes in order to serve him the EPO," a dispatcher said to me.

"He's right here, following me in his car," I explained, trying not to lose control.

I gave them my location and the direction in which I was driving. They told me to pull over and they would send a car to my location, but I was too afraid to stop. My phone buzzed endlessly and Kevin's number flashed on the screen. I declined every call. I made a sharp turn with one hand on the wheel and one on my phone, hoping I would go through a light just as it turned and that Kevin would get caught at an intersection. My heart was racing and my hands were clenched. I took a deep breath and checked my rearview mirror. Kevin's car had vanished. Traffic behind me was calm. Only random cars going to their destinations. I drove on for several minutes, checking the mirror, and realizing he was gone.

I returned to my mom's house, looking over my shoulder until I was safely back inside with the door locked. I called the police, who told me to stay in and they would notify me as soon as they had located Kevin and the EPO was served. I waited anxiously for my cell phone to ring, each buzz or notification making me flinch. It wasn't long after that I received a phone call from a police officer telling me they had served Kevin with the EPO. Kevin had been compliant, he said. Officers had escorted him home to get some of his things. He understood, the officer assured me, that if Kevin were to come within 1,600 feet, he would be immediately arrested.

"The EPO is officially in place now," he said.

My body and mind flooded with relief. I felt safe. For the first time in almost all of our marriage, I felt like Kevin couldn't hurt me, even if he wanted to. My relief was mixed with the recognition that I had been living my whole adult life on high alert, anxious and afraid of what would set Kevin off, what he would do, how he would hurt me. Now, he couldn't come near me. Sixteen hundred feet is a long distance. I had a week of safety under this emergency protection order. Then, I would need to apply for an extended one.

With Kevin gone, I took the kids back to the house so they could sleep in their own beds. As I tucked them in, I realized that when they had woken up this morning, they had no idea what their father had done to me. With the house quiet at last, I crawled into my bed. The house felt suddenly spacious, the air calm, with no feeling of fore-boding or that something was lurking. Nothing was going to happen to me. I could sleep, alone, and let my body fully relax. I replayed the incident from the night before. How Kevin had thrown me, quite literally, into freedom. My story was out now: my neighbor knew, the police knew, the kids knew. My secret was living outside me. The world hadn't collapsed because I had told the truth. My lawyer had believed me. My therapist had believed me. The courts had done their job to protect me. And here I was—still myself, still with my children, still with determination and fortitude driving me forward. That night I slept more deeply than I had in over two decades, finally beginning to believe that life could be different.

CHAPTER EIGHT

At the kids' swim meet, only a day after I received my EPO, I felt lighter and freer than ever before. I looked around the massive recreation center, which I had been to hundreds of times, but it was as though I was seeing it for the first time. Even though it was the same bustling place it had always been, there was a peace and calm that was somehow different, like a protective layer of silence encircling it. *Kevin can't come here*, I thought. He was forbidden from coming to the pool or the kids' school.

As I sat with my mom in the stands, I felt myself relax, a full-bodied exhale, a release of vigilance. I'd always loved watching West and Navy swim, and for the first time I wasn't worried about whether Kevin was going to make a scene on the pool deck, or yell at one of the coaches, or shamelessly flirt with the other swim moms while I looked on. My friend Lisa Streu waved and climbed the bleachers to sit next to me. She and I had become good friends serving on the board of directors of the swim club together.

"How's it going?" she asked.

"Okay," I replied. It was the truth. I was doing okay.

We made small talk for a while, catching up about her two daughters and all their activities. And then I found myself taking a breath and saying to her, "Kevin and I are getting a divorce."

She was taken aback by the news, but her face quickly turned sympathetic and kind.

"What happened?" she asked.

I pulled up my sleeves and then pointed to my chin and my cheeks. My face was still scratched from being thrown into the moving boxes. Finger-sized marks across my forearm were turning black and purple, and the large bruise on my shoulder showed where his fist had landed. Lisa gasped.

"I'm so sorry," she said. "I can't believe it."

Her words conveyed her shock and disbelief, but she did believe me. She listened intently as I explained that this kind of abuse had been happening throughout our entire marriage. I told her about the other night, the police, the protection order. I told her these things I had kept secret for so long.

Saying these things out loud used to be my greatest fear. Having someone know that I was being abused used to terrify me and fill me with shame. But the words cascaded from me like a dam had been released. The words flooded the air between me and Lisa. And she didn't leave. She didn't judge me. She didn't tell me I was crazy or wrong. She just listened.

A version of myself I had kept hidden suddenly came to life with these truths spilling out. It was deeply vulnerable and scary, but it was honest and it was real. I could feel myself growing lighter with each word.

Lisa's reaction to the news was not only compassionate and sympathetic, but also informative. I began to hope that others might respond like this too, believing my story and offering support. Maybe telling others might turn out differently than I had imagined it would for so long. Lisa didn't ask me very many details. It seemed she was still trying to process what I had told her. Like most people who knew me at the pool, she had seen me as the capable and fearless president of our large swim club, who didn't seem to take orders from anyone.

Over the course of the next few days, I would call my friends, including Nicole, Traci, and Stacey. I would tell them each that Kevin and I were divorcing, and the truth about why. I didn't hide any part of the truth from them. I didn't try to gloss over any of the horror that I had lived with and hidden from them for so long. That it had started at the very beginning of our marriage and had never stopped. Everyone expressed shock. They couldn't believe that what had seemed to many like an ideal marriage had been such a nightmare. It began to sink in that all the energy I had put into creating the facade of a happy marriage had only disconnected me from people who truly loved me and cared about my well-being. Nicole cried, pierced at having her earlier suspicions confirmed, and out of deep empathy for my pain. Traci listened quietly. After I told her the whole story and hung up, I was surprised to see her number appear on my phone just a short while later.

"Hi," she said sheepishly. "Sorry to call you back so soon, but can I ask you a question?"

"Yes," I said.

"How are you…" she began, searching for a word. "…so normal?"

"What do you mean?" I asked.

"I've known you for a long time. You've been one of my best friends and I know who you are as a mother, a leader, and a woman. Now, knowing what happened to you, I just…I don't know how you are the way you are. So strong and pulled together. So *normal*."

I didn't know how to respond. Traci's words struck me deeply and made me see the old dynamic with Kevin a little more clearly. Looking back, I always knew the abuse wasn't my fault. I knew that I didn't deserve the way Kevin had treated me and I was never to blame for how he behaved. But I did mistakenly believe that my purpose was to be the "normal" one, the responsible one, the one who could "fix" Kevin. Of course, that should have never been my burden to carry, but in the end, it's what kept me sane and high-functioning.

"It's a miracle," Traci continued. "How you've raised those kids and taken care of yourself, and how you've survived it all with the life that you've had."

I didn't know what to say. I knew there was much untangling to do about the life I had shown the world and the life I had lived in secret. All I knew in the moments of these truth-telling conversations was that showing all of me, not just part of me, was long overdue. I was excited to be open and authentic in all facets of my life now and I was done protecting Kevin at the expense of my own sanity. I no longer actually cared if anyone believed me.

I was acutely aware that Kevin had a talent for convincing people to accept his distorted version of events, and was likely to sway some who may have initially been inclined to believe my account. I suspected he would do what he always did: take responsibility for his actions while mixing in some fiction and a few facts to make himself the victim. By the end of the conversation, his story would be the most tragic and they would be comforting him. While they might hear Kevin's distorted version of events, that was no longer my concern. I knew *my* truth. I knew *the* truth. The more times I said the truth out loud, the more I could feel myself aligning with reality, the more solid I began to feel. The truth, even with all its ugliness and shame and fear, was out. The truth was mine to own, mine to share, mine to reckon with. And it was through the truth that I would finally be able to move forward. It was as if I could feel myself coming back to life with every word of the truth.

The swim meet ended, I said goodbye to Lisa, and I told the kids I would pull the car up to the entrance and wait for them to finish changing. As I waited in the roundabout, a car pulled up to my bumper. I looked in my rearview mirror and could see it was Kevin. He got out and walked toward me. My breath caught as I watched his face appear outside my window. He smiled slightly and raised a hand, not exactly in a wave but he gestured to me to roll down the window. He started talking to me through the glass, saying that he had something important to tell me. I cracked my window and said angrily, "What are you doing? You can't be here!"

"I know," Kevin replied. "I'm sorry. But thank you for talking to me."

"What do you want?"

"I don't want anything, Elaine. I'm just trying to help you."

"How exactly, Kevin?" I rolled my eyes.

"It's Karla," he said. "She's gone crazy. You're in danger."

"What does that even mean?" I asked. I knew Kevin would use whatever excuse he needed to in order to not stay away. Now he was suggesting that my life was in danger.

"You know she's crazy," he replied. "You know how she is. I think she might come after you. Stay away from your windows."

"Why don't *you* tell her to stay away from me?" I demanded.

"We broke up," he replied. "I've cut her out of my life."

"Then why is she coming after me?"

"She's mad," Kevin said. "She's mad because I told her I wanted to be with you, not her."

"Leave immediately, Kevin, or I'm going to call the police," I said.

And with that, Kevin turned and went back to his car, got in, and drove away. A predictable follow-up text arrived later that evening. *Thank you for talking to me. I miss you.* His antics weren't a surprise, but I did wonder if he was telling the truth. I knew Karla lacked boundaries and integrity. I knew she'd had a troubled past and I didn't doubt she could act irrationally. But I wondered if I was actually in danger.

On Monday, four days after my escape and before my week-long EPO expired, I went to apply for a year-long protection order. I went alone while the kids were in school. I knew that Claire would have come with me, but I chose to go alone. Partly it was because I felt strong and free and safe. However, a part of me still struggled with asking for help and letting go of my constant insistence that "I've got this!" I would repeat this phrase to myself, my mom, my friends, my kids, and anyone who needed anything at all: a side effect of my helpful nature mixed with a fierce independence.

And I got this done too. I had a full year of protection from Kevin, ordered and enforced by law. I got to determine the boundaries of his contact with the kids. I was in charge of how we moved forward. But before I left the courthouse, I made a stop on the third floor and changed my last name back to Hartrick. I was only a few days into my new life and shedding my old one couldn't happen fast enough.

The first few days after Kevin was out of the house, the kids slept with me, Navy in my bed and West on a mattress on the floor next to us. We kept each other company through the biggest change of our lives. Navy still sang herself to sleep. West still looked on the bright side and kept his calm demeanor.

The year-long EPO allowed Kevin to have the kids on some weekends, and only a few days later their first overnight visit was scheduled. As I helped Navy and West pack a bag, I realized the moment had now come that I had worried about since they were babies. Kevin would have them unsupervised and I wouldn't be there as a buffer between them anymore. What would happen without me as their shield, without me to see two steps ahead and know when Kevin was about to explode, and make sure that I took the brunt of his anger instead of them?

They got in the car and we set off to the hotel Kevin was staying at. I coached them on the drive over on what to do if Kevin got mad, making sure they knew I would stay by the phone in case they needed anything. The weekend went by quietly and I anxiously awaited their arrival Sunday night. When they came through the door, I greeted them excitedly, but Navy looked troubled and went straight to her room. West followed through the door, cheerfully saying hello, but he also went straight to his room and turned on a video game. Worried that my greatest fears had been realized and Kevin had abused them, I immediately went to Navy's room to help her get ready for bed and talk with her. As I was tucking her in, she started to cry.

"What's wrong, Navy?" I asked, worried about what she was about to tell me.

"Daddy says that he still loves you and he wants us to all be a family again. He says he knows he gets mad sometimes, but he promises he'll work on it and it's you breaking up our family."

"Navy, that's not okay. Daddy shouldn't be saying those things to you. I know this is hard for you and West, but remember why we're getting a divorce? It's because of the things Daddy does to me. It's not okay."

"He can change, Mommy, he really can. He said he can."

Navy then told me that Kevin had talked about the three children that he had with Beth. "You know how he never sees them, Mommy?" she began sadly. "He said that could happen to me and West too. He said he might as well pack up and move to Australia if we can't be a family anymore!"

She was distressed, talking to me as if she had the power to make everything better. West's story of the weekend was similar. It took a while to explain to both kids that while their dad was free to want whatever he wanted, that it wasn't right for him to put these grown-up issues on their shoulders.

"All I want you to think about," I said reassuringly, "is school, your friends, sports, swimming, and playing. There is nothing else for you to worry about, I promise."

Navy and West seemed to hear what I said and calm down, but inside I was aflame with rage at Kevin's cruelty and outright manipulation. Later, the kids revealed the extent of what Kevin had said to them over the weekend. That he would "never sign the divorce papers." That the only thing keeping our family from being together was me. That their grandmother was helping to "gang up on" him. That he wanted a "more fair" custody arrangement and that West, who prized fairness, should help make Kevin's time more fair. That he might as well move, at least to British Columbia, if we couldn't be a family anymore, and wouldn't it be terrible if he lost contact with Navy and West, the same way he did with his other three children?

I left a message with my lawyer as soon as the kids were in bed, desperate for some kind of legal action that would force Kevin to stop his manipulations. Hours after I had put the kids to bed, I heard Navy stop singing and creep softly out of her bedroom.

"What is it, sweetie?" I asked, looking at her at the top of the stairs.

"Could you give Daddy another chance, Mommy?" she asked softly.

Her question hurt so much I could feel my heart pounding. "I'm so sorry, Navy—I can't. I know it's hard to understand. I love you more than anything. Everything is going to be okay."

I wanted to make her happy and ached to take away her sadness, but I couldn't. Navy paused and nodded, pushing back the tears that were starting. But as she turned back toward her room she said softly, "Daddy said that he might not be okay if we can't be together as a family."

I looked at Navy and tried to process what she was telling me. Did Kevin really scare them into thinking he might harm himself if I didn't take him back? My fear of Kevin abusing West and Navy on their first weekend unsupervised had come true, but not in the way I had thought it might.

My conversation with Claire the next day was full of panic. The only remedy she could offer was a letter to Kevin's lawyer, laying out everything he had said to the kids and threatening to make his time with the kids supervised if this behavior continued. I then phoned

Kevin and chastised him for upsetting the kids and told him how distraught they were. His only response was that he meant what he said and that he didn't regret anything he told them.

"I do love you and I want us to be a family again. I miss you. This is just wrong."

I vowed to be the kids' voice of reassurance and calm. Whatever their father spewed at them, I would make sure they knew they were loved and safe when with me. I would make sure to shield them from any stressful details, and I would be the one to keep my emotions in check, never forcing them to shoulder what wasn't theirs to carry. I wished they had two parents who would do this for them.

It had been a little over a week since Kevin had confronted me at the pool and warned me about Karla. I found myself up late one night watching TV. Around 11:00 p.m., my doorbell rang. The kids were in bed and the house was dark except for the glow of the television screen. Alarmed, Swizzle leapt off the couch and ran to the door, barking loudly. I followed her, and saw a male figure running away from the house. The person scrambled into a car at the end of my driveway and drove away quickly. A few days later, I again noticed a car outside the house late at night. This time, I was upstairs, looking out the hallway window. A car was parked in front of the house, idling with its lights on. Then it pulled out and drove by slowly, only to reappear as if it had circled the block. After it made two more trips around, I called the police. But by the time an officer arrived, the car was gone.

Despite the appearances of strange cars at my home, there were no further incidents, and life did start to settle down. It was a stretch of time when I started making plans for the future. I decided to sell the house, which was far too big for us and still not entirely unpacked. Ultimately, the house meant nothing to me or the kids. It had been a dream, yet another way to try and paper over what was irreparably broken. But a dream house could never have made us happy because it would never have changed Kevin.

Incredibly, I found an available lot in a new residential development just half a mile away and our *new* dream was born. I would build a house and a home for me and Navy and West. It would be our fresh start, filled with love and hope for the future, never to be darkened by Kevin's manipulations or my secrets. I would sell most of our shared possessions, not only to downsize but also to clear out all the old gloom. So many of those objects bore the weight of my loneliness. I had picked them by myself because Kevin had never cared or bothered to help with making our home. The furniture and art of the old house were reminders of our split lives under one roof. But this new house would be the first thing of my own in twenty-three years.

Meanwhile, West was going through his own difficult transition. After school one afternoon, he came bounding in for his usual snack, but he seemed quiet and a little uncomfortable.

"How was school, sweetie?" I asked lightly.

"Fine."

"Anything interesting happen?" I pressed.

"Yeah, I got asked about you and Dad."

"What do you mean?" My curiosity was piqued.

The story came out in pieces as he stood beside me at the stove while I made dinner. He had been pulled out of class and taken to the office. He met with a man who asked him questions about his home. *Do you feel safe at home? Do you feel safe with your mom and your dad? Have you ever seen your parents fight? Have they ever hurt each other? Have you ever been hurt?*

My heart started to pound and my mind started racing, trying to figure out who would pull my son out of class and ask him questions that had nothing to do with his schoolwork.

"What teacher was that?" I asked.

"I don't think he was a teacher. I've never seen him before." West said.

My stomach sank and then it was on fire. *We're going to have to get other people involved and you won't like it.* My mind returned to the police officer who had answered my 911 call at my neighbor's house. He had made good on his threat with Child Protective Services. They had come to the school and interviewed West, alone, without my knowledge and definitely not my permission.

I was repulsed. *Don't you know who I am as a mother? You have no idea what I've gone through to make sure they have been safe, and it's now that their safety is in question?* I was insulted, offended, and furious. I then heard my own words echoing: *Yes, he's a danger to them. Now will you make him leave?* Then a new and terrifying thought came to me. *Someone else can be in charge of my children without my consent.* It was a strange, almost detached feeling that I wasn't going to tolerate— *no stranger is going to decide what happens in my children's lives.* I would protect them from that too, just as I had spent their lives protecting them from harm at all costs. I felt like all my sacrifices and my very motherhood were being scrutinized, questioned, cast into doubt.

I assured West that everything was fine, that the chat he had wasn't going to change anything about our lives, that he had done the right thing by telling the truth. When Navy got home, she told the same story about the man with the questions.

When they were both in their rooms doing their homework, I called the principal.

"Yes," he confirmed. "They did talk to West and Navy. I have the investigator's number and I think you need to give him a call." I hung up the phone, mortified.

I arranged to meet with the investigator in person the following week. He notified me that Kevin would be interviewed, too, but separately from me. When I sat across from him, I didn't wait for his report. I told him how inappropriate I thought it was to ambush my kids at school, while I hadn't been around. I recounted everything we had been through in the last month, everything I had done to get them to safety without disrupting their lives or losing my own.

He nodded slowly. "I believe you," he said. "I'm going to close your case."

Not long after that visit, I picked West up from school and while I was driving him to swim practice, I asked about his day. He responded quietly. I thought, *What now?* What could it be this time? Just when I thought he was getting back to his old carefree self.

"Something on your mind?" I asked.

"No. We just had health class today."

"Oh, that sounds interesting. What did you learn about?"

"Abuse." West's voice was almost a whisper and his eyes were fixed out the window. I let the silence hold us for a moment.

"Oh," I said softly. "That must have been hard to sit through. I'm sorry."

"Yeah," he replied.

"Do you have any questions for me?"

"No." After a moment, West continued, "I told my friend Ryan, from swimming, that you and Dad are getting a divorce."

"Oh?" I replied. "What did Ryan say?"

West looked at me. "He said that he wished his parents would get a divorce too. He said they don't get along at all."

"Sometimes married people have complicated problems, sweetie."

West didn't answer. He was quiet for the rest of the drive to the pool, but I could tell things were settling in. He was telling people about the big changes in our family and neither of us were afraid to tell the truth.

What are the Shadows in my life?

From when I was a little kid to last year
My Dad would beat my mom, My mom would
shadow me from the Sun (my dad) and say she
tripped or she ran into something. When I found out
I was really sad because of found out the truth
after something really bad happened.
I think a shadow is something that is able
to cover something up. It's like on Christmas day,
you take off the wrapping paper and it's
something disappointing or something you don't like

West, Social Studies Assignment, Ninth Grade

My mom and my friends surrounded me with their love and support. I continued to talk with my mom frequently, relying on her sensitive listening and thoughtful advice to get me through the thousand details I needed to figure out about moving forward with my life. My friends Nicole and Traci flew out to spend time with me. I even took the step of organizing a party to ring in the new year with just my best girlfriends. My church community offered their support as well, without any stigma or judgment. Meanwhile, I was deep in project mode with the new house.

Kevin agreed to have me sell most of our things, but complained about it nonetheless. After hosting a series of garage sales, one day I hauled an enormous load of Kevin's unsold old books to a used book-store in town. I left them to be priced and returned the next day to collect whatever they chose not to take. As I greeted the shop owner, she offered to carry the box and walk me to my car with the leftover books. Appreciating the extra customer service, I chatted with her about her quaint store, but when we reached my car she looked at me and paused, appearing to want to say something, but then nervously stopped. Instead, she handed me one of Kevin's business leadership books, positioned differently on the top of the pile.

"I just wanted you to know," she said softly, "that there were photos in this one."

I slowly opened the cover to find pictures of Karla, naked, legs spread, hands on her privates, and in all sorts of other vulgar poses. Slamming the book shut, I blurted out the only thing that came to mind, "That isn't me! She's blond!"

The shop owner was kind, if a little awkward. "This is just one of the reasons I'm getting a divorce," I said as I loaded the books and the photos into my car.

Secrets have a way of spilling out, sometimes in the worst places. I wondered what else I would find hiding as I packed up our old life and headed toward my new one. I thought I knew all of Kevin's secrets, but clearly there were ones I couldn't have even guessed.

At long last, the hardest year of my life came to an end. In the new year, I looked forward to building a house for us, finalizing the divorce, finding a new career path for myself, and slowly but very surely moving forward. But we were hardly two months into the new year before a new upheaval began.

"Can I stay for the whole week?" Navy pleaded into the phone. She and West had spent another weekend with their dad and were due to come home that night, Sunday, and get ready for the school week. "No, you have school," I said, holding my voice steady. *Not this again*, I thought.

"You can't do this!" Navy cried. "It's not fair. You're not being fair. Just let me stay!"

I took a deep breath. I tried to be understanding, since she and West were still adjusting to going back and forth from our home to Kevin's condo, which he had rented a few miles away from us.

"You need to come home," I continued. "You'll see your dad again in just a few days."

As Navy was growing more upset on the phone I quickly reached for a compromise.

"Navy, everything is okay. Maybe you can stay for an extra night. How does that sound? An extra night is fine, but not the whole rest of the week."

She said she would tell her dad and hung up. I waited for her to call back, praying that she was okay. I knew she was being told to ask for more time with her dad. Navy didn't call me back. Instead, Kevin's car pulled up with both kids and their packed bags inside. Navy's face was red and streaked with tears. As she opened the front door, she headed straight for her room.

"You're ruining my life!" she yelled as she stormed up the stairs. "Dad wouldn't let us stay an extra night with him because you wouldn't let us stay for the whole week." And then she disappeared into her room. West came in after her and went quietly to his room too. After a few minutes, I knocked on Navy's door. She was calm enough to talk to, but clearly still on edge.

"Navy," I began, "it wasn't fair for Daddy to do that. These arrangements were made by us as grown-ups, and we have to stick to them. I know it's hard. But it's not okay for Daddy to make deals with you about your time with him or with me."

She nodded but stayed quiet. I wanted to believe that she heard me. But Kevin was the one I really needed to hear me. I needed him to hear that it was damaging to talk to the kids about the divorce arrangements, or make them feel responsible for keeping him happy.

* * *

Another condition of the year-long EPO was that Kevin could call the kids once each night, just before bedtime, while I listened closely nearby. The kids could call him as often as they wanted, if they wanted. There were no restrictions, however, on his contact with me. His texts and emails alone were overwhelming in number, and began almost as soon as the first EPO was in place. From the moment we separated for the last time, Kevin was unrelenting in his campaign to get me to change my mind and stop the divorce. The version of Kevin who initially said he was happy about it was now nowhere to be found. With dramatic professions of his love and devotion, abject apologies, and promises to change, he was incessant in his effort to have me take him back. I ignored or talked past his messages, keeping my communications strictly about the kids.

He also continuously told the kids how much he loved me, how desperately he wanted us to stay married, and how I was the one choosing to break up our family. One of his most frequent tactics was to apologize to the kids for the awful incident back in October that caused me to leave, while downplaying its severity at the same time.

I noticed that the intensity of his efforts started to ease slightly right around the time that Navy had been shattered by his refusal to let her stay an extra night. But I discovered the reason when I heard Navy say on one of her nightly calls to Kevin, "Hi, Karla." My head snapped around, but I decided to wait until after their call to ask. I learned that Kevin was bringing Karla and her kids from Edmonton to stay with him almost every time Navy and West were over.

"How often?" I asked them as I digested this news.

"Most of the time," West replied earnestly.

"Sometimes Daddy is working and we just hang out with Karla," Navy added.

I roiled with disbelief and rage. The depth of Kevin's selfishness was stunning, even after all those years of catering to his deeply capricious nature. It was becoming ever clearer that his constant petitioning for more time with our kids and the barrage of complaints about the restrictions of the EPO wasn't even about the kids. He only got them every other weekend, and still couldn't manage to give them the attention they deserved. It seemed to me to be more about my *not* having them than him having them.

When they were with me, he texted them pictures of himself with Karla and her kids, Matt and Maya. He captioned them with *Wish you were here. This is so much fun!* Navy and West gazed longingly at their snapshots of the zoo, mini golf, the wave pool. The four of them looked like they were having the time of their lives and my kids ached with envy. *Wish we were there, too,* West texted back. *If you want to be here, just ask Mommy,* Kevin replied. Often he would add, *I love your mom. She chose this.*

Kevin's texts would send us into the same routine every time. The kids asked me if they could join Kevin and Karla on whatever thrilling adventure they had Matt and Maya on, and when I said no, they were crestfallen and grew more and more bitter. They wanted to be with me, but they wanted to be with their dad and other kids. Kevin wouldn't stop dangling these pictures in front of them, making them feel like they were constantly missing out, like he was living a new life with a new family, all without them. Sometimes Kevin would text pictures of himself and Karla, without the kids—selfies of them at a fancy dinner or out on the town.

But the ones that stung my kids the most were of their dad and Karla's family. And I was always the one standing in their way of their joining in. I always said *No, you need to do homework, go to practice, get to bed on time.* I kept the rules and the routine, doing everything to ensure predictability in their lives, and Kevin was using it to make me seem like I wanted to destroy their fun. I kept the kids in school, going to swim practice, attending church, and seeing their friends, trying to maintain the semblance of stability I knew they needed.

* * *

The change in Navy wasn't overnight, or even major at first. She had mostly maintained, miraculously, her sweet and tender self throughout these tumultuous months, and I felt just as close to her as ever. We texted each other like close friends, sometimes dozens of times each day, and often during school hours when Navy knew she shouldn't be using her phone. But she would text to say hi, to see how my day was going, to tell me some juicy news about the girls in her class, or how she had done on an exam she had been nervous about. Always effusive and expressive, she told me she loved me constantly. She told me I was her best friend. Her natural humor was irresistible, as it had been since she was old enough to talk.

But gradually, Navy became more and more defiant, refusing to clean her room, brush her teeth, or do her homework. At times she raised her voice or slammed a door. Her pushback was often repeating the line, "Daddy says I don't have to," as if to challenge my authority with his absent but looming undermining. And then she shifted to "I don't have to do that." It was like she absorbed Kevin's permissiveness, his disregard of my parenting. Eventually, after holding the line for long enough, I would make sure she did what I asked, even if it meant stony silence or outright anger from her. I knew all this behavior could be part of her adjustment or it could be part of being an adolescent. But with our lives thrown into such sudden change, it was hard to know what was normal or not.

As much as I tried to maintain a normal schedule and routine for the kids, Kevin seemed determined to disrupt it at every turn. Even though he was now fully with Karla, he continued with his incessant emails and texts asking me to reconsider the divorce. His pleas included declarations of love combined with vicious blame and accusations. His words were a storm of anything he could think of to either ply me back into his life, make me feel responsible for his happiness, or tear me down so badly that I would return to him out of some sense of guilt. One message would say, "I'm a loser," and "It was my evil that hurt you." The next would berate me for being "selfish" and "ruining his life." It felt like the same old gaslighting. Often, during our marriage, Kevin would talk to me like this until my head would spin. His verbal barrage was designed to confuse, offering compliments and shame in the same breath.

Then it was the texts about the kids. Kevin never texted me about co-parenting. Not surprisingly, we didn't communicate like I imagined divorced people would, keeping our focus on the kids' schedules and their lives. Instead, whatever the schedule was, he would sabotage my efforts to maintain a consistent and stable routine. Kevin told me repeatedly how miserable they were with me and how happy they were when they were with him. He painted a picture of my single-handed damage to them, without evidence or example, aside from his insistence that my "ego" was to blame. It felt like classic projecting from someone whose outsized ego drove his every move.

The texts between Kevin and the kids, which I gained access to much later, revealed the true extent of his manipulation. He talked to each of them about the other's behaviors, pitting West and Navy against each other, especially whenever one of them would advocate for me. He constantly burdened them with his emotions, and worst, he included Karla on everything. She began texting them and interacting with them on social media, actively encouraging any disparaging remarks about me and offering "sympathy" when they were angry at me. She endorsed and mirrored Kevin's manipulations and pushed the kids to think about *his* feelings. When I finally saw the extent of her complicity, my heart sank that someone with kids of her own would try to drive a wedge between me and my children.

I could sense a shift happening, but I couldn't put my finger on the change yet. I knew that with our separate households, I could not control anything between Kevin and the kids anymore. I could have faith that I had raised them to be honest and to act with integrity, and they could speak to me openly about anything on their minds. But I also knew that when they were with their dad, they could hear *anything* from him. A few months after I left, I had the kids at my mom's house on a Sunday. At the end of the evening, after dinner, I told Navy to finish her homework. She refused. I insisted she finish it for school the next day but she just turned and walked coolly into the next room. When she returned, she told me that she had just gotten off the phone with Kevin.

"Daddy says I don't have to do my homework," she reported.

"Well," I replied, still wrapping my head around the situation, "Daddy is not here. I'm your mom, and I said you need to go do your homework."

"He says I'm old enough to make my own decisions," she said even more boldly.

"Well, not about this," I said. "School is not optional and you don't get to decide to not do your homework."

Navy frowned and crossed her arms. "But Daddy says it's *my* life and *I* get to choose."

"Enough, Navy," I said firmly. You are old enough to make your own decisions about some things, but not everything. And there are things you have to do, like homework, that we are not discussing anymore."

"Fine!" Navy burst out with tears in her eyes and raging injustice in her voice.

She stormed off and I started to think about all the other moments of defiance that were becoming more regular in our lives. I would have never dreamed of interfering with Kevin's parenting in this way, or of putting my kids in the middle of some kind of parenting war. Deep down, I knew Kevin could care less about Navy doing her homework or not while she was with me. This all seemed like a way to use her, to cause a rift in our relationship. No matter how often I called and confronted Kevin about how damaging this behavior was, they didn't stop. My lawyer could do nothing but send letters to his lawyer, but there was nothing legally compelling Kevin to put his kids before himself, just as he didn't when he gave the kids detailed information about our divorce, or worse, asked them disingenuously for advice.

By the time the year-long EPO was nearly set to expire, it hardly felt like it held any weight at all. From the beginning, Kevin pushed and broke the boundaries of our custody arrangement. It was little things at first—an extra hour here or there, an extra night so the kids could attend a party or playdate at the zoo—so that Kevin could have them for longer. I wanted to say yes because I didn't want my children to suffer from the arrangement, stuck in the middle and losing out on fun activities. At least weekly, they were asking me to adjust our schedule, usually to spend more time at Kevin's. He never asked me himself; he always made the kids ask. When I said no, which happened about half of the time, the kids would be upset, sometimes in tears, begging me to change my mind. I was either the bad guy or the pushover. I couldn't win, ever.

What I didn't realize at the time was that I wasn't saying "yes" to the kids, I was saying it to Kevin. I relented and I gave in for the kids' sake, but it was sending Kevin the message that he could get what he wanted if he just had the kids push hard enough. Once, when I put my foot down about a youth group activity the kids had planned to attend, Kevin poisoned them with a rant about how he hated church and how I cared more about church than letting the kids spend time with him. Soon, they began asking me if they had to go to church at all.

I could almost understand it if Kevin were spending every extra moment with them, but in reality, from what I could gather, he had Karla over almost constantly and the kids rarely had any alone time with their dad. He also regularly disrupted their scheduled time with him. One weekend, Karla's two kids were supposed to join them for some time together. Instead, after Kevin and Karla had another of their frequent and tumultuous fights, Kevin canceled on *our* kids. Their entire weekend was off because the fight meant that Kevin didn't want to see Karla's kids at all, which meant that no one could come over.

It was as if he thrived on pure chaos as much as he did sabotaging my relationship with the kids. And yet, while West and Navy were with me, Kevin continued to barrage them with calls and texts. "I miss you," he would say, multiple times a day. "I'm lonely without you." They consoled him, assured him that they missed him too, and promised to see him soon. They were taking on the role of his emotional caretaker while always being kept on edge about his affections.

"Does Daddy tell you to ask me to let you stay longer?" I asked Navy one day. It was quiet and calm and I asked it as casually as I could.

"No, not exactly," she replied.

"What do you mean?" I asked.

"He just says things like, 'I wish we could have a movie night. But your mother expects you to go to her house. If you want to stay with me, you should probably ask her.' He says, 'Your mom's trying to keep you from spending time with me.' It should be equal."

I was furious at how he was using them, controlling them. The next day, I called Kevin.

"You can call me," I told him firmly, "if you want more time with the kids. Stop making them ask. It's not fair to them."

"What?" he asked. "If they want more time with me, why shouldn't they ask you for what they want?"

"You know why," I snapped. "You're putting them in the middle and trying to make me the villain. We're the parents. We're in charge of the schedule."

Kevin's voice softened and grew pleading, a tone I knew all too well. "I never wanted this, Elaine. These are my kids. We're destroying their lives. It's awful for them to not get both of us all of the time. You know how you can make this right?"

"No, Kevin, I don't," I replied, knowing exactly what he was going to say.

"We can be a family again. We *are* a family. We should be together. I'm sorry for everything I've done. I'll do whatever I can to fix it. Then we can stop torturing our children. It will be so much easier and better for everyone. Don't you want that too?"

Kevin's duplicitous maneuvering went beyond words. In July, right when our custody mediation hearing was being scheduled for later that month, he moved Karla and her kids from Edmonton to Calgary, just three blocks away from the house I was building. When I tried to sell our last home that we had owned together, I learned that Kevin had secretly placed a lien on it to pay for Karla's new house. I was furious. Despite this outrageous situation, Kevin and I still had to work out a new custody agreement before our year-long emergency agreement expired in October. Claire told me that I had a good chance of getting the arrangement I wanted, which would allow Kevin to have the kids for four days every other weekend and splitting summers and holidays evenly. Had Kevin been the father I had envisioned and hoped for for my children, I would have easily agreed to equal time between us. However, with Kevin's history I was not open to that arrangement.

The day of the mediation hearing, Claire told me reassuringly, "As their primary caregiver, now and throughout most of their lives, I think the mediator will favor your having primary custody."

I hoped she was right. I was also hoping for a legal reset. I wanted firm boundaries put into place, spelling out our time with the kids in black and white so that Kevin would finally stick to them. But when we arrived at a downtown high-rise with our lawyers and sat across from each other at a long conference table with the mediator to our side, Kevin's lawyer didn't hesitate to jump in.

"We're seeking full custody," he said sharply.

My jaw dropped. "Absolutely not," I snapped back. I was ready to lunge across the table but the mediator jumped in.

"I don't think that's a reasonable request, given that Mrs. Sykes is the one who currently has primary custody."

I was furious from the start. I had anticipated that Kevin would angle for more than he deserved, but this kind of bald-faced attempt to take my kids from me entirely was truly shocking. Over the next several hours, we argued over Kevin's outrageous requests, first for full custody, then for 50/50, despite the kids considering my home their primary residence, and despite my being the one who still did everything for them. Kevin had no idea what it was like to be a parent who was responsible for more than taking West and Navy to swim practice and drive-thru dinners. He hadn't done it while we were married; why should I believe Kevin would be any different now? I believed that Karla was only invited to Kevin's parenting time to take care of the children's basic needs—a role that he had no real interest in fulfilling himself. Kevin's petition, I believed, wasn't because he wanted to be a full-time parent; it was about winning the contest between us. But for me, the stakes were as high as possible: my children's happiness, and even safety, were on the line.

In mediation, I yet again had to argue for my work and worth as a mother, for my kids' best interests, for my right to be with them. It felt like talking to Child Protective Services and the EPO court all over again. However, I stayed calm through the absurdity, even conceding that of course I wanted the kids to be able to see their dad, and that I had no intention of keeping them away from him.

But it was when Kevin made a grab for my mom's money that I nearly lost it. When our house finally sold, we planned to divide the assets, except for the money that my mom had loaned us in order to make a down payment—which I planned to pay her back in full. But Kevin said he was entitled to half of it. Tears of rage began to flow as I thought about all my mom had sacrificed for us, only to have Kevin make a selfish claim on her generosity. She was a retired nurse on a pension and Kevin made four times what my mom did. Our voices began to rise and soon Kevin and I were yelling over each other.

"Why don't you both step outside for a moment to clear the air," the mediator interrupted.

Shortly after we came back in, the mediator made her decision, which was final. Kevin would see the kids every other weekend, from Thursday night to Sunday night. We would split holidays and summers. It was exactly what I had asked for. I had won. And Kevin was furious. He slammed his things together and stormed out of the room. I thanked Claire and headed out. I couldn't believe that finally, after all the fighting I had done for my kids, a decision had favored me.

Claire and Kevin's lawyer must have gone a different way because I found myself alone in the lobby waiting for the elevator. Suddenly, Kevin appeared next to me. His face was red and contorted with rage. He loomed over me. It was all too familiar, his posture and his threat. But I wasn't at home where no one could help me. I was here, in a public building, and I had just won our custody agreement. I stood my ground. I didn't flinch. I stared right back into his menacing eyes.

"You," he seethed, his face nearly touching mine, "may have won here. But I promise you, I will win in the hearts and the minds of our children."

Without another word, he barged down the stairwell and left me to wait for the elevator in the now-deserted lobby.

I thought about the menacing words of his threat, of how often during our marriage Kevin would threaten me, how he could talk and talk until I was left turning in circles. But I was the one who knew every detail of West and Navy's lives. They were loyal and loving and if their father told them wicked lies about me, surely they could never believe them. Not after I had brought them up with rarely a hand from Kevin, showered them with love and affection, and had been there for every important and unimportant moment of their entire lives. As their primary parent, I had made sure they could share anything and everything with me, that they could count on me to know their friends, their favorite foods, and what would make them feel better when they were sick. I had taught them right from wrong, and the importance of being honest, kind, compassionate, and responsible. While Kevin was, without a doubt, powerfully deceptive, my kids knew me and they knew the truth. I went home that afternoon buoyed by the fact that Kevin was taking up less and less of my life, and that I had so much to look forward to at last. Looking back, I wish I had realized the depth of his rage and the validity of his threat. That mediation hearing was the last time I ever believed the law was on my side.

CHAPTER NINE

In September, a month before our new custody arrangement was set to begin, the kids texted me to ask for more time with their dad. It was only minutes before Kevin was supposed to pick them up at the pool. I said no. It was a school night and they had already had extra time with him that week. But just then my phone rang, with Kevin on the other line having a full-on tantrum. I had no idea what started it but maybe it was because he hadn't been able to exploit the mediation and custody arrangement to his benefit. I could hear that he was driving.

"I'm done! You can have the kids. I'm never seeing them again. They're not my children; I'm bringing them to you. Where are you? Right now, Elaine! Where are you?"

"Stop it, Kevin. Quit being ridiculous. What's the problem?"

He didn't respond, but instead kept yelling and repeating himself. Then he hung up. I called him back to see where the kids were, but he didn't answer. I started to panic. My phone chimed with a text from him: *I'm done. You can have the kids.* His texts echoed what he had spoken on the phone. *I'm never seeing them again.*

Then, a text from Kevin's phone typed from Navy flashed across my screen. *Mommy, I need my backpack!*

I gasped. I didn't realize West and Navy were *with* him in the car. I thought they were still at the pool waiting to be picked up. If Navy had Kevin's phone, she not only saw his cruel words, but both she and West were in the car listening to Kevin behaving hysterically and threatening to never see them again.

I texted Kevin back, telling him to calm down before he caused irrevocable damage. He continued to text me. *They're not my children. I'm seriously done. Don't ever bring these children near me again. Have a nice life. I'm done.*

I tried calling again, and this time he answered.

"Just bring them to me," I said, trying to keep my voice level.

"I'm bringing them now," he seethed. "I'm coming. You can have them because I am done. I'm seriously done. I'm not seeing them again. I'm on my way," he repeated.

"Stop it!" I yelled, now knowing the kids were in the car with him. "What is the matter with you?"

The kids were quiet when Kevin arrived at my house. They crept out of the car without a word and rushed inside and Kevin turned and sped off. Inside, I gave Navy and West a few minutes to settle in before calling them into the living room.

"I'm sorry you had to hear your dad say that," I began.

"It's not fair," Navy jumped in before I could say more. "We should be getting more time with Dad."

"It should be fifty-fifty," West added. "That would be fair."

These were the same words Kevin had been using since we separated. The kids sounded like little tape recorders repeating back his words.

"This is the arrangement," I explained. "These are the rules about your time with me and your dad. We have to follow the rules."

I tried to appeal to their sense of rule-following, which was especially keen in West.

"Do you think Daddy will ever see us again?" Navy asked softly.

"Yes, for sure he will," I assured her. "Your dad was just upset. He didn't mean what he said."

I found myself trying to explain away Kevin's behavior, smoothing over his damage like I always had. I couldn't stop myself from protecting my kids from their dad's dark side. For their entire lives, I tried to ensure they had a good image of their father, to spare them from the devastation of knowing his true character. I believed that knowing the truth about Kevin would cause them to hate him, and that hating your own father would damage anyone.

And then, there was the added layer of my own need to protect them from any kind of harm. I wanted so badly for my children to be happy. I thought it was possible to be the mom who provided them with a childhood free from distress. They were so innocent, so pure, so loving and good, that it seemed terribly unfair for them to be hurt or to have their hearts broken. They didn't deserve emotional scars. But then, who does? None of us. We can't really do anything to avoid the everyday pain of life, not even to completely avoid the enormous pain of betrayal or abuse. It would take me a long time to come to terms with the fact that my children, resilient and strong as they were, would experience hurt and nevertheless overcome it.

Kevin apologized that evening over the phone. "I didn't mean it," I heard him say to the kids. "I was mad. I'm sorry."

Kevin had never been short on apologies after his horrific behavior toward me, and whatever remorse he expressed never actually changed his behavior. His apologies always started with him sorrowfully voicing responsibility but shrouding it in half-truths and excuses. His words of remorse were laced with professions of guilt, but ultimately he would end up blaming others. Now he was using those same words on the kids after hurting them. Once, back when we were still married, I overheard Kevin say to my mom, "You can do anything you want. You just have to apologize afterward." Kevin would then move on as though nothing had happened and appear confused or angry when others couldn't move on as quickly as he had.

Throughout our separation and divorce, his message was consistent and recurring: "This is just wrong. I will never get over that your mom divorced me. We should all be together. I've changed and she won't forgive me. She chose this."

He tried to convince the kids that their lives were in ruins because of their mom. I told them later that no matter how angry you are, you shouldn't say hurtful things, and you shouldn't blame your behavior on anyone else. I did everything I could to control Kevin's damage and his attempts to blame me for his failings. I underestimated him.

* * *

The new custody order was finally in place. On my days with the kids, Kevin could still drop them off or pick them up from school or practice, yet he never stopped complaining to me about how unfair everything was. Thankfully, his first official weekend with the kids seemed to go smoothly. There were no calls for more time, no abrupt changes in the schedule.

A few days later, however, Navy arrived home after Kevin dropped her off from swim practice. "Daddy wants me to swim with Matt and Maya."

"Like for a playdate?" I asked.

"No, on their team, in their club. I swam with them today. Dad took me to swim with their club today instead of taking me to our regular pool."

Since moving to Calgary, Karla had enrolled her kids in a swim club at a nearby pool, with whom our club competed. "I want to do it," Navy continued. "I want to swim with them. Daddy said I could."

"Wait, Navy," I began. "You already have a place in our swim club," I said firmly.

"But I want to. Daddy said it's a better club than the Patriots and he says that Joy is a terrible coach. He says it will be more fun, too." Her voice was bright and hopeful.

"Honey, you can't change swim clubs," I repeated. "You have a spot on your team and this is where you swim."

Navy's face fell. "Then I have to quit," she said mournfully.

"What are you talking about?"

"Daddy said if I don't move over to Matt and Maya's club, then I can't swim at all. Also, why can't I just move? Daddy says I'll like it better there. He said Joy doesn't pay enough attention to me and she doesn't know what she's doing."

"Let me sort this out, sweetie. Don't worry," I tried to reassure her. "You're going to be able to swim."

"That's not what Daddy said."

My first call was to our head coach, Jamie. I was still the president of the Calgary Patriots, where West and Navy swam and I knew the coach well. I couldn't calm myself enough to call Kevin yet and I needed to sort things out with Jamie first.

"Yeah," Jamie said on the phone. "I got a call from the other head coach, Mike. He's a good friend of mine," he explained. "We looked after it. Mike told your ex-husband that Navy isn't allowed to register at his club because she's already registered here. Well, it sounds like Mr. Sykes didn't take that well."

"Thanks for your help," I said.

Kevin and I argued on the phone later that night. How selfish could he be to not see that Navy was upset and confused over where she belonged and who she should try to please? In the end, Navy stayed with the Patriots, as did West. But a spark went out of her after this. She dragged her feet to practice after years of boundless enthusiasm.

She complained about her coach and her teammates. She asked to quit. Swimming had been poisoned for her, ruined, taken away. What could Kevin's motivation possibly have been? What could he be trying to get from her or from me with this game? Maybe it was because Kevin knew that if my kids didn't swim for the Patriots then I would be out of a volunteer job that I loved. He'd never made it a secret that he resented that I was the president there.

Kevin resumed inflicting chaos on the kids' schedules. Instead of leaving after he dropped them off at a swim meet, he would find a seat in the bleachers just close enough to me and my mom to make his presence known. He would arrive early to pick West up from the pool and take him to his house when he knew I would be looking for him. When I arrived at the pool one afternoon to find West nowhere in sight, I texted Kevin frantically. He replied that West was at his house, showering, as if this were perfectly normal and my response was a gross overreaction. *Bring him to the pool. I'm here, waiting for him. He's supposed to come home with me.* My text was met with, *Goodnight*. No matter how I insisted that his behavior was wrong, he responded with feigned innocence and shock at my emotions. A text followed from West, making excuses for his dad, acting as peacemaker and promising that I could pick him up at swimming the next day as usual.

I found out from the kids that Kevin continued to ask for their advice on the divorce. More than once he gave legal papers to West to hand off to me, instead of getting them to me himself or through his lawyers. West and Navy knew the details of every document. They would talk about their dad, commenting on which strategies he thought *they* would win with.

Meanwhile, I was doing my best to protect them from too much information. I hardly talked to the kids about the details of the divorce because it wasn't information they needed to know. As an adult, it was my job to handle things and their job to do well in school and all their activities and be with their friends. And this had been my role for the kids' whole lives—protecting them from Kevin. But now they would be with him two long weekends a month, eight entire days without me as a buffer or shield. I couldn't control what he filled their heads with or what he demanded of them. I had no idea what he said about me, but I could guess.

The divorce continued to be painted as my fault because it was my idea. Since the day I showed the kids my bruises, Kevin had campaigned hard to wipe it from their memories and shift the narrative to be instead about me as an "unforgiving" wife. He constantly questioned them about whether they had ever seen him harm me, and when they said no, it only further supported his campaign against me. After all those years protecting them from witnessing the abuse, was it possible that the cruel irony was that their dad could now convince them that it was all a lie?

What made October bearable was my newly finished house. After living with my mom for months, the home I had designed for myself and the kids was finally complete. It would be our refuge, our fresh start. And it would be all ours. To help us move in, over fifty of my friends from my social and church community came with willing hands and open hearts, lifting dozens of boxes, assembling furniture, and bringing us hot food. I marveled at their willingness to put our new home together, filling it with generosity and love. They made the work go so quickly and smoothly with all those hands. It was truly a good, old-fashioned barn raising.

By evening the house was lit up with people and music and laughing. Friends continued to arrive as others left. As I opened the front door to welcome more of my neighbors, I saw across the street, parked in the shadows, Kevin's car. I could make out his figure hunched in the driver's seat, and then I saw his arm waving me over. I refused to get anywhere near him and went into the house. A minute later, his number flashed across my phone. I didn't answer. He called repeatedly, more than ten times in the space of a few minutes.

"What do you want?" I asked angrily after finally answering.

"What are these people doing here?" he demanded as soon as I picked up.

"They're helping me move in, obviously," I replied, still angry. "Go away, Kevin. Why are you even here?"

"What are they doing with my things?" he asked, his voice rising. "What are they doing with my kids and my kids' things?"

"Stop it, Kevin. Leave and go home," I barked.

Before he could go on, I hung up. My phone continued to light up as he called me back several more times, until he finally gave up. I looked out the window every few minutes and could still see his face pressed against his car window, seething as he watched the festivities throughout the evening. I was relieved when he finally left. This was my new beginning, my new house, and my new life and I was not going to let him ruin it.

A few days later, the house furnished and settled, I saw fresh sidewalks being poured out front. I watched men in orange vests carefully smooth the tops of the dark gray squares. As soon as they left, I threw on my shoes and walked down to the damp sidewalk, grabbing a small stick on my way. I knelt down and looked at the perfectly level concrete, how clean and crisp it looked, how new and ready for our footsteps. Very carefully, I took the stick and carved out all our initials: EWNS for Elaine, West, Navy, and Swizzle. Our little family. Together and safe. Then, with the stick, I surrounded all our letters with a heart.

The next weekend, the kids came home and said, "Daddy is upset about our house." When I asked them why, they told me Kevin wanted to know why he wasn't allowed to help.

"We should have invited him," West sighed. "It wasn't fair."

As usual, I tried to ease their worries, hating that they felt responsible for Kevin's feelings and were trying to manage them for him. I wish now, in hindsight, that I had empowered them to tell Kevin to not talk about these things with them. I wish I had given them age-appropriate words to stand up to their own father's manipulation. Their entire lives I was so consumed with protecting them from Kevin, I wonder if I could have armed them better with what they needed to protect themselves. I now better understood Kevin's ability to make anyone believe anything he told them—all the more easily with his own children, who trusted him completely. I'll never know if I could have ever taught them enough to protect them from his machinations.

* * *

The kids were supposed to be with me on Halloween, and I looked forward to trick-or-treating with them like always. But this year, there was something even more important.

"I'll let you have the kids for Halloween," I told Kevin on the phone in early October, "if you switch November 6 with me. Just that Saturday night," I clarified. "You can still have the rest of the weekend."

"Why should I?" he replied.

"I'm serious," I insisted. "This is important to me."

It was, I explained, the church talent show that I had been in charge of organizing over several months. It fell on Kevin's weekend with the kids and I wanted Navy and West to be there for the show. I knew my kids loved me and that our relationship was strong, but I was growing more concerned about what Kevin's words were doing to them. Kevin relentlessly painted me in a negative light, as the parent who wanted to ruin the kids' fun, who was unfair and unforgiving. At the talent show, they would be with their friends and they would see me in a way that pushed against Kevin's narrative.

I was feeling particularly concerned since the new custody arrangement had been implemented, and Kevin had the most unfettered access to them he'd ever had. Navy seemed especially vulnerable to Kevin's tactics and the shift in her attitude toward me was becoming more and more apparent. Just a few days before the talent show, Navy was again angry with me. She had requested more time with Kevin because he had texted her that he was lonely and wanted her to come over, but I had said no. The next day, after she had calmed down, I shared with her in a text that I was afraid I was losing her. She texted back a funny selfie with her hands making a heart shape. *I love you, Mommy. You're my best friend. You'll never lose me.* Her loving response was so characteristically Navy that I felt some relief and hope that maybe I was worrying unnecessarily.

The talent show was a smash. While I oversaw getting all the acts onto the stage at the right time, I kept peeking over to where West and Navy were sitting in the audience. Their faces were beaming and I hadn't realized until then how much it meant that they were proud of me.

Around 8:30 p.m., just halfway through the talent show, Kevin texted West to say he was coming to pick them both up. West rushed backstage to show me his phone.

"No, sweetie," I said, trying to sound reassuring. "Tell your dad the show isn't over, and that you're supposed to stay with me tonight."

West texted Kevin back that the show was running late and he would text him when it was over. Then he showed me Kevin's response. *Be ready to go. I'm picking you up in 10 minutes.*

West replied, *The show isn't over yet. Mom wants us to stay.*

Kevin responded, *Too bad. I'm coming now.*

Caught in the chaos of the show's dozens of moving parts and players, I didn't realize that Kevin had shown up, called the kids from his cell phone, and told them to come out immediately. When I had a chance to catch my breath, I saw that their seats were empty. I tried to console myself with the fact that they had seen part of the show and had enjoyed themselves. But I was fuming at Kevin's deliberate sabotage of my time, especially when I had given up Halloween, one of the best nights of the year with the kids. I'm not sure why I had believed that Kevin would follow through on our arrangement. Maybe I had hoped that just this once, he would surprise me.

I got home late that night. It was after 1:00 a.m. and I was ready to collapse into bed. As I went to put my phone away, I realized that Navy had an early morning swim meet. It was in six hours and I knew I was too exhausted to make it. I didn't even know if I'd be able to make it to church in the morning and I very rarely missed a Sunday. I texted Navy an apology and let her know that I wouldn't be there in the morning. She didn't reply, but it was late and I soon fell into a heavy sleep.

Late the next morning, I saw a text from Navy when I woke up. *Mommy, you missed it. I had my best time of the entire year.* I texted back that I was so sorry. And I was. I had made it to nearly every other meet and practice and I loved watching both kids swim. This was one of the rare times I wasn't able to go. I didn't hear back. An hour later, a text from Karla came across my screen. *What kind of a mom misses her own daughter's most important swim meet of the year? A lousy mom.* I knew better than to let Karla get under my skin. She had sent awful texts to me before and I needed to be the bigger person despite how cruel she had been to me so many times before.

That night, Kevin dropped off the kids. I had plans for a quiet Sunday evening to get them ready for school the next day. He pulled up in front of the house and as I opened the car door to bring the kids inside, Kevin said, "Oh, I forgot their coats."

"You'll need to go back and get them," I said. "They'll want their coats tomorrow."

As I was about to shut the door, Kevin said, "Get in."

I raised my eyebrows at him.

"Just come for a ride, Elaine. We'll run back and the kids can grab their coats and then I'll bring you right back here."

Reluctantly, I got in. I really wanted West and Navy to experience their mother and father interacting as regular divorced parents might, even if infrequently. While the kids were getting their coats from Kevin's, we started discussing what had happened the night before.

"Why did you pick the kids up early?" I asked. "We'd had a deal."

"They saw your g*ddamn show. You got what you wanted."

"No, I absolutely did not. We had an arrangement. You got them for Halloween and I was supposed to have them last night. Why do you continue to exploit situations like this for your benefit and, as usual, put the kids in the middle where they know if they don't do what you say that you'll be mad at them? Then I cave so they aren't upset, and they know I won't get mad at them the way that you do."

We were still arguing when the kids returned with their coats. We continued to exchange heated words, but then Kevin's old, familiar rage started to surface. I recognized the contortions on his face and the flush of red under his skin. It was a dizzying flashback to all the times he had grabbed me, choked me, and thrown me into walls. Immediately, I pivoted, lowering my voice and trying to calm him down.

We made a right turn onto my street and I could feel Kevin's rage building. I was afraid. Only a half a block from my house, Kevin slammed on the brake and cranked the steering wheel hard to the left, almost coming to a stop and making a U-turn away from my house. He hadn't accelerated yet, so I quickly unlatched my seat belt and threw open the door before he sped up. With one foot on the ground and the car moving, I jumped out onto the road, spun around and grabbed the door handle to the back seat where West and Navy sat, stunned and terrified. I frantically shouted to them to hurry and get out. When I did, Kevin hit the gas and the force of the car caused me to lose grip of the door handle and toppled me to the ground. I watched his car speed off down the street with the rear door swinging open, West and Navy still inside.

I ran to my house and furiously tried calling Kevin but it went straight to voice mail. I called West's phone and then Navy's. Neither answered. I quickly called Kevin again but then saw his car pull up in front of the house. West got out first and ran into the house, his eyes downcast. Navy didn't move from the back seat. I could see her shoulders shaking. I walked around to her side, opened her door and bent down to talk to her.

"Come inside, sweetie," I coaxed. "Everything is going to be okay."

She was heaving and sobbing uncontrollably. When she finally caught her breath, she screamed in a voice I had never heard from her before, "I can't take it anymore!" She repeated herself, hysterically crying and rocking back and forth. "I can't take it anymore!"

"It's okay," I reassured her. "Just come in and we'll get everything figured out."

But Navy didn't move and continued to sob. I knew exactly what it was that she couldn't take anymore, and the agony I felt from seeing her in so much pain was almost more than I could bear. She was being tortured by the situation and I felt helpless to know what to do. When I conceded to Kevin's demands, every inch turned into a mile until my time was becoming less than his. When I called him out on his behavior, it would escalate into something so horrific that I would concede to anything to stop the pain it would inflict on my kids.

"Just let me stay with Daddy. I need to be with Daddy," she cried, pushing her hair out of her face.

"Daddy is fine, Navy."

Kevin stayed in the front seat of the car, staring straight ahead, listening to our conversation but saying nothing.

"He needs me. I need to look after him."

"Navy," I said, more firmly now, "Daddy is a grown-up and he can take care of himself. It's our job to take care of *you*."

"No, he needs me. He's not okay without me!"

The last thing I wanted to do was let her stay with Kevin. I wanted her to be home, safe, with me and her brother. I wanted to make it better for her, like I had when she was a baby and would cling to me when she was hurt. When she was small, I was able to calm her and make everything okay. My touch and my voice could dry her tears and put her at ease. But now, nothing I could say or do seemed to help. Relieving Navy's suffering was the only thing I cared about, and so I said she could spend an extra night with Kevin. It remains one of my biggest regrets.

* * *

West stayed with me while Navy went back with Kevin. I trusted that time would help us move past this together. But when I texted Navy on Monday to let her know that I would be picking her up from school, she replied, *Don't come. I need to figure things out. On my own.* I had no idea what she needed to figure out. I wracked my brain, trying to understand what, other than my missing her swim meet, she seemed so devastated about. Like all preteens, Navy saw most things in black and white and took things hard. *Just leave me alone. You're hurting me. I'm not coming home.*

Over the next day, I reached out to Navy with increasing panic. Kevin wouldn't take my calls. Navy barely responded to me or to West. She felt so far away and unreachable. It had only been a week earlier that she had told me I was her best friend and now I couldn't get her to come home. Over the course of the day, I texted messages that were encouraging, apologetic, and sympathetic. I wanted to make some kind of connection, however small. But all I got in response was

I don't know or *I want to stay with Dad.* She didn't call when she said she would. She wouldn't pick up when I called her. I was at a loss, utterly confused, sick with worry, and deeply anxious. She stayed with Kevin through Tuesday, then Wednesday. I asked her to talk to someone, offering a therapist, a friend's mom, anyone who could ensure she wasn't alone. Her texts grew less frequent. *Whatever. IDK. Buzz off. Nope.* I felt her slipping away.

And then her texts stopped altogether. An entire day passed with no contact at all. Then another. By the end of the week, I hadn't heard from Navy for five days. I hadn't seen her in seven. Beside myself, I called Claire.

"He's keeping her from me," I said, my voice raised and shaking. "I haven't heard from or seen Navy in a week."

"Call the police," Claire replied.

When the officers came to my house the first thing they asked me was, "Do you have a police enforcement clause?"

"What is that?" I asked, completely perplexed.

"It's in the parenting order of your divorce agreement. Do you have one?"

Not only didn't I have one, I had never heard of such a thing. But I learned that they weren't standard in a divorce agreement, trusting that the majority of parents respected custody arrangements, even if they didn't like them. Without a police enforcement clause, I couldn't force Kevin to abide by our custody agreement if he broke it. I had no power, without the clause, to compel him to give me the kids on my days. He could keep the kids from me and cut off all communication, and the police could do nothing without this clause. How could he keep my child from me but not be breaking the law?

Claire got to work quickly, but it would take three weeks for us to finally get in front of a judge who could put in an Order of Enforcement to compel Kevin to honor our custody agreement. While

I waited for the paperwork to go through, I needed to see Navy. I felt unmoored without her in my life, not knowing if she was well or not, not knowing where she was, if she was happy or sad. I was still desperately confused about her silence, understanding that I had let her down by not making it to her swim meet, but bewildered by the outsized reaction.

On Monday, after nearly a week without seeing Navy, I went to her school. It was lunchtime. It wasn't uncommon for parents to pick up their kids and take them to lunch, and I myself had done it before on special occasions. The secretary asked me to wait while she called Navy down from her classroom. When Navy walked toward the door of the school office where I was standing, her face went ashen. She looked utterly panicked and backed a few steps away from me. I convinced her that I was just there to take her to lunch, nothing more. I wasn't going to take her out of school; I wasn't going to get her into trouble.

"I don't want to go," she said nervously.

"We'll go to the Mongolian Grill, the one you love," I said. "And then I'll drop you back off at school."

Navy stood silently, looking down at her shoes.

"I promise," I said.

She reluctantly walked out the front doors of the school with me, got into the car, and I took her to the restaurant as promised. She kept quiet for most of our lunch. I apologized again for missing her swim meet. I asked her how she was doing. I asked her to come home.

"Even West misses you," I said lightly, hoping to see her smile. When she didn't respond, I said, "I love you, Navy. It's not okay for your dad to keep you from me. We will sort this out. I will do anything, everything I can to make things okay with us."

Her shoulders settled a little and she ate her lunch, seeming to relax. I could tell she was listening, but she still appeared frightened. Back in the car, she turned to me.

"You're taking me back, right?"

"Yes," I answered, dumbfounded that she was so fearful of me. "Of course I'll take you back to school."

Navy turned away from me and leaned her head against her window as we sat quietly at a red light. I felt the weight of the air between us, this invisible wall keeping me from my daughter who was sitting right next to me, who just a few days ago said I was her best friend.

"I'm so confused," she said very quietly. I saw that she was crying. "I don't know what to believe."

Witnessing her pain was excruciating. I also felt sick. Sickened by what Kevin must be saying or doing to my beautiful daughter to make her so tormented. I would have done anything to take it away, to feel it for her, to set her free. Instead, all I could do was return her to school as promised and watch her slowly disappear behind the doors, back into a life where her dad was keeping her from her mom.

Another week went by and Navy was still staying at Kevin's, refusing to come to my house. West, meanwhile, dutifully went back and forth on his assigned days. He was, as ever, concerned about doing what was right and fair. Regardless, I lived in fear that without warning, he could also just not come home. I knew having Navy in his control wouldn't be enough for Kevin, and when I saw a text exchange between him and West, it confirmed that my worst fears could be realized. Kevin was urging him to follow his sister.

Navy is brave enough to take a stand for what she believes and wants. West, being complacent isn't always the right thing. I would hope if you ever felt the same way she does, you would be brave and know that I would support you also.

West replied, *She's standing up for the wrong reasons.*

Kevin went full-court press on his son. *I completely disagree. She knows exactly what she wants. Navy wants to be respected, loved and treated as a person with opinions and beliefs. Navy has power.*

West continued, *You might think that, but she doesn't help anybody including herself by leaving. She is always loved and respected, mom was making special french toast for her when she left."*

Kevin responded, *Is mom typing this West? Or feeding it to you?*

She doesn't even know I'm texting you, West texted back.

I miss you, Kevin texted.

Please don't feel sad dad, that will make me feel sad that I'm not with you, love West.

On social media, Navy was vocal about her misery. "MY MOM IS THE BIGGEST JERK 2 WALK THE EARTH" said one post. Her brother tried to push back against her posts, sounding just as confused and concerned as I was. But she wouldn't be reached.

"I don't understand what's going on with her," West told me, when I asked if he had any idea what was happening with Navy. "It's like she's gone crazy."

The days passed while I awaited the call from Claire to notify me that we had a court date set to revise the parenting order. I continued to be at a loss as to what I could have possibly done to warrant the anger and vitriol I was experiencing from Navy. I asked God, morning and night, to help Navy, and to help me understand.

Then one morning, my laptop chimed. I had received an email from my friend Lisa Hardie, who was a schoolteacher at the local junior high. I could see it had links and attachments at the bottom.

Elaine,

Are you close to the internet right now? Something just came across my desk and I thought of you. When I have a few more minutes, I'll email you more info but I wanted to get this to you ASAP. Have you heard of Parental Alienation Syndrome? I just (like minutes ago) heard about this. It sounds like what you're going through with Kevin. It is a sign of child abuse. I know you're going to the lawyers on Wednesday. Perhaps some of this info can help?

I just googled it and there is lots of information on it on the internet. Let me know. Very serendipitous that it came across my desk. That will keep you busy reading for the afternoon.

Love,

Lisa

I clicked on the links and as I read through what she sent me, tears streamed down my face. I could hardly believe what I was reading. It was exactly what was happening to me, and West, but especially Navy. It was like I had written the description myself. For the next several hours, I was lost in research about parental alienation, and the syndrome it caused in a child, a term introduced by child psychologist Richard Gardner.

According to Gardner, "PAS is characterized by a cluster of eight symptoms that appear in the child. These include a campaign of denigration and hatred against the targeted parent; weak, absurd, or frivolous rationalizations for this deprecation and hatred; lack of the usual ambivalence about the targeted parent; strong assertions that the decision to reject the parent is theirs alone (the "independent-thinker phenomenon"); reflexive support of the favored parent in the conflict; lack of guilt over the treatment of the alienated parent; use of borrowed scenarios and phrases from the alienating parent; and the denigration not just of the targeted parent but also to that parent's extended family and friends."[1]

Gardner and others divided PAS into mild, moderate, and severe levels. In severe cases, children were found to display most or all of the eight symptoms and refused to visit the targeted parent, possibly threatening to run away or engage in self-harm if forced to visit the

[1] Richard A. Gardner (2002) Parental Alienation Syndrome vs. Parental Alienation: Which Diagnosis Should Evaluators Use in Child-Custody Disputes? The American Journal of Family Therapy, 30:2, 93-115, DOI: 10.1080/019261802753573821

other parent.

As I read, my alarm grew more intense. The explanations read like a mirror of my life. Another expert on PAS, Dr. Amy J.L. Baker, Ph.D., wrote about the five alienation strategies by the alienating parent: "(1) poisonous messages to the child about the targeted parent in which he or she is portrayed as unloving, unsafe, and unavailable; (2) limiting contact and communication between the child and the targeted parent; (3) erasing and replacing the targeted parent in the heart and mind of the child; (4) encouraging the child to betray the targeted parent's trust; and (5) undermining the authority of the targeted parent. Taken together these parental alienation strategies foster conflict and psychological distance between the child and the targeted parent."[2]

I learned that if the child expresses any love, fondness, or affection toward the targeted parent, the alienating parent will withhold love from that child and threaten expulsion from their lives. This pattern of behavior continues until the child can't decipher the difference between their own thoughts and what they are being told.

I then read cover-to-cover what was reported to be the most acclaimed book on parental alienation, *Divorce Poison*, by Dr. Richard A. Warshak.

Suddenly, everything made sense. I felt a wash of relief as my confusion over Navy's behavior toward me now made sense, but terrified about what it could now mean. Kevin's bizarre emails and texts, his accusations that he was freeing Navy from my control, that the kids never asked about me when they were with him, how I was a terrible mother who only let my children down. It was as if a single slip-up—missing her swim meet—had suddenly become the focal point of his campaign against me. All of this behavior is designed, as

[2] Baker, Amy & Fine, Paul & Lcsw,. (2008). Beyond the High Road: Responding to 17 Parental Alienation Strategies without Compromising Your Morals or Harming Your Child.

the name suggests, to alienate the child from the parent.

It also became clear that his scheme had started over a year ago, when Kevin had West and Navy alone for the first time, the week after he threw me out of the house and I had called the police. He had threatened to move away forever if West and Navy couldn't convince me to give him another chance, and said that I was solely responsible for the disintegration of our family.

Navy's personality, in particular, made her the ideal target for Kevin's manipulation of her thoughts and emotions. I remembered when her teachers and I talked about how pure-hearted and empathetic she was. I thought back to a time when Navy was around seven years old and my mom was watching a documentary about undernourished children in underdeveloped countries. When Navy came to her looking for a snack, the images of emaciated children on the screen caught her attention. Rather than thinking about her own hunger, she asked my mom why the children in the pictures were so thin and then asked, "What can we do about that?"

And then there was Karla's role. Her emails and texts had grown vicious, unhinged, and deliberately cruel. I never expected her to be kind to me, nor did I give weight to her name-calling or outrageous accusations, but her attacks were shocking nonetheless. *Fat pig. Pathetic loser. Lazy. Poor excuse for a mother. Child abuser.* This is only a sanitized fraction of Karla's texts and emails to me, sometimes directly from Navy's phone. I learned later that many of the most cruel and vile text messages I would receive from Navy were sent by Karla masquerading as Navy, after Navy had gone to bed. When I would run into Karla in person at a swim practice or school event, Karla would refer to me as "muffin" or call out to me sarcastically, "Look, it's the mother of the year."

OMG [Angie] its hilarious [Navy] told me she only posts stuff from when she wasn't a fat pig!! She cuts [Kevin] out of pictures because she doesn't have any recent skinny ones!! How's [Ed] did he have fun? I'm teaching 5 classes a week and westside. BTW [Kevin] and I started hot yoga AMAZING.. Call me later!! Love ya.

I know and now a video from years ago so everyone will validate her pathetic existance... Still no Job what a loser

No [Navy] still hasn't gone home and won't I feel so bad for her.. We love her though and she calls me Krum.. [Karla] and Mom...

Elaine I just noticed [Maya] opened up u and not my friend [Angie] these were meant for [Angie] but I do belive u are a fat lazy pig and a poor excuse for a mother.... Have a great day [Karla].. The one that raises [Navy].

A series of texts from Karla, sent to me sequentially as pictured, allegedly intended for her friend, Angie.

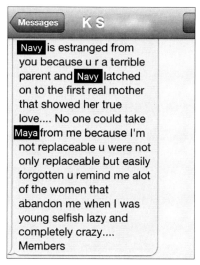

Karla texting me that no one could take her daughter away from her.

Text from Karla after I asked her to return Navy to me and to stop encouraging her to run away.

This was what Navy was being exposed to constantly, relentlessly. How could a child be expected to have any defenses against her own caretakers manipulating her in this manner? It would have been horrifying if Kevin and Karla had talked about *anyone* in Navy's life this way, let alone her mother. Learning about parental alienation, I felt some relief knowing that Navy's abnormal behavior had nothing to do with a missed swim meet, but I now had even greater cause for concern. I read of very few circumstances where the child voluntarily comes back into the "healthy parent's" life, and if they do, it often isn't until they are adults. The articles said that parental alienation could cause a lifetime of psychological harm to a child, and have long-term effects on that child's future relationships. There was also a high rate of drug and alcohol abuse, promiscuity, and even suicide among children that are caught in this circumstance, often into adulthood. It was going to be critical that the police enforcement clause return Navy to me.

The next day, Claire and I appeared in court and the clause was finally set in place. Officers were dispatched to Kevin's house to collect Navy and deliver her to me. It was November 24, seventeen days since Navy had been home.

I waited frantically by the door, in disbelief that my daughter was being dragged home by the police because her father refused to comply. When the police car pulled up, I raced out the door to meet her. But Navy didn't even look at me as she ran straight inside. There was nothing, not even a screaming fight. Just silence and a wall I couldn't penetrate. I noticed she was holding a cup, a Slurpee from 7-Eleven. The officers came in behind her. West came down from his room and we all sat together on the couch. These officers, who had to force my daughter to come home to me, spoke to Navy and West kindly.

"You both have to go along with your parents' custody agreement. You have to follow the schedule, go with your dad on his time and your mom on her time. Do you understand?"

West nodded. Navy did too, but almost imperceptibly.

West spoke up. "My dad says that the time should be equal."

Then Navy angrily chimed in, "It's not fair that my dad only gets us every other weekend."

The first officer nodded, then looked Navy directly in the eye. "That almost never happens," he began. "I see a lot of custody cases, some of them just like yours. It's extremely rare that custody can be split perfectly evenly. This is the agreement that your family has. It's what your dad agreed to also. It's the law that everyone obeys that agreement. Okay?"

Navy didn't respond.

"This is your mom's time with you. You need to be here when it's her time. It's not right that you stay with your dad and don't come here."

Navy didn't move, but she looked like she was listening. The officer who was speaking then offered to go upstairs with West and play video games while the other stayed and talked briefly with Navy and me. He explained that they had indeed stopped to buy her a Slurpee, gave me his card, and told me to call him any time.

I was grateful for the officers' compassion, and that Navy got to hear from someone other than me that what was happening was wrong. I didn't know what would sink in or what would change. I let Navy go to her room, my heart anxious about what she was thinking, feeling, and going to do the next day.

Later, in her room, I tried to help her understand that it was Kevin who was keeping her from me.

"No, he's not," she snapped. "This is my life. It's my choice. I'm choosing where I want to live, where I go, and when."

"No, sweetie," I responded. "You're not choosing. Your dad's not letting you choose. He's controlling you."

I couldn't tell her everything I had read about parental alienation. I didn't want to risk overwhelming her. All I knew at that moment was that my daughter was home, with me, with her brother, and away from Kevin. I didn't know how I would keep her safe or undo the damage that had already been inflicted. I prayed hard that night that Navy would see the truth, that my love and our deep mother-daughter bond would win out.

CHAPTER TEN

The next day, after Navy had spent her first night in my home in weeks, I dropped her off at school and told her I would pick her up at the end of the day. She had barely spoken a word to me all morning, but she seemed calmer, less agitated than the night before. But that afternoon, she wasn't at school when I went to pick her up. I watched the crowd of kids streaming through the school gate, and searched for Navy, growing more frantic as the crowd thinned and there was still no sign of her. I picked up my phone and called Kevin.

"How dare you?" he screamed into the phone. "You're telling me you lost my daughter?"

"She's not your daughter; she's our daughter. And I didn't lose her. She's not here. It's probably because of whatever lies you've been filling her head with."

Next, I called West. A friend's mom had given him a ride and he was already at home.

"I'm coming to pick you up," I said.

We drove around the neighborhood first, scanning every sidewalk, every front porch, every car that passed for a sign of Navy. West began texting and messaging Navy's friends on social media, asking if anyone had a clue where she was. Navy's friend Olivia responded: *She might be at Alise's house.*

"Do you know where she lives?" I asked.

"Yes," West replied.

Alise's mother answered the door. She kept her distance and seemed nervous. I told her who I was and that I'd been looking for Navy all afternoon.

"No," she said, her demeanor still strange and unnatural. "She was here, but she's not here now. She and Alise left and I don't know where they are or when they will be back. Sorry."

West and I climbed back into the car and we continued to comb the neighborhood. All the while West was texting Navy, her friends, his friends, anyone he could think of. The sun was beginning to set. Where was she? I was frantic that she would be cold or afraid. We circled back around Alise's house, this time along her back fence, and then I saw Navy through the fence slats, standing with Alise in her yard. I stopped the car and leapt out.

"Navy!" I called.

Both girls bolted out of sight as soon as they heard my voice. I raced back into the car and drove around the front, trying to keep an eye on Navy as she darted between houses and cars. But I lost her. She disappeared from sight, into someone's yard or alley. I felt completely powerless. I couldn't keep my daughter safe. I couldn't keep her with me. I was chasing her in my car and all she wanted to do was get away from me. It was one of the worst moments of my life. I sat outside Alise's house for what seemed like an eternity, thinking they would eventually come back. I went back to the door two more times asking for Navy. Alise came to the door with her mom the second time I knocked and told me she didn't know where Navy was.

As I made my way home slowly, still scanning the streets that were now cloaked in the shadows of dusk, Kevin called.

"Karla has Navy," he said plainly.

"What do you mean?" I demanded. "Bring her to me, now!"

"I've already told the police," Kevin said, ignoring me. "They know we've found her and that she's safe. Stay away from my f**king daughter. She doesn't want to be with you. Don't show up at her school again. Leave her the f**k alone. She doesn't want to be with you, Elaine."

"She is twelve years old, Kevin," I insisted. "You've brainwashed her to hate me!"

He hung up on me and I drove home with West in silence and filled with deep dread. I decided to let Navy stay with Kevin for the next several days while I tried to figure out my next move. I couldn't bear to call the police again and have them drag Navy from Kevin's house to mine, knowing how traumatic it was for her to be placed in the back of a police car and forced to return to me, regardless of how badly she was being manipulated into saying she wanted to stay with Kevin. I was also worried that Kevin's false narrative, which he was telling to the police, the courts, and everyone else, would be believed: that Navy was afraid of me, didn't want to live with me, and would only come home if forced to.

When my next custody day came around, I texted Kevin. *Bring her here. It's my time with her. I don't want to have to call the police again.*

He replied with a barrage of texts. *Sure, put your daughter in a police car again. You are the absolute worst mother possible. An absolute monster. Get it through your head. Navy doesn't want to see you.*

Navy had now been gone for a month. Her room sat empty. West came and went on his days. I was lost and desperate not to lose him too. "I love you," I told him every chance I got. "Remember, I'm picking you up today. You're staying with me tonight," I reminded him as I watched him leave for school in the morning, continuing to be terrified that I might lose him too. I didn't want to pressure him for information, but he was seeing his sister at Kevin's and I was desperate. He was my only line to Navy. I tried to make his life at my house as normal, fun, and loving as I could. It was hard to do with this rift hanging over us all. On his phone, I noticed a text from Karla: *Start calling me Krum, okay? It's Karla + Mum!*

A few days later, after I dropped West at school, I stopped by the grocery store for a few things. In the produce section, I noticed some overripe bananas, perfect for making Navy's favorite muffins. I would make them regularly for her snack between school and swim practice. I reached out to put the bananas in my cart, and then it hit me in a way it hadn't until that moment: Navy wouldn't be there in the morning to pack a swim bag for. She wouldn't be there for dinner tonight. She wouldn't be there to tuck in. The idea of never getting her back didn't fully sink in, but it started to enter my thoughts, just around the edges. I slowly pulled my hand back from the bananas and gripped the handle of the cart. A tidal wave of pain radiated through my body. Would I ever get the chance to make muffins for Navy again? Worse yet, would I ever even see Navy again? I walked through the store feeling like a ghost, reaching for my daughter who also felt like a ghost.

The police brought Navy back a second time in the last week of November. Out of options, I had resorted to calling them again. It was the same as before. She arrived full of hatred and hostility. She told me she wanted to be with her dad. Her choice was to be with her dad. I couldn't stop her from doing what she wanted. It was her life. I couldn't get through to her. I couldn't find her behind the script that she wouldn't stop repeating, the words that I knew were Kevin's and not her own.

* * *

The text was clear as crystal. Kevin to Navy. *Just walk out the door. We'll come pick you up.*

I was frantically searching Navy's phone, scouring her text messages to find out if she was planning to flee the morning after she was brought back by the police again. I gasped when I saw what her dad had been sending her around midnight.

I can't. She's awake. Navy didn't want to sneak out. Kevin was pushing her to. *Just go. Get out the front door. Leave.*

She never left because I had been up late. She could hear me moving around late into the night. It felt like a test of her loyalty. It reminded me of how he had pushed and tested *my* loyalty when I was his wife. I could see the parallels of how Kevin was shifting the emotional and mental abuse he had inflicted on me onto Navy now. How far would he push her to make sure that she was on his side? Before I had the chance to sort anything else out in my head, Navy was gone again.

I called Claire, hoping for some legal recourse.

"The police can't make her stay with me," I said. "They can't make Kevin stop turning her against me. She's gone. Again. Kevin is the one who told her to sneak out!"

Claire had no solutions other than calling the police. "They're there to enforce the custody agreement," she explained. But there was no real weight behind the custody agreement or the enforcement clause. The world was spiraling out of control. I was losing my daughter. She was already gone and I was out of options.

December crept in with cold and wind, marking the second month without Navy. I couldn't bear the thought of Christmas. This year, the kids were supposed to be with me for the holiday and then with Kevin and Karla for the new year. Earlier in November during one of Kevin's weekends, before I lost contact with Navy, Kevin had "surprised" her and West with the news that he was taking them to Hawaii for Christmas, causing a massive upheaval. They were supposed to be with *me* over Christmas, I reminded him again and again. He was going to have the kids from December 27 through the new year, and he could take them wherever he pleased on those days. The kids, of course, were ecstatic about the thought of going to Hawaii, until I told them that it was my time with them and it would be with me and their Grandma in Calgary. I was placed squarely in the middle, a roadblock to their fun and happiness yet again. However, despite wanting to concede so they wouldn't be angry with me, I was immovable against Kevin's attempt to maneuver Christmas away from me. Eventually, he said he would take them on his days to Arizona to visit the Sykes family.

But now, the holiday seemed not only distant but impossible. How would we celebrate Christmas like this, broken into separate homes and estranged? My soul was exhausted. I was losing faith.

The next day, I sat in the car after dropping West off at an early-morning church group. As I waited for him in the parking lot, in the dark, with the car running to stay warm from the frigid temperature outside, my body was flooded only with dread and terror as I contemplated a future without Navy. The reality of that nightmare scenario had, at that moment, fully hit me in a way it hadn't before, even at the grocery store.

I was also facing this all on my own. Until I experienced what we had gone through over the last year, I could never have imagined that the legal system wasn't going to be there for me, or for my kids. Kevin would never relent and he would never be reasonable; he would never do what was best for Navy if it meant not getting exactly what he wanted, which seemed ever more like it was simply to hurt me. Navy would be a mere casualty of his crusade. I sobbed for what felt like an eternity with my head on the steering wheel, my shoulders heaving and my heart collapsing under the weight of it all.

* * *

My plan was simple. I would take Navy away. My hope was to be gone for two weeks, ten days of which were my legal custody time. I knew two weeks would be the most I could get away with before Kevin had any leverage to force us back. My plan was to get Navy out from under Kevin's control. It was called "deprogramming" and recommended by experts in Parental Alienation Syndrome as one of the only ways to undo a child's brainwashing and alienation. I needed to get Navy away from Kevin and Karla, to stop their narrative filling her head, to free her from their grip and return her to herself. I called Traci, who already knew about our situation and how it was growing worse by the day. She lived in a tiny town in rural Wyoming, a fourteen-hour drive from Calgary.

"Of course you can come stay with me," she said immediately. "I have plenty of room and everyone would love to see you both. Stay as long as you want." Then she added, "Only a mother's love would compel someone to drive nine hundred miles in the dead of winter. I'll be praying for you constantly."

I had no idea how I was going to get Navy to come with me, how I would get her away from Kevin, or how I would get her in my car. But I picked a date, a Monday during my scheduled time with Navy. I was filled with adrenaline as I prepared for the trip, trembling as I finished up some laundry. I packed a suitcase for us both, as well as lunch, snacks, and several other things we might need in case we had trouble driving through several mountain ranges and icy roads.

I waited until midday, knowing she would be in school and I could pick her up without Kevin knowing. I arranged for my mom to pick up West; he'd stay with her while we were gone. She and Traci were the only people who knew about my plan. I knew that I couldn't tell West exactly where I was going, knowing Kevin would mine him for information. If he knew nothing it would be easier on him. I dropped him off at school that morning knowing I would be gone by the time he came home, my heart heavy but determined.

At dismissal time, I arrived at the school. Before I got out of my car, I said a prayer. I prayed that Navy wouldn't want to cause a scene at her school, in front of her teachers and friends. I prayed that I could just get her in the car and start driving.

I walked in and saw Navy just as she was leaving her classroom. Her face betrayed terror as she looked at me, just like she had the day I had come to take her for lunch.

"Hi, Navy," I said. "I just want a few minutes to talk."

"No," she said. "I don't want to."

"Let's just walk outside. I just want us to talk. That's all."

She paused for a moment and then walked behind me out to the parking lot. God seemed to be moving her legs and getting her closer to the car. I could hardly believe what was happening.

Navy climbed into the car without a word. I slowly pulled away from the school. She was here. I had her. This was going to work. My stomach was churning with hope and fear all at once. Then Navy glanced into the back seat and saw the bags I had packed for both her and myself. She whipped her head around and demanded to know where we were going.

"Where are you taking me? What are you doing?" she screamed.

"It's okay," I said. "We're going on a little trip, just for a few days, just the two of us."

"No!" Navy was thrashing wildly now, hysterically kicking and flailing her arms.

I locked the doors and tried to drive steadily on. I was terrified that she would try to jump out of the car while it was moving.

"We just need some time together, Navy. I promise it's going to be okay," I said, holding back tears of my own.

She wouldn't stop crying or kicking. She couldn't calm down or find a way to control herself, seeming to fight as though her life depended on it. I tried to steady her with one hand while keeping the other on the wheel, but she balked and threw herself against the door. Just as I was getting on the highway, she slid down low in her seat, curling up into a tight ball. Suddenly, she let out a yell and kicked her legs straight up, shattering the mirror on the visor.

"Navy!" I cried, as glass shards fell all around her. "Please calm down! We're going to be okay, I promise!"

For two hours, Navy crouched in her seat and wept, refusing to talk to me. I tried to make light conversation, asking her about school and her friends, but she said nothing. Several critical junctures were approaching. We would have to stop for gas, and for bathroom breaks, where I feared she would run and I wouldn't be able to catch her. I was also worried she would call out to a stranger and pretend she didn't know me, or even lock herself in the gas station bathroom. My imagination was running wild, but I knew the most critical moment of the trip was coming. We weren't far from the Sweetgrass, Montana Port of Entry and we would have to cross the border into the U.S. I feared agents would peer into the car and be alarmed at the sight of a distraught child, that she would tell them I had kidnapped her, however true that might be. I also knew that crossing an international border with a child required a letter of permission from the absent parent, and I definitely didn't have one of those.

I kept talking softly to her. I promised her that we would be together and that after a few days of quiet and rest, we would go home. She would see her friends again. She would see her dad and her brother. She would go back to school and everything would be fine, but in the meantime, she could have fun playing with Traci's kids, and we had all kinds of exciting activities planned. She was silent as we neared the border. How was I going to get her across? I prayed harder than I had ever prayed for anything in my life. *Just let us get through. Just let me get her to safety.*

I glanced over at Navy, searching for words that would keep her calm. But her head was slumped against her window and her shoulders were rising and falling steadily. She was asleep. I held my breath through the checkpoint. I slowed the car as gradually as I could. I chatted breezily with the border agent, telling him that we were on a special mother-daughter holiday, headed for southern Wyoming to see friends there. I told him how long we would be gone, and showed him our passports. He waved us through with a smile and a nod. Navy hadn't moved. She had slept through everything—the car's change of speed, the window rolling down, and the less-than-quiet conversation I had with the border agent. He didn't even ask for a permission letter. I sped up and finally exhaled, thanking God for another answer to my pleading prayers that day. I settled in for the next eleven hours of our drive.

Navy woke up shortly after we got through the border, and aside from muttering, "It's my life, I get to do what I want," she barely said a word to me.

"Navy," I began gently after a long period of silence. "I know this situation between your dad and me is really hard. I know how confusing it is for you and how stuck in the middle you've been. That is the last thing I would want for you. I love you so much."

"My dad and I need each other," she replied flatly. "He needs me and I need him."

I was again reminded of the parallels, how he was making her responsible for his happiness just like he had done to me our entire marriage.

"I understand," I said patiently. "Of course you need each other. But West and I need you too. We all need each other." After a pause, I continued. "You know that I have always taught you and West to be forgiving. I want you to know, sweetie, that I forgave your dad many, many times for how unkind he was to me while we were married. But he didn't change, no matter how many chances I gave him. I didn't feel like there was any chance he would change and there was nothing more I could do. It was going to have to be up to him. Navy, it's been hard for me to understand why you've been so angry at me, but I now know it's because your dad is angry at me. He is angry at me about the divorce and it's made you angry too. I know your dad has also told you we should be sharing time with you and West equally. But, Navy, I also know that eventually, it wouldn't be enough for your dad. If I changed the agreement so you and West spent half the time with each of us, he would still push until you and West weren't coming to my house at all."

I knew she was listening. I hoped my words were sinking in. But then she replied, "It's my choice." Then, after a short silence, she blurted out, "I know I've been a bad girl and I may be going to hell, but at least I'll be there with my dad."

I was shocked. I didn't even know what to make of her words or of her blind loyalty to Kevin. I shuddered at what he must have done to turn her against everything and everyone but him. Kevin was isolating her, forcing her to depend only on him as her single source of affection, security, and love. At twelve years old, she couldn't see what was happening to her. She was afraid of losing her dad's love, which is what he'd been threatening all this time. I could tell she was scared to death that he would abandon her. She was so scared that she was willing to abandon everyone else in her life, including her mother.

Then she announced, "I'm Grandma Sykes favorite. Dad told me I was."

Kevin's mother loved Navy, of course, but she lived several thousand miles away in Arizona, and had more than forty grandchildren and multiple great-grandchildren. I was doubtful that his mother had told Kevin that Navy was her favorite. Then she piped up, "I'm Dad's favorite too. He told me that he loved me more than any of his other kids." I couldn't believe what I was hearing, but then again, nothing was shocking when it came to Kevin. It all seemed to be part of his master plan to pull Navy entirely into his world.

Our long stretches of silence gave me a chance to wrap my mind around what this time away would hold for us. All I wanted to do was hold her and make her believe that she was safe. I wanted to free her from her father's web of manipulation and lies. I imagined untangling her one strand at a time from the asphyxiating grip of parental alienation, to show her that I was not the monster he made me out to be; that I was the mom she had always known and loved and that our bond couldn't be broken.

We spent the night at a small roadside hotel. Navy was already beginning to relax a little. She wasn't trying to run away. There was nowhere for her to go, but she was also no longer frantic and terrified. She followed me into the hotel room and started opening the bag I had packed for her.

That morning, I'd sent the email I had composed to Navy's principal explaining why I had taken her out of school and how long we would be gone. I told her some of the history and hoped she would be understanding and compassionate. Sharing my situation with others continued to be difficult. I was filled with embarrassment that my children and I could somehow be in a circumstance like this. I hoped she would be sympathetic and I promised that we would keep up with Navy's schoolwork during her time away. The principal responded with abundant kindness, offering to share the news with Navy's teachers and assuring me she would do everything she could to support us. She commented on the kids' unusual number of absences and wondered if something had been going on.

Next, I texted West. He was home with my mom and sounded worried about us. I apologized for the suddenness of our trip and the mystery of it all. Finally, I emailed Kevin telling him that I was going to be gone with Navy for two weeks and that I would be back before Christmas. Then I switched my phone off, and put it in my bag along with Navy's phone. I knew Kevin would call and text. We needed to sleep, and I didn't want to hear his barrage of messages. I would deal with them in the morning.

Kevin's messages were there to greet me when I woke up. He demanded to know where Navy was, accusing me of kidnapping her. He threatened to call the police if I didn't let him talk to her. I replied that Navy was perfectly safe and that since this was my time with her, I didn't need to explain a thing or put her on the phone. He and Karla filled their social media accounts with posts claiming that Navy was missing. I turned off my phone again and then turned off Navy's. Going dark was the only way to make this work.

Traci's house is in the village of Lyman, tucked in the southwest corner of Wyoming near the Utah border. The town is surrounded by open plains and scatterings of pine, spruce, and cottonwood trees. The land felt vast and the sky stretched on endlessly. There was birdsong and flowing water, clear air, and soft breezes. It was the perfect place for us to decompress and start to heal. Traci and her husband, Jason, who was the town's chiropractor, welcomed us warmly, making us meals, including us in their kids' activities, and giving us plenty of space and time to be together. After two days, I started to feel almost normal. We would get up and make breakfast, go for walks, explore the land, gather for lunch and dinner, and watch movies. It was all so ordinary and miraculous at the same time.

By day four, I was starting to see a change in Navy. Her posture was unclenching, her body language relaxed. She laughed and played with Traci's two daughters, while their younger brother tagged along. Navy talked to me. When I said, "I love you," she answered, "I love you too." The sweetness returned to her voice and she seemed to grow young again with the burdens of her father lifted from her shoulders.

I was becoming reacquainted with my daughter. One week later, the police called.

"Is this Elaine Hartrick?" said an officer.

"Yes," I replied.

He questioned me about where I was located, and when I left. He asked me why I left my son behind, and who I was staying with. I could hear Kevin's voice in his questions, and was angry that Kevin and Karla were now going to know where I was.

"Why did you take your daughter across the border?" he demanded.

"She is my daughter, these are my custody days with her, and I can take her on a trip if I want to. That's not a crime," I replied.

I gave the officer the exact day we would be back. I told him to go ahead and call Navy's school principal, who knew all about our trip.

"We're taking note of your return date," he said, threateningly. "If she's not back by then, we will be issuing an AMBER alert."

"I am her mother," I insisted. "She is not missing."

I was fuming. Kevin had, yet again, duped the justice system to make it seem like I was the one breaking the law, when he had been going against police orders for weeks. I also learned that the day after I left, he had gone to my mom's house and taken West, even though it was during my custody time and I had arranged for him to spend time with her. I was filled with dread imagining the things he and Karla were filling his mind with while they had West all to themselves.

On our last night in Lyman, I sat on the edge of Navy's bed as she folded clothes into her suitcase. The entire trip, I had kept things light and fun, hoping that Navy could simply relax and return to her old self. Every day that had gone by I could see her mind uncoiling the twisted sense of reality that had been imposed upon her. We didn't talk much about what was happening. I was grateful that the strategy of getting her completely out of Kevin and Karla's hands was working, but I knew it would be a tall order to keep it going once I returned to

Calgary. I was desperately wishing that I could have kept her away for longer. I wished that the law could see what I was trying to do and be on my side.

"When we get back, can we go visit Grandma?" she asked.

"Of course," I said, thrilled that she was thinking about the future, that she knew what she wanted. "We can have Sunday dinner at her house, just like we always have."

"I don't want to go back," Navy said.

She said out loud exactly what I had also been wishing. Except that I couldn't believe it was her saying it.

"I understand, sweetie. It's not going to be easy." I took her hand. "Your dad is not going to be happy when we return. He's mad that I took you on this trip. But it'll be okay."

Except that I didn't know that it would be okay. In fact, I was very concerned that it wasn't going to be. Navy didn't answer. I could tell she was concerned about how Kevin would feel. She had been trained to put his feelings first and she seemed nervous about his anger. I had shown her that we were still mother and daughter, that this is what care and love should look like. I wanted her to know that love didn't demand that you cut off someone in your family, or that you needed to worry about one person's feelings above all others, even your own. I hoped beyond hope that this time away would stay with her when we returned, acting as a shield against her dad's emotional manipulations.

We packed up our car and said goodbye to Traci and her family on Saturday, December 18, and would arrive back in Calgary the next day. The car ride home was completely different from the drive out to Wyoming. We were getting along almost exactly like we always had. Navy was laughing, smiling, telling silly jokes, catching me up on all the news of her school and friends on the phone I had somewhat reluctantly given back to her. I listened patiently while she described what Karla's kids, Matt and Maya, were up to, and how much Navy was looking forward to opening Christmas presents with them when she got back. I had given her money while we were in Wyoming to buy gifts for Kevin and Karla, Karla's kids, and West. She was excited for them to open what she had picked out.

But a few hours before we arrived home, Navy showed me Facebook messages from Kevin and Karla. A picture was posted of them, along with West, Matt, and Maya in front of their Christmas tree. They wrote in the comments that they missed Navy and there were presents under the tree waiting for her when she got back. Everyone had already opened their presents. *At the Christmas party you were supposed to be at,* wrote Karla. *We missed u.* Navy was devastated. And yet, she strangely took all the responsibility onto herself, which is not at all uncommon for a child being manipulated into alienation. She replied, *I don't feel left out…it's my own fault but I promise you I really wanted to be there. I'm so so so so sad. I really wish I was there.*

Karla's words said they missed her and wanted to be with her, but I could see that their messages were intended to evoke rejection and jealousy. And it worked. Navy was miserable and helpless. Their cruelty was hard to believe. Navy desperately wanted to be with them, to be included and feel like she was a part of the family too. It was only six days before Christmas, and I was sure that Kevin and Karla had intentionally had their gift-opening early to exclude her. Navy couldn't see that they were taunting and manipulating her. No child wants to believe that their own father could do such a thing.

During the car ride, Navy got increasingly anxious to see her dad, Karla, Matt, and Maya before they left to see Kevin's family in Arizona on the 21st.

I had held my ground on West and Navy spending Christmas with me as scheduled, so Kevin decided to take Karla and her kids and go visit his family without West and Navy. He could have waited until the 27th when my kids could join them, but instead, he ignored his scheduled time with them and left the country. As we got closer to home, Navy and I could see the big city lights of downtown twinkling in the distance. I told her to call Kevin and said that we could go straight over to his house so she could spend the next two days with everyone before they went away. "You can open presents at your dad's house before they go," I suggested.

I smiled at Navy, feeling genuinely excited for the holiday together. But when she got Kevin on the phone, he refused to see her.

I heard him say, "No, Navy. We're good. Enjoy this time with your mom. We'll see you later."

Navy started to cry. She then tried texting Karla but got the same response. *We'll be back soon. Talk to you then.* When Navy begged them to let her come, they ignored her calls and texts. My heart shattered. She desperately wanted to open presents with her brother and Karla's kids. She wanted to give them the presents she had carefully selected for them. *No*, they said flatly. *We'll connect with you next year.*

The realization was almost more than I could believe Kevin and Karla were capable of. They were punishing this child. The message to Navy was clear: *We'll withdraw our love and affection. We'll ignore you. We'll make you regret not fighting hard enough to get away. You've been disloyal, Navy. You've broken our trust, Navy.*

We pulled into the driveway after the long road trip, and she tried calling Kevin again.

"Please, Daddy, please!" she cried. "Please, can't I come over? Why can't I come? I have a present for you. And for Krum, and Matt and Maya. Please!"

But she was met with a wall. The answer was no, they would see her in the new year. Instead of enraging her, it terrified her even more deeply. She would never again do anything to displease Kevin or Karla.

I spent the next couple of days trying to keep Navy's soul from being completely crushed. We went shopping, cooked her favorite meals, and prepared for Christmas festivities. But I could tell she was sad, confused, and lost. Meanwhile, Kevin and Karla, long after that Sunday when they opened presents with West, continued to post dozens of pictures of that day. Navy felt abandoned and betrayed, and she had been. The pain she was in made my heart pound so hard I could feel it moving in my chest. The magnitude of the cruelty being inflicted on this twelve-year-old was unfathomable. Eventually, I took Navy's phone again to stop the flood of photos calculated to hurt her.

The only good news was that I got extra time with Navy and West, during what was supposed to be Kevin's scheduled time. West had arrived home on the 21st and we tried to make things as normal and festive as possible. We followed all of our little family traditions that the kids had loved since they were small. I sprinkled the snowy lawn with oats and glitter to show Santa and the reindeer how to get to our house. Since we didn't have a fireplace, we hung a special house key for Santa on the outside doorknob so he could get in. We set out cookies; I hid a glass pickle ornament in the tree and whoever found it first on Christmas morning got to open the first present. It was all wonderful and magical, but it was never going to feel like enough for Navy, who knew what she had missed out on. It was becoming clear that the progress we had made in Wyoming was quickly becoming undone.

"Your dad shouldn't be doing this to you, Navy," I told her. He's punishing you for going on that trip with me. But you know you didn't have a choice to come or not. You didn't do anything wrong. You know that, right? I am so angry. It isn't okay for them to do this to you, Navy."

She didn't say much but she looked like she was being tortured. She wanted to be with her dad, she hated what was happening, but she couldn't quite shift her mindset and place the responsibility squarely on Kevin, where it belonged. She still believed it was her job to protect his feelings and to make him happy. No amount of telling her the truth would make her believe that she wasn't to blame in any of this. However, on Christmas Eve and Christmas Day, her confusion began to turn to anger, directed at me. Instead of enjoying what should have been a fun and celebratory time together, she stayed in her room most of the time and interacted with me as little as possible. When she did, she was sullen and cold.

Having more time to myself than usual over Christmas, I had recently taken an interest in learning about mental health disorders and how to identify them. It was precipitated by a long conversation my mom had recently had with a friend of hers. The woman had a PhD in psychology, and knowing I was desperate for help with Navy, my mom confided in her about my situation. My mom told this doctor that Kevin was keeping Navy from us, making her deathly afraid of me, and manipulating her to the point that she wouldn't leave her dad for anything.

"She listened to everything. I told her in detail about what was happening with you and Navy and a lot of what you had gone through while you were married to Kevin," my mom recounted one evening after dinner.

"What did she say?" I asked eagerly.

"She asked me if I had ever heard of people having personality disorders," my mom replied. "Based on everything I told her, she thinks Kevin fits the description of someone with a specific kind of personality disorder, or possibly more than one."

She reached into her purse where she had written on a scrap of paper, Mixed Cluster B Personality Disorders.

"It's this," she said, pointing to the note.

"Thanks," I said.

I spent hours on the computer reading everything I could about personality disorders. I learned that there were four different ones under Cluster B, including Antisocial Personality Disorder, Borderline Personality Disorder, and Narcissistic Personality Disorder. There were several traits that crossed over so someone could have a mix of them, rather than just one. Just as it had with Parental Alienation Syndrome, the pieces fell into place as I read. It was like reading a case study specifically on Kevin and his behavior. I had thought for many years about the gnawing sense that maybe something was actually wrong with Kevin, that there was more to it than just bad behavior. Compulsive lying is a common characteristic of several of the disorders, but that didn't come as a surprise to me. I had already been coming to grips with the fact that anything Kevin had ever told me may have been a lie. I was never able to fully explain what was off about Kevin, his desires, his inability to connect his actions to consequences on other people. It had only been a month since Kevin stood on my doorstep after dropping West off, wanting to speak to me about something.

"Can I ask you a question?" he said. I waited in silence. "Why did you divorce me?"

He appeared genuinely puzzled. I stood there, wide-eyed and dumbfounded. He seemed to honestly want to know the answer. Could he possibly not know? No wonder he was so good at convincing people of his innocence: maybe he really believed it himself. After several speechless moments, I asked him to leave, without responding.

Kevin was such an immensely complex person, this all got filed away under something else that I needed to figure out but didn't know how. My relief mixed with dread the further I delved into the topic. These toxic personalities rarely change, they just change victims, I read in one study. It all resonated. I had been Kevin's victim and now Navy was. Worst of all, what was happening to Navy and West was my nightmare coming true. What I had tried to protect above all else—the kids' emotional well-being—was now in jeopardy.

It didn't seem like anything could be done to repair a personality disorder, and certainly not if the person doesn't acknowledge that there's a problem, which I learned happens most of the time. People with these disorders routinely live in a world where they may speak about taking responsibility for their actions, but they don't ever actually believe they are to blame. Instead, they believe they are the ones being victimized. Accomplishing their personal agenda, whatever that may be, is their primary goal, and, with no reluctance, they will even hurt people they love, including their children, in order to achieve it. Learning about even just a few of these characteristics was enough to know that I wasn't crazy and neither was Navy.

When Kevin and Karla returned from Arizona, they switched gears, and in a flash they turned on the affection with Navy once again. After stony silence and leaving her behind, suddenly they were texting her with warm messages, saying they couldn't wait to see her, to give her her Christmas gifts, that they had missed her terribly. *We can't wait to pick you up and see you tomorrow*, they wrote effusively. *We'll make up for what your mom did to you*, they promised. It was an easy sell. Navy had already accepted the idea that their rejection of her had been my fault. They told her how unfair it was that I had confiscated her phone and they offered to buy her one she could keep at their house. After their long and tortuous neglect, there they were, back in her life as if nothing had happened.

It was now December 30, and Kevin and Karla were flying back into Calgary around midnight. I had let West and Navy know that I would take them to Kevin's first thing in the morning. But I could see on Navy's phone that she was already getting texts from Kevin telling her to not wait until they arrived home that night. They told her that as soon as she got the chance, to walk out the door to the nearby pharmacy at the mall and Karla's forty-year-old brother, James, would be waiting to pick her up. They had made arrangements for him to meet her there. Later that evening, Navy came downstairs from her room dressed as though she was going out, including her small gold purse hanging from her shoulder.

"I'm leaving," she said.

"Navy, I know you're anxious to go and your dad and Karla are anxious for you to leave. I'm happy to drive you wherever you need to go, but let's wait until your dad gets back into town later tonight. I will take you over as soon as they get there. You don't need to wait until the morning when I'm going to drop West off," I offered.

"No!" she said, and then ran out the back door of the house. I ran after her but couldn't catch up to her. I called her cell phone but she didn't answer. I texted her to come back, but she didn't return. I then texted her and told her I would come by wherever Karla's brother had taken her just to say goodnight and to make sure she was okay. She refused. I had no idea where Navy was, and she was now with this forty-year-old man whom I knew nothing about. I watched as the entire week in Wyoming and all of the progress I had made with her simply evaporated. It was like we never went, like she never started to recover, like we were back to the deepest kind of alienation.

At midnight I texted Kevin and asked him if he had Navy. He told me that he did, and I told him how angry I was about what had happened. He stopped replying to my texts. The next morning, rather than waiting for me to drop West off, Kevin came and picked him up early. On New Year's Eve, I called West and Navy to wish them a happy new year. Neither of them answered.

Two days passed and Navy and West were due to come back to me. Kevin refused to return them to me so I went to his house to pick them up. West got in the car, but Navy stood on Kevin's porch.

"You're a lazy, fat loser and I'm never coming to live with you again!" she yelled from over the balcony. "Go ahead and call the police but I'm not coming back!" she added angrily.

I returned home with West and did call the police. They retrieved Navy and dropped her off at my house. Her body language and her expression were completely deflated. She looked afraid of me, like she desperately wanted to get away. It was 1:00 a.m. when the officers left, and I told her and West to go up to their rooms to get some sleep. I saw on Navy's phone the next day that she had texted Karla in the middle of the night and pleaded with her to come and get her. Karla had refused. Karla told her that she would come and get her at 2:00 p.m. the next afternoon and to plan on sneaking out then. Seeing the email exchange between Karla and Navy and now knowing that Navy was going to run away at 2:00, I called my mom to come over and help me. She came right over.

"I don't think I can keep her in the house," I said. "She's going to try to run away again; how do I keep her here?" I was particularly concerned because it had snowed heavily that day and the temperatures were frigid.

"We'll find a way," my mom said, ever the reassuring presence in my life that I needed.

Just then, at five minutes before 2:00, Navy came bursting out of her room and toward the stairs. She had a bag of things in her hands and told me she was just going outside for a few minutes.

"I know what you're planning, Navy, and you're not leaving," I said.

I darted toward the front door, and as Navy tried to get past me, I shouted to my mom, "Go to the back door!" My mom did as I asked and caught Navy just as she was trying to escape out the back. "I can't hold her!" I heard her shout.

I raced into the kitchen to see my mom with her arms locked around Navy's waist, and Navy thrashing to get free, fighting and pushing against her grandmother with all her strength.

"I can't hold her, Elaine!"

I tried to get my arms around Navy so that my mom could let go, but she broke free from both of us. We managed to grab hold of her again. She began flailing her arms, hitting me in the face and kicking both me and my mom with her winter boots. My mom lost her grip on her as Navy continued to try and wrestle herself away from us. Holding her as tightly as I could, she and I both lost our balance and fell down onto the hardwood floor. She then tore off her winter boots, threw them at me, and ran upstairs. She stopped at the top of the stairs, turned around, screamed, "You're a f**king piece of shit and I hate you!" and slammed her bedroom door. I stood doubled over at the bottom of the stairs, trying to catch my breath.

"This can't go on," I said to my mom. "I don't know what to do."

I sat down on the bottom step, in such shock that I couldn't even cry. I didn't know this child. In only two short months, her mind, body, and spirit had become complete strangers to me. My mom and I talked quietly, wondering what could possibly be done to set her free, to put my family back together.

After a few minutes, my mom offered to go upstairs and try to talk with Navy. "She might listen to her grandmother," she said hopefully, and headed for Navy's room. A second later, my mom's voice called out, "She's gone!"

I raced upstairs to find Navy's bedroom window open, the tall screen removed, and a line of footprints along our snowy roof to the ledge. She had somehow managed to get down the icy slope of the roof and jump from the edge almost twelve feet onto the ground, in only her socks and a T-shirt. I raced outside but there was no sight of her. I walked back into the house and my mom looked at me in total disbelief. "Well, she's nothing if not resourceful," she said. It was true. Navy was so determined to not be with me, it was obvious she would resort to whatever it would take to get away.

Knowing Kevin and Karla were down the street waiting for her escape, I called Kevin and asked him to let me know when he had her. Within a few minutes of that call, he was on my doorstep raging. He pushed his way into my house and screamed at me, threatening to call the police.

"Get out of my house!" I screamed, as I tried to push him out the door. He pushed me back and I screamed at him again to leave.

"You assaulted Navy and I'm calling the cops!" he yelled.

"I did not! She's lying!" I said. "Leave right now!"

He finally went out the door and I locked it behind him. Almost immediately, I heard a large bang on my door. I looked out the peephole but couldn't see anything. I waited a minute and then slowly unlocked it to see what had happened. For Christmas, I had hung a large fresh evergreen wreath on my door for the holidays. But the only remnants of the wreath that now remained were smashed pieces of green pine all down my steps and sidewalk. The thick metal curve on the bottom of the wreath hanger was bent almost flat from the force of Kevin pulling the wreath off and breaking it. My heart was racing as I walked down my sidewalk to survey the mess. When I walked around the corner to my driveway, I saw Kevin pull away from the front of my house. Navy was with him, in the front seat, where she had watched the whole thing.

A short time later my doorbell rang. It was the police. Kevin had called them.

"Did you assault your daughter? Did you knock her to the ground?"

"Absolutely not!" I said, enraged by Kevin's twisted version of events. In fact, this is what my ex-husband did," I added, gesturing to the wreath's debris. "Her grandmother and I were trying to keep her from running away again, which she only does because he's telling her to."

"It sounds like your daughter doesn't want to live with you," the officer said coldly. "Maybe you should stop calling us."

I froze, taking in his words. There was no law that could make my daughter stay with me. There was no threat that would make Kevin abide by our custody agreement. I felt, at that moment, like it might all be over. I didn't know what more I could do to bring Navy home. With devastating clarity I could now see the immensity of the obstacles before me. My efforts felt pitifully futile, like I was trying to break down the walls of a mighty fortress with a pocketful of pebbles.

* * *

Kevin and Karla continued to encroach on my life, mimicking it in strange ways. The house they had bought in the summer was less than a mile from my house. They had taken swimming and triathlon from me, and now they were shopping at my grocery store, filling prescriptions at my pharmacy, enrolling Matt and Maya at the same schools that I had carefully chosen for my kids. Kevin had even started attending our church again, where Karla became a baptized member and joined him each week. Yet they kept Navy from seeing me. Karla continued to bombard me with texts and emails. She would stick her middle finger up at me when she saw me, or if she was close enough to yell, she'd shout, "You're still fat!" and then laugh. I couldn't understand what she was gaining from the unrelenting and unprovoked verbal assaults when she already had Navy. *Retard, you don't deserve to be called a mother* or *Navy is never coming back to you, we'll raise our daughter now.* Her texts and emails were always signed, *Karla, the one who raises Navy.* My world felt like a waking nightmare. Nothing felt right or real.

Just after the new year, unprepared to give up my fight to get my daughter back, I had to come up with a new strategy. Forcing Navy back clearly wasn't working. Taking her away for deprogramming hadn't worked either. I needed a different plan. I continued to research Parental Alienation Syndrome, learning everything I could to see what others had tried. Reading other parents' stories was horrifying and comforting at the same time. At least I wasn't completely alone in my nightmare.

Online, I came across a PAS expert who worked with parents. He guided them through different strategies of staying connected with the child who was alienated, and even sometimes how to reunify. He seemed extremely knowledgeable and experienced. There was nothing to lose, I thought. All my legal avenues were closed. I sent him $5,000 and hired him to help me. For several months, he consulted with me on the phone, confirming Kevin's alienating behavior and assessing Navy's level of alienation as severe and West's as moderate. We focused on what I could do to help Navy.

This was the lowest period of my life. Nicole flew in to visit me and help see me through it. She had come right away, after I had called her with an update. Other friends, who also knew my story and how deeply lost Navy seemed to the alienation, hadn't responded like Nicole had. *I don't feel safe coming to your house,* one close friend had said. *My husband won't let me* was another's reason. While I knew that Kevin was unpredictable, I still felt abandoned. I was yet again paying the price for his outrageous behavior, this time in the form of some of my lifelong friends.

One day, during Nicole's stay, the PAS expert recommended that I install a special software onto my phone so I could record Kevin's phone calls, with the goal of gathering evidence against him to use in court, or in a police report. I couldn't even count the number of conversations where Kevin had berated me, called me vile names, or threatened to abandon the kids. Maybe, I thought, gathering evidence would finally show the courts what they had been unable to see because of Kevin's convincing courtroom performances. But it was now the new year, and not once in the fifteen months since I had left Kevin had the police or the courts taken his behavior seriously—either because they didn't witness it or perhaps simply because they refused to believe me.

I stood with Nicole in a strange spy tech store, in disbelief that this was what it had come to. Before a salesperson could help us, I turned to Nicole and said, "Let's go."

We hurried out of the store and back into the bright sunlight. I shook my head as we walked away. "This isn't going to help. The law just isn't on my side. No amount of phone evidence is going to change that."

I was grateful for Nicole's visit, and our time together had lifted my spirits. I was struggling with worsening depression so having her come to spend time with me and care for me had been an enormous help. She cooked dinner, did laundry, cleaned my house, took me shopping and out to a movie.

Saturday morning, after dropping her off at the airport, I was looking forward to going home and enjoying some one-on-one time with West. We played some games, watched a movie, went out for lunch, and read a book together that night. I got up Sunday morning to get ready for church, and woke West up so he could also shower and get dressed in time. When I went into his room, he pulled his pillow over his head and told me he didn't feel like going. I told him it was okay, that he didn't have to, and I left on my own.

When I returned around noon, I had expected to find him doing his homework or playing video games, but the house was empty. After searching his room and the yard, I saw the note taped to a wall near the front door. I had come through the garage when I came home and hadn't seen it. It was in West's handwriting but I couldn't figure out what was misplaced about it. Then I realized that it was written in crayon, the letters thick and offering a version of his younger self I hadn't seen in years. *I'm going to live with Dad 50/50 so he won't be so mad at me all the time. This is the only way for things to be fair, so this is how it will be now. I will be leaving on Sundays from now on. West.*

From the time that the new custody arrangement had been put in place in October, there had been unyielding pressure from Kevin for West and Navy to leave me. When Navy left, the pressure on West intensified, and I had been terrified that this day would come. There had been many texts from Kevin to West about needing to be brave like his sister, and even more about West not being a man because he wouldn't walk out of the house and leave. West had finally surrendered to Kevin's coercion. Kevin had played on West's deeply ingrained sense of fairness and now, having all but lost Navy, West was being pulled away from me too. I texted West immediately and asked him to come home. But he said he would stay at his dad's and see me next week. *7 and 7 is fair,* he replied, meaning one week with me and one week with Kevin. *I'll see you next Sunday, I promise. I love you.*

CHAPTER ELEVEN

It was when I found a Parental Alienation Syndrome support group that I was able to feel a real sense of consolation. Once a month, I drove over an hour to sit in a little community room inside a shopping mall, surrounded by other parents who'd had their children alienated from them by the other parent. The group was overwhelmingly men, fathers whose former wives or partners had manipulated their kids into little or no contact, sometimes for years. We shared our heartbreaks, listened openly, sympathized, and felt less alone. It was the smallest shred of comfort I could find while I ached for Navy, and now for West too.

This was the one place I could be honest about the turmoil and what felt like ongoing torture. These parents understood how expensive legal help was, how I was watching my savings and my mom's savings drain away with no results. I later learned that this is common behavior for an alienating parent: to represent themselves in court and push back against every legal agreement in an effort to drain the other parent's bank account with fees, so they have no resources left to fight for their children.

Over the course of several meetings, I shared about Kevin changing the kids' names on legal and school documents, changing Navy's middle name from Elaine to Marjorie, after his mother. He'd also removed Hartrick as West's second middle name. He even told me that Navy was using the last name Shepherd—Karla's last name. I told them about all the times I had sent little gifts, cards, and notes to Navy, only to have them returned to me unopened, placed on my doorstep or handed to me by a downcast West on his days with me. One of the returned gifts included a note from Navy telling me to quit trying to buy her love, like I had all those years that I organized her birthday parties and bought her presents.

I even shared about the memory book I created for Navy, filled with pictures of her and me throughout her childhood, which, after wrapping it and quietly dropping it off at their house, got torn apart—the photos of Navy by herself were kept and the remnants of the memory book and all pictures of me with Navy were thrown into a grocery bag and returned to the doorstep at my house. At our February meeting, I shared that on Valentine's Day, I had dropped off a pink stuffed heart shaped pillow that was covered in small pastel-colored hearts, along with some of Navy's favorite candy. That evening I saw, tagged on Navy's Facebook, a picture taken by Karla of fluff and fabric—the bear torn to shreds in a pile with the caption "Look, Navy gave my dog Jersey a new chew toy."

But one of the most difficult stories I shared was when Navy began riding in the car when West got dropped off at my house, only to sneak into her room, grab her things secretly, and dash out of the house with them, leaving a stray sock on the stairs or a hair tie for me to find near the door. During one of these furtive visits, she took from the fireplace mantle a small, silver double picture frame of herself and West that I had treasured because West had painstakingly chosen it for me as a little boy years ago during a school trip specifically for parents' Christmas gifts. Another member shared about his own heartrending attempts to keep in contact with his estranged young adult daughter, leaving her letters and gifts as often as he could under the windshield wiper of her car at her work. He even went so far as to sneak into the open house of their family home that his ex-wife was selling, just to wander around his daughter's room and feel close to her.

I hated belonging to this club of anguished parents, all trying to find a way forward through their confusion, grief, and rage. But comfort still came from sharing space with people to whom I didn't have to explain why my kids wouldn't have anything to do with me. Outside of a room of people like us, no matter how you tried to describe it, it was hard for people, even friends, to understand why a young child would cut a parent out of their lives. Often the look on their face and subsequent questions revealed what they were really thinking— *You surely must have done something to make your child hate you.*

Months went by with no contact from Navy and week-long absences from West. Mother's Day had come and gone with no call or acknowledgement that I even existed. That Sunday, it was poignantly highlighted by a young girl sitting with her family in the pew in front of me at church. Several times throughout the service, the little girl with white-blond hair and pink bows would slowly twist herself part of the way around and shyly look at me out of the corner of her eye. It was difficult to be there that day, to sit alone at church listening to messages from the pulpit honoring motherhood. I tried to stay focused on my own mother, rather than on *being* a mother. Shortly before the service was over, the young girl twisted around again, slid her hand up and over the back of the wooden bench, and handed me a small slip of paper. I took the paper and wept as I looked down at the beautiful pencil sketch of a flower she had drawn for me, with the words *Happy Mother's Day* written on it. It was just the comfort I needed to make it through the day, and I couldn't help but wonder if somehow this young girl had understood the pain I was in. My life had become a nightmare. I didn't know how to make things right, how to make the truth prevail.

Around this time, June of that year, I received documents in the mail showing that my divorce had become final. It was a quiet afternoon, and I stared at the declaration that I was no longer married to Kevin. It felt monumental that we were no longer joined legally, and yet he still held everything over me, including my kids' minds and their time. I remember thinking that twenty-five years of marriage were at long last over, that it had taken two whole years to actually divorce him because he had dragged his feet and refused to cooperate with any part of the proceedings. Being legally free from Kevin had not solved any of my problems, however.

Along with the divorce came Kevin's sudden refusal to continue paying spousal or child support. He claimed that since the kids were with him most of the time, there was no call for child support, despite the fact that I was providing West with food, clothes, school supplies, and other necessities for swimming and piano lessons. We appeared in court, yet again, and this time Kevin stood up and held out the keys to his BMW in one hand and his shiny Rolex in the other, and claimed that he was broke and would need to sell his possessions to keep up his payments to me. My mouth gaped open in shock when he actually seemed to push out tears as he was talking.

In a lifetime of knowing Kevin, I had never seen him drop a tear, not even at his father's funeral. He claimed poverty despite the fact that I had heard from his former colleagues at a recent cocktail party that Kevin was doing well at his job and making upwards of $300,000 a year. This didn't include the sizable income that I knew Karla was contributing to the household, which I learned about when Kevin accidentally divulged it at one point during our legal battles. Kevin's colleagues shared that Kevin would come back to the office after our court appearances, bragging and laughing about what he got away with in front of the judge again. Kevin found the most success representing himself, which he did after having fired three different attorneys. This time, the court granted his request and all financial support for me and West ended immediately.

Suddenly, I could no longer afford tuition at Mount Royal University, where I was earning my degree in Travel and Tourism. I was forced to drop out mid-year. I had already lost my daughter. I was in the process of losing my son. And now my future was no longer secure. The depression and weight gain that had started during the final part of my marriage began to overwhelm me. I struggled to be able to construct any kind of future for myself. I was sleeping more and more, sometimes the whole day while West was at school, though I always managed to drop him off, pick him up, and take him to practices and activities. I had trouble cooking and keeping the house clean so we ate a lot of take-out and pizza, and my mom came over a few times a week to help me keep the house in order. I was starting to neglect myself too, showering less frequently, continuing to gain weight. Nicole continued to fly in whenever she could to lend a hand and make sure I was at least surviving.

Finally, one day, my mom said, "I'm worried about you, Elaine. I can see that you're not taking care of yourself. You need to see a doctor. You're depressed."

I didn't say anything.

"You really need to see a doctor," my mom insisted, "and get some medication."

"I don't want to," I said.

"Why?" She asked.

"Because then I'll feel like Kevin won."

"What do you mean?"

"Going on antidepressants means I couldn't fix it. It means that I couldn't solve my problems without external help. It feels like evil won over good."

"It doesn't have to be forever," she said. "It'll just help you get through this terrible time so you can get a job and support yourself and keep fighting for West and Navy."

"That feels impossible right now," I said, barely able to form the words. "I feel like I've lost everything."

Ultimately, I listened to my mom and went to see Dr. Heide, who had known me nearly all my adult life. She had been there when I found out I was pregnant with my babies, and had been their doctor their entire lives too.

"What brings you in, Elaine?" she asked.

"I think I'm suffering from depression. My mom sent me, actually." Dr. Heide was my mom's physician also.

"Oh," she said, looking surprised. "Is there something that has brought it on?" she asked.

When I told her the reason for my visit, I didn't hold back about the divorce, the abuse, and Kevin taking the kids. She was extremely compassionate. As I told her my story and why I needed medication, she began to cry.

"They are such beautiful children," she said, and then apologized for the unprofessionalism of her tears. I was moved by her emotional response. I knew she saw the stark change in me, having been my doctor since I was a teenager. She had seen me at my healthiest, youthful and glowing, and now I was sitting in front of her at one of the most dismal points of my life. Her devastation on behalf of my situation was a profound moment for me, magnifying the tragedy of my circumstance.

I did begin taking antidepressants, and at first I suffered from side effects like fatigue and brain fog. I felt very unlike myself, but then again, it had been a very long time since I'd remembered feeling anything like my old self. After about a month, however, I remember leaving West's swim meet and suddenly feeling like I was going to be okay. My mom continued to provide me with emotional support. Her training specialty as a nurse had been in mental health so it was always helpful to talk things through with her. She even told me one day, in the midst of all this, that she had begun fasting each Sunday.

"Every week for as long as I need to," she said. "So that Heavenly Father will bring Navy back to us."

Fasting from all food and water for twenty-four hours was something we would do once a month as part of our faith, for anything special or at any time we might feel in need of something important from God. However, fasting every week with no end in sight was a monumental sacrifice. I joined her as often as I could, willing to try anything and everything to bring my children home.

* * *

It was nearing the end of the year, and the parental alienation expert I had hired in the spring had yet to provide any solutions for getting my kids back. I decided to go back to my attorney, Claire. She advised that I might have one final avenue for reunification with my children through the legal system. It was something called a Bilateral Parenting Assessment or Practice Note 7 Intervention. Essentially, I could hire a court-appointed mental health professional to assess our family situation, at the cost of $15,000. His report and recommendation, however, would be final. There would be no appeals and the court would adhere to his advice. Several members of my support group warned me against this route. They cautioned me that in their personal experience with the Practice Note 7, the court might find parental alienation, but they likely wouldn't act on it. *It's an expensive and very long process*, they said. *Don't waste your money.*

"I have to," I said, grateful for their concern but determined to exhaust every avenue. "Even if I'm unsuccessful, I have to be able to lay my head on my pillow at night and know that I tried everything to get my kids back. Absolutely everything."

That December, Dr. Shoemaker, a court-appointed psychologist, began a series of home visits and interviews. He talked to me, to Kevin, to Karla, to the kids, and to my mom. He even joined us for family dinners. His assessment would take an entire year. My mom and I pooled together our very last pennies and paid for the assessment ourselves, without any contribution from Kevin. As a last resort, I sold all of my jewelry. I was happy, though, to include my wedding rings in the sale.

Christmas was drawing near and I knew I would have to spend it without Navy. The ache in my chest was almost unbearable and I worried about how I was going to provide a Christmas for West. So I was stunned when my doorbell rang one evening and I opened the door to find the bishop from my church standing there with a giant red Santa sack in his arms. It was full of food, treats, a box of oranges, a whole turkey, and all the fixings to make Christmas dinner. Everything had been purchased with donations from our congregation.

Twelve days before Christmas, my doorbell rang again, but this time no one was there. Instead, a large reindeer-shaped wall hanging made from felt was left on my step along with a bouquet of beautiful fresh-cut seasonal flowers. On the wall hanging were twelve small pockets, one for each of the remaining days before Christmas. Tucked inside each pocket were gift cards worth hundreds of dollars to grocery stores, the movie theater, and West's favorite electronics store. I had no idea who could be this generous, but I was so overwhelmed with gratitude I couldn't stop crying—nor could my mom when I called to tell her about it.

My neighbor, hearing I had a talent for arrangements and design, hired me to create corporate gift baskets for his clients, and the money I earned buoyed me through the rest of the season. West came home the day after spending Christmas Eve and Christmas Day with Kevin.

I was thrilled to provide him with a modest but beautiful and enchanting Christmas that my mom joined us for. But then I learned what had happened over the holiday at his dad's house.

"They had a fight," West told me. "Karla drove off, then Dad followed her. They were gone all night and the next day."

"You mean, they left you—and Navy and Matt and Maya—all alone? Over Christmas?"

"Yes," he said, almost chuckling and brushing it off like it was no big deal.

But it was a big deal. It was beyond belief. Why, I wondered with outrage, would Kevin fight to keep my kids from me, only to abandon them to his dysfunctional relationship? It only confirmed further that he didn't really want the kids: he wasn't interested in being with them, only in hurting me in the worst way possible. I committed to keep fighting for my kids, to somehow try and protect them from their dad's mania. All my hope was riding on Dr. Shoemaker and the Parenting Assessment.

By spring of the next year, I was applying for jobs and landing interviews. I was excited to go back to work, but also nervous. I had reached out to several of my previous travel industry contacts and hoped to find something in management at a hotel. I got a call back from the Fairmont, one of the most prestigious hotels in Calgary, for a position as their corporate sales manager. The interview had been fantastic and I knew I had done well. It had been with Daniel Woodsen, the director of sales, who would be my boss. We discovered that we knew several of the same people, and, in an even bigger coincidence, his daughter and West went to the same high school. Daniel and I got along famously and he all but said the job was mine.

But days went by, then a week, and I heard nothing. When I called to follow up, he suddenly wouldn't take my calls. Finally, I reached him and he told me that the hotel wanted to go in a different direction.

I was upset and confused. I couldn't figure out what had happened to make him have such a change of heart. A few days later, I received a cryptic email from Karla. *Ran into a friend of yours recently. So sorry, but you won't be getting that job after all.*

West told me the whole story a few weeks later, as I was still reeling from this abrupt rejection. Karla had been attending one of Matt's hockey practices and chatting with a fellow parent in the stands. West had stopped by after school to watch Matt play. He sat by Karla and introduced himself to the parent Karla was visiting with.

"West?" the parent said. "That's not a name you hear every day. I'm pretty sure I just met your mom."

"Oh, really?" West perked up.

"Yes, I'm in the process of filling a position on my team and I had a chance to chat with her about it," Daniel shared.

"That's cool."

West watched for a while, then grabbed his backpack, told Daniel that it was nice meeting him, and said to Karla he would see her at home. He thought nothing of it as he headed out of the arena, leaving Karla and Daniel alone together.

I can imagine what she said to him and how convincing she must have sounded to get him to change his mind, despite having met me, despite not knowing Karla at all. What were the chances in a city of over one million people? It was too random and yet too precise a coincidence. Where, I asked, was God in all of this?

I rallied from that experience and applied for more positions, eventually landing an interview at another five-star hotel. This was an all-suite property with the most expensive rooms in the city. My interview with the director of sales and marketing, Erica, went perfectly and I was even more excited about this sales manager position than the one at the Fairmont. We parted ways warmly, with all but a job offer. After days of hearing nothing, I drove down to the hotel and asked to speak to

Erica, but she wouldn't see me. I dropped off a gift and left her several messages, but she still didn't respond. And then another email from Karla. *You won't be getting that job either.* It was all too sordid to be true. I couldn't believe she was capable of sabotaging me twice. And how?

With more determination than ever, I set a meeting with Erica and vowed to straighten out whatever mess Karla was trying to make of my career and my life. Erica received me graciously and explained the situation.

"The Fairmont and our hotel are owned by the same management companies," she said. "Daniel is a friend and colleague of mine and I ran into him at a company event last week. I told him I was excited about a new manager I was about to hire. When he asked more about you, he told me he'd also met you. I don't like to get involved in people's personal affairs, but apparently he's acquainted with your ex-husband's partner and she told Daniel some things about you that would make me nervous to bring you on. I'm very sorry, Elaine."

"Thank you for sharing that with me, Erica," I began, training myself on staying calm and professional, even though I felt like screaming at the top of my lungs about the injustice of it all. I wondered how much worse my luck could get than Daniel and Erica knowing each other, or that I happened to come up in conversation the week she was deciding who to hire. I continued, "I understand that you may have heard some unpleasant things about me, but I assure you they are all fabricated. I have excelled in this industry and I am the best person you could hire for this position. If you give me a chance, you won't regret it. I promise."

I don't know what it was that changed her mind, but Erica offered me the job. I felt vindicated yet inflamed with anger at Karla's deliberate attacks on me. It was one thing to keep my kids away from me, but to try and ruin my chances of making a living was a new low, even for her.

I arrived at the hotel on the first day of my new job to find a bouquet of flowers on my desk welcoming me to the team. I immediately loved my work, which included travel to Ottawa and Toronto, where I got to see Nicole regularly. Yet weeks and months went by, and I still had no contact with Navy. The summer came and with school out and activities over, I looked forward to at least more time in the evenings with West. But on the days when West was due to come to my house, Kevin and Karla would arrange for some dubious family vacation that overlapped with my time and there was no equalization when they returned. My days with West just became fewer.

In September, West turned sixteen. Kevin bought him a brand-new luxury truck, equipped with all the extras. I wanted to be happy because West was happy, but I was angry and resentful at all the milestones I was missing. With West's new truck came new driving responsibilities. He started missing more of his days with me because he was charged with driving Navy, Matt, or Maya somewhere. Kevin and Karla had made him their caretaker and chauffeur in exchange for the truck, and West spent hours before and after school and on the weekends shuttling them around to activities and friends' houses.

"I can't come today. I have to drive Maya to cheerleading," became a refrain when he missed a day with me. "I have to pick Matt up from hockey," became the reason he had to leave my house a day early. I could see the control Kevin was exerting on West, holding his thrilling new truck as a privilege he barely even got to enjoy for himself, and keeping him so busy looking after the younger kids that he started seeing me less and less.

Looking for his gym clothes a few days after his birthday, and realizing he'd left them at my house, West called me. I offered to bring the clothes by, but he declined.

"Dad's just going to get angry," he said. "He doesn't like that I see you at all. You can't come here. He will lose it."

"What do you want me to do?" I asked.

We made a plan for me to drop his clothes off, wrapped in a plastic grocery bag, in the parking lot of his school. "Once you've brought them, text me a picture of where you left them, please," he said.

I tucked the bag between two fences near the football field so it wouldn't be spotted easily. I held up my phone, took the picture of precisely where I'd placed it, and texted it to him. He retrieved the bag at lunch and let me know he'd found it.

It had come to this kind of sneaking around. Yet none of it felt new. We had always danced around Kevin's temper, his feelings, his needs, his insecurities, his likes, dislikes, and wants, no matter how outrageous.

After West had missed several days with me, yet again, I called him.

"It's our time together, West. Your dad or Karla can drive the others. You're supposed to be with me," I said.

"I can't come," he said, his voice low and a little mournful.

I knew his sense of fairness was bothering him. He and I both knew it wasn't right to be cutting into my time with these driving obligations. And we both knew that West did not want to give up his beloved truck.

"It would just be easier," he said, "if I stayed with Dad."

What I didn't know is that Kevin had forced West to choose. In a series of texts over the span of four days, he accused West of not being loyal and "taking your mom's side." West, bewildered and panicked, was about to be left out of their family trip to Vancouver, in which he desperately wanted to be included. He begged, pleaded, and promised to do whatever Kevin wanted.

You will have to choose to be with her or me, Kevin had texted. *West, I am no longer supporting your decision to go back and forth. Could you be happy living with just us? You need to really think about that. Navy does not miss Elaine and she cannot see a day where she would EVER return. If you want to be part of our family the timing isn't up to you. You seem to think the world revolves around what you want. I have a lot of stress, West. Do you ever consider the complexity of my life?*

No, the world doesn't, West responded. *I'm just not the type of person to abandon people like that. So it's really hard for me to do things like that. Could I please go to Vancouver?*

You think it would be bad to abandon Elaine? I don't understand your values, West. Kevin typed.

I heaved and felt my stomach drop to the floor. This was it. It was happening all over again. Only West wasn't even angry with me. He wasn't afraid of me. He hadn't been brainwashed, not exactly. His life had just become wrapped around Kevin and Karla's demands and he couldn't sustain it all anymore. He was being forced to choose something he knew was neither right nor fair.

> K⬛⬛⬛⬛⬛   3/17/11
>
> ⬛West⬛, can I trust what you tell me?
> Are you saying that at the end of the
> school year - you will commit to living
> with us? I perceive that u often get
> caught trying to make ur parents
> 'happy' ... Could u be happy living just
> with us? U need to really think about
> that? ⬛Navy⬛ does not miss E and she
> cannot see a day where she would
> EVER return. ⬛Matt⬛ just said to tell u
> that he misses u and its too bad u will
> miss his hockey tournament this
> weekend.
>   You will have to
> choose to be with her or me on your
> return ... You will no longer be
> welcome in my life as you are now.

Text from Kevin to West (on Messenger)

Kevin had managed to fulfill his promise from that day outside the mediation room, when he said he would win in the hearts and minds of our children. I couldn't quite bring myself to believe he had done exactly that. Not yet, at least. But what did it matter when both my kids were now no longer living with me, when one of them had cut me off completely and the other barely had time to see me anymore? It broke me to think that Kevin had won. I was alone with nowhere else to turn except for my one last resort—the results of the Practice Note 7, which came the very next month.

We gathered in a courtroom to hear the results of the year-long assessment of Navy, West, and our family. The room was empty, except for Kevin and me. The judge emerged from chambers, carrying a large banker's box full of papers. He slammed the box down on his bench and without hiding his contempt, turned to face us and said, "Well, you two certainly can't seem to get along. This is one of the worst files I've ever seen."

He brought out the Shoemaker report, reminding us that the recommendations for where Navy and West live would be upheld by the court.

"You have exactly fifteen minutes to read it, and you'll read it together," he barked. He held up a single copy, several pages thick, and motioned for both me and Kevin to come forward. When I asked for my own copy to read over at my table, the judge refused.

"Oh," he continued. "Neither of you will be taking this report home. It's a closed case. You are forbidden to share it with your children."

"I can't anyway. I don't have my children." I stated.

"That's not what I asked you!" the judge screamed.

Kevin came to my side of the courtroom, where we sat side by side and read it. This was the first circumstance in a very long time that I had been this close to Kevin, and feeling his body invade my personal space was suffocating and infuriating. The shock of the judge's demand that my violent ex-husband sit beside me was beyond any explanation I could come up with. Feeling Kevin's hip against mine, his elbow bumping me when he turned a page, felt unsafe and humiliating. Then, I read the final recommendation: the children could decide for themselves who they wanted to live with. They were old enough to choose for themselves. The psychologist noted that both of them said they wanted to live at Kevin's house.

The strange truth is that everything changed in that moment and nothing changed. Navy and West were already choosing to be with Kevin, and they had already slipped away from me. But this report brought official and legal permanence to the situation. The law said I would retain written legal custody, but the law also said they could stay with Kevin. The law said they never had to see me again if they didn't want to. The law gave me no rights at all to see my own children, who were still minors. I was, at that moment, completely out of options. My support group friends had been right. However, this was what I had needed to do. I walked out of the courtroom that day fully confident that I had tried everything, spent every last dime possible, asked for help in every way I could have. I was going home without my kids that day, but a year had already gone by without Navy and now more than a month without West. I wept openly on my drive home, but felt no discomfort about the effort I had made to get them back.

Unbelievably, things got worse. Kevin filed for a reversal of our child support arrangement. He not only refused to pay me anything at all, but he demanded that I now pay him, since the children were living with him full-time. No one checked Kevin's income, only mine. In our court system cases may be assigned to any available judge at any time, so another judge ruled that I was now responsible for paying $1,100 every month for West and Navy. One small consolation was that this particular judge made the ruling apologetically, almost regretfully. Kevin earned more than six times what I did, but a third of my income now went to Kevin, with no guarantee at all that he would use it for the kids.

Within weeks, West stopped coming over entirely. He responded occasionally to my texts, but rarely took or returned my calls. The response I did get were excuses for why he couldn't come see me. He had to drive the kids somewhere; he had to babysit; he was too busy.

I tried to keep myself busy by keeping in touch with my friends, either on the phone or going for the occasional lunch. Most of them had kids West and Navy's age so we now struggled to find things in common or make conversation. "I feel survivor's guilt," as one friend put it, not wanting to ask about my kids, and feeling bad about talking about hers. I would sometimes be with a group of friends, some of them single mothers, and listen to them complain about their plight. One talked about how exhausting it was to look after her ten-year-old son by herself with all the housework and other responsibilities she had on her plate. Another complained about her ex-husband picking the kids up late so she'd had to miss her hot yoga class that night. They would carry on about their car pools and laundry, to-do lists and science projects, with no husbands to give them a break until it was their turn to take the kids. I listened quietly, attempting to be sympathetic, but couldn't help saying to myself, "Be grateful."

I tried throwing myself into work and I still liked my job, but I was a shell of my former self. Any reserve will or energy I'd had was drained by the court proceedings. Because of my weight, which was now over 250 pounds, I had little to no energy. My body had become permanently bent, slumped over, beaten down so far that I couldn't stand up straight. I looked so much older than I actually was, and my feet were chronically sore from plantar fasciitis, crying out under the weight they had to carry around. I was late to work more than I care to admit, and some mornings I didn't know how I was going to get out of bed at all. When I came home at the end of the day, it was with a bag of take-out in my hand. I headed straight for the lounge chair in my living room, turned on the television, placed the food and my little dog Swizzle in my lap, and ate until I was numb. The next day, I would repeat the process.

One night after work, I wandered through both of the kids' rooms. I looked at their beds, their books, the photos in frames on their dressers. We had furnished and decorated their rooms together, in their favorite colors, with their personalities in mind. Navy had spent perhaps a month in total in her room, but otherwise it had sat empty. West had taken most of his things to Kevin's house and his room looked just as unlived-in now.

Me, eating

I smoothed their bedspreads, which didn't need smoothing, and thought about how much hope this house had once contained. It was meant to be our refuge from the divorce, mine and theirs to share. But it was now nothing more than a mortgage payment that I could no longer afford. It was just four walls and possessions that didn't belong to my kids anymore. It felt like a house for ghosts.

Staying in the house, I began to realize, would turn me into a ghost too. I couldn't go on like this, barely able to function, living a shadow life. But I wasn't sure where else to go or what else to do. All my heart knew how to do was long for my children. In wanting to end their suffering, I sometimes even found myself wishing they had died instead of having been kidnapped. I knew they were being abused, and I knew their abuser. They were being manipulated and emotionally tortured. It broke my heart. I missed them as if they *were* dead. They were gone from my life completely. I was in the agonizing position of mourning for my children who were still alive.

CHAPTER TWELVE

Less than a month after the Practice Note 7 Order was entered into the court record, I put my house up for sale. I didn't yet know where I was going, but I knew I couldn't stay there any longer. The weight of it and the torment of all my unfulfilled hopes and dreams were too much to carry around. My children were not coming back. I began to absorb this horrific truth.

What I did know is that there is a small hope that children who have been alienated may return, after maturing and realizing what the abusive parent has done to them. I hoped this might be true for me someday. And if it were a possibility that in a matter of a few years, West or Navy would find their way back into my life, they couldn't find me as I was. They couldn't begin to heal from their extensive traumas with a mom who was in a state of shock, grief, and poor health. If there was going to be a chance for them to come out on the other side of all this, they would need a mom who was healthy, strong, and able to support them as they processed all that had happened. I was going to become that mom. I was going to heal myself so that I could be there to help them heal too, whenever that day might be.

I knew enough to know that I couldn't lose the weight I needed to—over a hundred pounds—by myself. I couldn't find emotional healing alone. My support group had been wonderful throughout this awful year, but I needed more intense and dedicated help. I couldn't remember the last time I'd felt like myself. I knew I had to get back in alignment with that person I once was, however long ago she existed.

My auntie Anne, my mom's older sister, said to me on the phone one day as I was contemplating what was next, "Well, you've been to the top of the mountain." Indeed, I had. And the good news was that I had received an entire education on that climb. I would never be the same, and I now got to choose what to do with the broken and almost unrecognizable Elaine who stared back at me in the mirror each morning. I needed to find meaning in this suffering. For West and Navy I wanted to be an example of strength and perseverance, because they now had their own paths to forge. If I didn't embrace the growth that could come from this, then what was the point?

I knew for sure that looking after my physical self first would contribute significantly to my mental and emotional healing, so that's where I wanted to start. I began researching and was led to a fitness resort that offered lodging, meals, nutritional counseling, exercise regimens, and educational classes on everything from emotional eating to stress management. For the first time in a long time, I could envision doing something to help myself. I was even sort of excited. I'd been so beaten down by all that had happened, a surprising wave of relief came over me when I thought about dedicating myself full-time to healing. My future was still not entirely clear, but I would have enough from the sale of the house to resign from my job and pay for an extended stay at a resort. Selling my house and quitting my job to throw myself entirely into the hard work of moving forward with my life was exactly what I wanted and needed to do.

I made the calculations and read everything I could about all the different fitness resort options around the world. I wanted to be able to take my car, and the closest resort to me geographically was in a small resort city north of Las Vegas, on the Utah-Arizona-Nevada border, called St. George. In my research, this one seemed to have everything I was looking for and I could get there in just over a day's drive. I was familiar with the route because it was on several of the same roads that I took to Wyoming when I had escaped with Navy. Suddenly, I wasn't afraid to confront my own pain anymore. There was simply no avoiding it any longer.

Shortly after I had made my decision, I got a call from Navy. After months of complete estrangement, she called and asked me to pick her up.

"Where are you?" I asked, leveling my voice.

"At a convenience store," she responded. "I need a ride back to Dad's house. Please."

"What happened?" I asked, trying not to sound panicked.

"I just needed to get out of the house for a while," she explained.

"Stay where you are. I'll be right there."

I raced to the address Navy had texted me. It was a good fifteen-minute drive from Kevin's house. I knew Navy was adept at using public transit, but she was completely alone and it was after dark.

"I do this sometimes," she explained softly after we had gotten in the car. There had been no hug, no greeting of any kind. Just a strange and stilted meeting in the parking lot. Navy continued, "Sometimes I sleep away from home, in a train or a bus station. There's also a tree-house I like that's not too far from here."

"Thank you for calling me," I said.

My mind was racing but I stopped myself from asking any of the one thousand questions I wanted to probe her with. I kept my expression steady to not reveal the level of my horror and dismay at how unsafe she felt at home and how much less safe than that it was for her to sleep unsheltered. It was clear Navy was deeply unhappy. What else would cause a fourteen-year-old child to sleep in a train station? I so badly wanted to ask what was going on but stopped myself. What she needed most right now was an adult who was calm, steady, and compassionate. She needed someone to feel safe with.

"I'm sorry," I said. "Is there anything I can do?"

"Karla hates me," Navy replied, looking out the window. "She was nice in the beginning, but now she just hates me. Her nickname for me is c**t. She and Dad fight a lot. Sometimes when they're fighting they come and wake me up in the middle of night. They tell me I'm the reason they are fighting and expect me to fix it. Karla drinks a lot, too. But it's the worst when she's been using cocaine."

Navy seemed anxious and fearful, and terribly sad. We were nearing Kevin's house and I would have to let her go in a moment. There was nothing I could do to help her, to change Kevin, to fix her situation. "Karla and Dad told us a few weeks ago that they are expecting a baby and it was going to tie our whole family together; we've all been really excited." She went on, "But I guess she lost the baby and they told me it was my fault because I bring so much stress to the house."

I was speechless.

"You can call me anytime," I said as I pulled up to the house. "Anything you need, just call."

She got out of the car without a word and walked into Kevin and Karla's house. The next day I texted to check on her and was met with stony, clipped phrases. *I shouldn't have called you. Leave me alone.* The opening I thought I might have had was gone. Navy would continue to endure Kevin and Karla's dysfunction and emotional torment, endangering herself by sneaking out alone. But I couldn't help her if she wouldn't let me. Slowly, I was seeing my own human limits: what and whom I could actually control; what I could hope to fix, and what lay completely beyond my control. It was me, and me alone, that I could fix. The only behavior I could control was my own.

I returned home and redoubled my efforts to sell my house, which had been on the market for over a month. Ultimately, it would take until nearly summer to get it sold, but I got a fair offer and finally had enough money for the fitness resort and whatever would happen after that. In the weeks I spent packing up my things, some to give away and some to store at my mom's house, Navy graduated from ninth grade and West was nominated for Student Athlete of the Year at his high school.

My friend Stacey sent me pictures of the graduation from her daughter's Facebook page, and told me how "yucky" it felt to be sending me pictures of my own daughter. I was grateful she had, though. Navy looked beautiful and so grown-up in her bright pink graduation dress and strappy sandals with a heel. I wondered which store she had picked everything out from and if it had been Kevin or Karla who had taken her. I attended West's award ceremony in secret, slipping in and sitting alone and unnoticed off to the side of the auditorium. I texted him afterward to say that I had seen him win third place, and how proud I had been. He still contacted me occasionally, but I received most of my scant updates from other parents who tried to help me stay connected while I sat outside my kids' lives.

In May, I finalized the sale of my house and started making plans to go to the fitness resort in St. George, Utah. Around that time, I was driving out of the grocery store parking lot and found myself maneuvering around two girls on their scooters taking advantage of the downhill slope. I slowed down to make sure they could get past me safely and when they got closer, I realized that one of them was Navy. I rolled down my window and called to her with a mix of hope and caution. To my surprise, when she realized it was me, her face lit up and she squealed out a big "Hi!" She immediately ran over to my car and gave me a big hug through the window.

Then, in a flash, her expression and demeanor shifted completely. She drew away and her eyes darkened. I could tell that she had just remembered that I was a forbidden person in her life, and I could see the gears turning in her young brain, casting about for the ramifications at home if Karla or Kevin found out that she had talked to me. I said goodbye, she went off with her friend, and I continued driving home, somewhat heartened to see Navy's immediate and genuine reaction. She had actually been happy to see me. Without the years of manipulation ingrained in her, she would have not only hugged me, but also put her head on my shoulder and filled me in on all the details of her life, just as she had once done every day of her life. But now she was shrinking away from me fearfully. I tried to contain my sadness over how far away she had become.

Just before I was ready to close up my house and resign from my job, I attended a hospitality conference in Ottawa. I was looking forward to my last work trip before I let Erica know of my plans to resign. After the gala on the last evening, I went back to my hotel room and rented a movie while I was packing. It was called *The Impossible*, a true story of a family that had been on Christmas vacation in Thailand during the 2004 tsunami. Since losing my kids, I was particularly choosy about what books I read or movies I watched. I didn't need to spend time immersed in any reality-based stories of misery and loss, since I was living my own painful trauma that wasn't just *based on* reality, it *was* my reality. The trailer seemed benign enough. After I finished packing, I lay down to watch the rest. I was riveted by the harrowing tale of a mother, Maria, who, with her son Lucas, got separated from her husband and other two sons when the December 26 tsunami engulfed them as they were lounging by their hotel pool. When Maria saw Lucas drowning, he called out to her to save him. She was badly injured by rubble and sharp objects when she swam over. I was gripped by the struggle of this mother and son. The final scene showed Lucas standing over his mother before she went into surgery. He had brought his dad and brothers over and told her that everything was going to be okay, that it was his turn to care for her because she needed help now. I watched, overwhelmed by this tender moment as they looked at each other, without any words, and knew that they had saved each other.

I lay paralyzed in my hotel room bed. I could hardly breathe. I couldn't even take in enough air to let out my cries of grief. I had lost Navy so abruptly. She had been with me one day and the next day she wasn't. I had lost West so gradually, and I had been so numb from everything that had led up to him not coming back, that I hadn't fully processed that he was gone. West was *gone*, just like Navy. I couldn't stop crying for my son, my firstborn, my heart walking outside my body. I cried until my pillow was soaked, until early morning. Then I got dressed, went to the airport, and caught my flight home. It was time for me to say goodbye. Goodbye to my job, goodbye to my home, and goodbye to the life that I knew. My new start had to begin now.

* * *

I hadn't told many people about my plan. My mom, of course, was deeply supportive. In addition to her, I told only my closest friends and my bishop. I certainly didn't tell Kevin or Karla. I didn't even tell West or Navy. Because of the vicious and unprovoked texts I was still getting from Kevin and Karla, with a lump in my throat, I changed my phone number. I had to sever their ability to get to me, even if it meant severing it from my kids too. Right before I did, I emailed West with instructions to contact my mom if he or Navy needed me for anything. By the beginning of June, I had given notice at my job, packed the rest of my belongings, and was picturing myself in the vast desert landscapes of Utah. I loaded my car and began my long drive south.

At the resort check in, each guest was weighed and measured, and I was terrified. I had arrived in Utah without much of a plan. Maybe I would just take it week-to-week. Maybe I would stay until I got my weight back down to 140, a number that symbolized a return to a youthful, happier me. Kelly, the resort's life coach, greeted me warmly.

"So, why are you here?" she asked.

I had so many answers but I wasn't sure what to share with this stranger. I decided to go with "I'm here to change my life."

Kelly nodded with understanding.

"I need help," I continued. "I need to heal myself emotionally. I've been turning to food to fix my problems, but I can't do that anymore."

Kelly was kind and encouraging, and promised to help me achieve my goals emotionally, not just physically. We visited until I got called in to stand on the scale. It was there that I met Sherry, one of the hiking guides. "Share-Bear," as she was also known, also helped with checking in new guests. She guided me gently to the scale. It read 276. It wasn't a complete shock, but the number still hit hard. I had been medicating with food for a long time. I had been depressed for even longer. And this was what it added up to. Share-Bear then asked me the same question as Kelly had.

"Why are you here?"

"I quit my job and sold my house and I'm going to use the equity to stay here as long as I need to to get my life back," I declared.

"Wow," she exclaimed. "That's quite a commitment. I don't think I've ever heard of anyone doing that before. Well, way to go!" she cheered. "I'm one of the hiking guides here. It'll be fun to have you out on the trail with us."

The thought of a hike made me laugh. I hadn't walked around the block in a year, let alone gone on a hike in the hills. I hadn't been to a gym in who knows how long. Filled with excitement and trepidation, I finished my check-in, then headed to the dining room for my first dinner followed by orientation.

Once orientation ended we all headed to our rooms to prepare for the next day and get a good night's sleep. On my way, panic overcame me. I was convinced that once morning came and I began the program, I would never be able to eat anything "good" again. I pulled my keys out of my purse and instead of going to my room, I walked to my car and drove to the local Dairy Queen. If this is going to be my last day of freedom to eat what I want, I might as well make it a good one, I thought. I ordered a Peanut Buster Parfait and since it was surely going to be the last ice cream I would ever have, I took a picture of it with my phone. I then sat alone in my car and ate it.

The next morning, we were on the trail by sunrise. I was terrified. And it was going to be over a hundred degrees that day. Although not unusual for a summer day in St. George, Utah, it was completely unlike my home in Canada. The trail looped uphill and down. The guides were extremely patient with me, kind, and encouraging as I painfully made my way along the trail. My body was not used to exerting itself, to the hot and dry air, or to carrying around my weight for more than a few minutes at a time.

At the resort, everyone hikes for two and a half hours and each guest gets as far as they can in that time. There were different hikes for different fitness levels and everyone was assigned to a group based on their ability. I was in the beginner group, and other than having to push aside my ego over how unfit I had become, I was happy to be with others like me. By the end of the hike I was completely exhausted, my hair looked like I had stuck my finger in an electrical socket, and my face was as red as a tomato from the heat. But I had walked farther than I had walked in years. I was proud of myself and it didn't seem as hard as I thought it was going to be. We arrived back at the resort after the hike, had breakfast, and when I looked at the schedule and realized I had five fitness classes to attend that day, I wondered if I'd been out of my mind to come here. I knew I had come to a boot camp, but there was no way I could have prepared myself for how hard it was going to be. I also knew, however, that I could do hard things.

The days were filled with communal meals, cardio and strength training classes, nutrition seminars, motivational speakers, and a lot of time to get to know my fellow guests. They were from everywhere and every walk of life and most were financially successful. But they, like me, were there out of a desire to close the gap between who they were now and who they used to be, or wanted to be. There were people hoping to lose two hundred or even three hundred pounds. There were others who had very little weight to lose, but felt themselves getting off track so they had come for a simple reset. Some had come for deeper reasons. There was a doctor who had no weight-loss goal, but wanted to confront his debilitating depression, which he had learned to manage with exercise. There was a guest recovering from leukemia, a mother and daughter who wanted to spend quality time together after their husband and father had died in the twin towers on September 11, and a man who had turned to food and alcohol to cope with his abusive childhood. There were chain-smokers, addicts, and survivors, and we were all together with a common goal of caring for ourselves, facing our demons, and receiving help. Our struggles bonded us and I would come to learn that these relationships would make all the difference in my journey's success. Wendy, one of the veteran hiking guides, would often refer to us as modern-day warriors. We were people going into battle every day for the sake of our very lives.

The second day's hike was worse than the first. After an exhausting first day, adjusting to my new surroundings, and doing more exercise in one day than I had ever done before, my tank was empty when I woke up. I got moving anyway. With thirty minutes left to go on that second hike, my body shut down completely. I couldn't move another inch and I wouldn't be able to finish. Dennis, my guide that day, walked back to where I had stopped in the middle of the trail and encouraged me to just put one foot in front of the other. He walked with me the rest of the way, as slowly as I needed to go. *Can I possibly hit rock bottom on only the second day?* I wondered, as we hobbled down the trail together and back to the van where all the other hikers were waiting for us. I had no idea what rock bottom even looked like anymore, not after losing first one child, then the other. Physical collapse was nothing compared to my own heart collapsing twice.

When people asked me how long I would be staying there, I said I didn't know. Maybe I would leave when I hit my goal weight. Maybe some other time. I kept my plans open and let myself work at my own pace, savoring the environment of total support and love without any rush or deadline. I extended my stay by a week, and then another. My full-time job was now looking after myself and living a life that I would be proud of, and that my kids might be proud of someday. It was completely freeing. I fell into a steady and even enjoyable routine, and my stay stretched into the fall, then into the winter.

Every night, after a long, regimented day of exercise, classes, and healthy meals, I collapsed onto my bed and often caught up with my mom or my friends on the phone. I'd heard nothing from West or Navy, and they hadn't tried to contact my mom either. I thought about them every day, plotting their activities as the calendar moved forward—what they would be doing for the holidays, how their exams might be going, and their swim practices. Part of Kevin's alienation had been to sever ties with all the adults in the kids' lives that had any connection to their previous life, from their pediatrician and dentist to their piano teacher. I'd heard that Navy even switched junior highs. Any person whom they knew while still living with or seeing me was completely cut off. I was being erased from their lives entirely.

While I made great progress at the resort, there were many down days as well. I lamented how long it was taking to lose the weight, how much it hurt, how tired and how emotionally spent I was. I questioned whether I had been realistic about my goals in the first place. I went through several plateau periods, when despite strenuous and continuous exercise, I didn't lose any weight at all. My coaches assured me that this was normal, that my body was trying to hold onto the weight and that I just needed to stay present and push through. They were right each time.

On Sunday, October 27, I weighed in and was down fifty-four pounds. I was feeling stronger every day. A new crop of guests arrived that evening, and after dinner and the meet-and-greet portion of orientation, I met a guest from Texas by the name of David House. He had been a guest before and had returned to continue working on his weight loss goal. He was tall, warm, and extroverted and had already formed a group of friends, myself included. He approached me as the evening was wrapping up.

"Hey, Elaine! I'm getting a group together to run the Snow Canyon Half Marathon. I want you to join us."

Snow Canyon was the state park near the resort where we went on a lot of our hikes.

"A half marathon? I think I'll pass. Thanks, though," I said with a little laugh.

"C'mon, you can walk it. It's only twenty-one kilometers and you are already on your feet that much in a day here," he said.

"I have never done any running, though, and I would need time to train. When is it?" I asked.

"It's on Saturday," he said.

"This Saturday? Like, in six days?" I laughed out loud. "No way."

David finally gave up trying to persuade me and I went back to my room to get ready for the next day.

Tuesday after dinner, David approached me again.

"Elaine, the deadline is tonight at midnight to register for the race. C'mon, I really want you to join us."

A few other guests whom David had managed to convince joined in on asking me to come. I finally surrendered and agreed. As David suggested, I could walk, and it would be good exercise for that day in place of the regular hike.

On the day of the run, I waited at the starting line with all the others, including David and the half a dozen other guests he had urged to come. I looked around at the hundreds of people preparing to run and thought to myself, *I have no business being here. These are real athletes. How did I get myself into this?* But I was committed now, and I reminded myself that I was there to get a workout. Walking 13.1 miles would definitely be that.

The starting gun went off and as happens at a road race, everyone started running. I got caught up in the excitement and started running also. I decided I'd go just a few feet and then walk. It was challenging and I wasn't enjoying it, so I kept telling myself that I would stop and walk any second now, as soon as I didn't feel like I could run any farther. I kept making mini goals for myself: just run to that tree, that sign, that fence—but giving myself permission to walk whenever I wanted to. I crossed the finish line 13.1 miles later, having run the whole thing. I couldn't believe it. At just over three hours, I hadn't broken any land speed records, but I had done it. I was even a bit tickled that I beat David House, much to his chagrin. It was the most physically challenging thing I had ever done in my life, and one of the most surprising. *What else can I do?* I wondered.

My belief in myself soared. By Christmas, I had been at the resort for five months. I was the only guest who had ever stayed that long and the staff felt like family to me. I bought them all small gifts and cards. In my notes to them, I finally told my story and explained what I was trying to heal from. It was the first time I had shared with them about my past, about my marriage, divorce, and alienated children. Along with shedding pounds, I was also shedding a lifetime of secrecy. By January, I was thinking more and more about the future. I was ready to make plans, feeling braver, feeling almost invincible as my body grew strong and capable of feats I had never imagined.

Snow Canyon Half Marathon

CHAPTER THIRTEEN

As I approached the six-month mark of my stay, I was still spending seven hours a day, six days a week, exercising. Perhaps this amount of exercise was not unlike what an Olympic athlete might do in training, I thought. The best part was that I was loving getting reacquainted with the me that had gone missing years earlier—physically, mentally, and emotionally.

While on a hike one morning, I was thinking it might be time for a short break. I wanted to make sure I could continue on for as long as I needed and wanted to. Despite not having lost any days to injury, the exercise had taken a toll on my feet in particular, I thought a trip somewhere might be nice. But where? I then remembered that from the time my mom was a little girl she had always wanted to go on an African safari and fly in a hot-air balloon over the Serengeti. I had some travel points saved, and with no work commitments, the timing seemed right. The next evening, on our usual call, I said, "Let's go to Africa. I know a great travel agent who specializes in Africa. I'll call her and arrange the whole thing. Just you and me for two weeks. We'll do it next month."

She was surprised by my sudden decision but agreed quickly. "I'm game!" she said.

My agent booked us a tour through Kenya and Tanzania for early February. We were both very excited. I was now down seventy-six pounds and feeling great.

I continued my time at the resort through January, both in the gym and on the trail. I had grown especially fond of one of the cardio classes called Mt. Kilimanjaro. I liked it because it was less interval training and more endurance focused, which I learned was a strength of mine. I was participating in the class one morning on the treadmill when it dawned on me that Mt. Kilimanjaro was in Tanzania. I went back to my room that night and did an internet search about the climb. From my research I learned that, while hard, it wasn't very technical and could be done by anyone who was fit enough. The thought occurred to me before I could stop it. I was going to climb one of the iconic *seven summits* and the tallest freestanding mountain in the world.

My mom didn't try to talk me out of it, but she absolutely refused to join me. "Have a nice hike," she said, laughing, and added that she would meet me at the bottom for the safari when I was done. I immediately contacted my agent and booked an extra week to allow me to complete the climb.

One evening after I got back to my room, my mom called to tell me about a feeling she had had. "We should invite Navy to come with us," she said.

The suggestion stunned me. I'd had little or no contact with Navy for three years. She was fifteen now.

"What? Navy? There is no way she'll come, and even if she wants to, Kevin will never agree to it," I said.

My mom felt strongly about it. She had been praying about the kids a lot. "I still think we should ask her."

I reluctantly agreed. It meant having contact with Kevin, even if indirectly. I had enjoyed months of no contact from him or Karla. So that Kevin wouldn't learn my phone number, I asked my mom to text Navy. She wrote, *Your mom and I are going to Africa, we want to know if you'd like to come?* The next day my mom's cell phone rang. It was Navy and Kevin on the phone.

Kevin began, "I understand you're going to Africa. Navy says she would like to go. I will be providing you with a list of conditions if I allow it."

"Okay," my mom replied.

Navy had to call and check in daily, Kevin would have a say in our itinerary, and there were some other items that he wanted to control. But he would let her come with us. My mom called me to tell me he had agreed and that Navy was coming. I couldn't believe it. It felt too good to be true. But I also felt uneasy. I was excited about the trip, about this time with my mom, about my climb. However, I was now going to have a fifteen-year-old girl with me whom I didn't know, who didn't know me, and whose every interaction with me since going to live with Kevin had been full of hatred and venom. I was also concerned about sharing anything about myself with Navy, including my phone number, knowing it would likely get back to Kevin. I would have to watch everything I said. After this time of peace and healing I was terrified about allowing Kevin and Karla to seep back into my life.

I couldn't then, and still can't now, presume to know why Kevin said yes. Maybe he was completely confident in Navy's alienation and had no fear of her spending time with me. Maybe things had grown too difficult at home and he was more than happy to get her out of the house for three weeks. Whatever his motivations, I was wrapping my head around it all. I had so many emotions about not only seeing Navy but spending an extended period of time with her. One thing I had decided for sure was that Navy would climb Mt. Kilimanjaro with me. I sent her a packing list of things to bring, only letting her know we were hiking while we were there and giving no further details. I didn't want Kevin vetoing my plan.

In February, Kevin dropped Navy off at the airport, where she met up with my mom and they flew to Las Vegas. I met them there and we flew together to Tanzania. Navy was tall and slim and seemed so grown-up. It was so wonderful, yet so strange to see her. Our conversation was awkward and strained at first. It felt like getting to know someone else's child. Navy was nervous, even a little agitated. I wanted so badly to take her in my arms, but the last thing I wanted to do was move too fast and frighten her. The flight was thankfully uneventful, and we arrived safely at our destination. I'd had my agent arrange for my mom to go on a small safari while Navy and I were climbing Kilimanjaro, and my mom had arranged to volunteer at an orphanage later in the week. This would be the first time in years Navy and I would be alone together.

We signed in at the bottom of the mountain and met our lead guide, Attley, and our tail guide, Thomas. They would be responsible for getting Navy and me to the top. They spoke little English, but we made do and enjoyed learning some Swahili along the way. We took the Machame route, which was thirty-seven miles to the top and passed through so many different climate zones that it was said to be like walking from the equator to the North Pole. Our first day was beautiful and warm. We were going to climb to 9,990 feet to settle into our first camp. We met several people from all around the world as we made our way up, including three very fit thirty-something Chilean brothers who would run to the top each day and always arrived at the camp first. We also met another Canadian, a girl in her twenties named Robyn, who was climbing alone. Navy and Robyn quickly hit it off, so we spent much of the day with her and enjoyed getting to know each other.

We settled into our first camp at the foot of the massive, iconic volcano. Along with our guides, there were porters to help us on our climb, carrying up our food, tents, and equipment. The mountain's summit was at 19,341 feet, and it would take five days for the ascent and one day for the descent. We would be sleeping at various campsites along the way, and by the time we reached the top, there would be half the amount of oxygen there is at sea level. The guides had arranged for Robyn to join us at mealtimes. Our dinner on the first night consisted of boiled hot dogs, white bread, and scrambled eggs served on a small card table at which we sat on folding chairs. When we had finished our meal they brought some popcorn for us to snack on.

"You two have such a great relationship," Robyn commented. "You seem more like friends than mom and daughter."

I was taken aback by her observation. Navy had spent most of the climb talking to Robyn and she and I had barely spoken more than a few pleasantries the whole day. Navy also looked surprised by what Robyn said and didn't take her words as a compliment. "We're not friends," she said darkly. "I haven't lived with her since I was twelve."

My body grew hot with embarrassment and rage as Navy began telling this girl that in fact, I had never done anything for her and that I was a bad mother who had abandoned her. She turned her chair toward Robyn and continued speaking, making no eye contact with me. "My brother doesn't live with her either. We've had nothing to do with her."

She was talking as though I wasn't even there. Robyn looked uncomfortable. I was speechless listening to her spew out other hurtful, cruel, and untrue statements. I was doing everything I could to not cry, and before she could say any more I finally interrupted and stood up.

"I'm going to bed," I said sharply, and retreated to the tent Navy and I shared. Without getting ready for bed, I slid down into my sleeping bag and began to sob. A few moments later, Navy came in and got into her sleeping bag too, without saying a word. I held my breath and my tears for as long as I could.

"Why did you say those things about me to Robyn, Navy?" I asked in the darkness. I was almost shaking as I said this to her. Navy didn't answer. I had wanted to give her space and freedom to be with her friend. Since my separation from Kevin, just as I did when we were married, I protected my kids from the ugliness of our relationship, and the ugliness of Kevin. In doing so, I hadn't always defended myself or explained how heinous Kevin and Karla had been, how abusive and wantonly cruel. But I had just been through seven months of long overdue self-care. I wasn't the same person any longer and I now wanted to maintain some boundaries, even with the daughter I missed dearly.

I continued, "I know it's hard to understand everything that has gone on in the last three years, and we haven't spoken in a very long time, but please don't do that again, Navy. Your dad—"

She cut me off quickly. "My dad has nothing to do with this! My dad is amazing and all those things you think about him aren't true. You think that he abused you. If he really abused you, why have I never seen him abuse Karla?"

I didn't have an answer, except to say that Navy had never actually seen her dad abuse me either. I realized that there was no way I could help her know the truth or undo what Kevin and Karla had done to her mind and heart. I didn't want to put her in the position to defend her dad, so I laid there in silence, not knowing what else to say. My fifteen-and-a-half-year-old daughter was a stranger to me.

My emotions swirled but one emotion stood out more than all the rest: fear. Strangely, despite everything I'd been through, I felt more fear at that moment than I had ever felt before, and it was surging through me. I was afraid of the dark volcano we were on, of the enormous distance between me and everything that was familiar in the world. I was afraid *of Navy*. I could hardly breathe; I was over-whelmed and panic-stricken, and about to take on what was likely the hardest physical test of my life. My body was jet-lagged and sick from the altitude. I felt more alone than I had ever felt before. I wanted to talk to my mom, who represented safety, and I certainly felt unsafe. I lay in the green vinyl tent wondering how I could get myself out of this situation. It was past midnight, but maybe I could find Attley and insist that he take me down the mountain. But I was afraid of that, too. I was afraid of everything.

I managed to speak through my fear. "Navy," I started. "I know you're angry. You have every right to be. You have been through so much. I want you to know that I love you. I have loved you every day of your life and will love you every day of my life."

"You're right. I am angry," she declared.

"Can you tell me why you're angry?" I asked.

"Yes," she said. "I've had to be angry. Because being angry at you has been easier than the guilt I've felt since choosing my dad over you when I was twelve."

I was astounded at what she had taken on as her responsibility, as her fault. And at how she had been trying to cope with going to live with Kevin all those years ago. I was enraged at how Kevin and Karla had deceived and exploited her when she had been so vulnerable. And yet, I was astonished at how deeply wise my daughter was.

"Navy," I countered. "You didn't choose. You didn't have a choice. You can't choose one parent over another when you're only twelve. Your dad—"

She cut me off again. "Stop!" she said. "My dad didn't do anything. I chose; it was my choice. I don't want to talk about this anymore."

"Okay," I said quietly. "Goodnight. I love you."

Camp, and our green tent

She didn't answer. I heard her breathing grow deep and steady. But I lay awake for hours. Even though I felt that maybe a small crack had formed in Navy's hardened exterior, I still had no idea how I was going to get up in the morning and climb hundreds of feet up a mountain, or somehow keep Navy and myself moving toward some kind of healing.

My thoughts were all over the place. On the long flight to Africa, I read a review of the book *Outliers: The Story of Success* by Malcolm Gladwell. Although some have since disputed Gladwell's premise, his book famously popularized the notion of the 10,000 Hour Rule, where the key to achieving expertise in any skill is to practice it for 10,000 hours. *If you do something for 10,000 hours you will be an expert at it,* he wrote. The number struck me as I thought about the fear I was experiencing. I did the math in my head. I knew that I had lived in a state of fear for *at least* 10,000 hours in my life. All the years of being married to Kevin, and then losing my kids: it had actually been many tens of thousands of hours. *I am an expert in fear,* I thought to myself.

Staring at the tent ceiling, I then thought back to a proverb I had once read about courage and fear being brothers, without either of whom the other wouldn't exist. My thoughts began to shift. Courage exists because of fear, achieved by persevering through fear, and overcoming it. Perhaps, then, I was also an expert in courage. Perhaps I could say that I was equally as experienced in courage as I was in fear. I thought, I'm an expert in being brave. I began to appreciate how bravery and fear were yoked together, and that I already possessed the resources and experience to face anything that lay before me, including the peak of Mt. Kilimanjaro. I realized that the fear of climbing that mountain, or facing whatever challenges lay ahead for Navy and me, could be conquered. Regardless of the number of hours required to claim to be an expert in something, I knew I had experienced both fear and courage more than enough to realize, and fully understand for the first time, that I was already an expert in both. I had needed to be courageous for all the metaphorical mountains I had previously climbed, so I was sure I could be just as courageous for a real one. Looking back, coming to this realization was a profound turning point in my life. With a feeling of peace and new-found confidence in my ability to handle anything that could come my way, I would never again let fear hold me back. I resolved that I would get up in the morning and climb.

Our second day began early. We packed our things and our porters broke down the tents and carried them ahead of us. That day, Navy walked with me instead of Robyn. The higher we climbed the colder it became, so that evening, Navy and I sat bundled up in our tent. She began asking me questions, tentatively at first, but I could tell she was desperate for information.

"Why weren't you there for us?" she demanded. "Where were you all that time? Why did you leave us?"

Navy

I was incredulous that she thought that I had chosen any part of our separation. She continued. "A mother should be there when her daughter tries on makeup for the first time, gets her period, graduates from ninth grade, and all the important stuff. And where was grandma for everything?"

I knew I couldn't tell her the truth as it really was, so I tried, with difficulty, to respond without mentioning Kevin or Karla. My responses became, "It was a very difficult time for everyone," and "That's a complicated question to answer, but I love you and I promise I wanted to be there."

Telling Navy that there were too many details and too much damning information about her father, I realized, wasn't how I should respond. But I sensed Navy needed to ask the questions more than hear my answers.

On our third day, bodies weary and hearts heavy with the exchanges between us, Navy seemed somewhat lighter and freer. She turned to me as we began our ascent, hoisting her backpack up. "Can I walk with Robyn today?"

Her question startled me. It took me a moment to realize why. In the last year that Navy had lived with me, she had rejected my authority completely. Her mantra was that she was in charge of her own life, she was making her own choices, and she could do what she wanted. I realized that I hadn't heard my fifteen-year-old daughter ask me for permission for anything in almost four years.

"Yes," I answered. "Of course you can."

"Thanks!" she called as she trotted ahead to catch up with her friend.

We walked separately for part of the day, together for part of it. We ate together, talking sometimes and sitting quietly at others.

Our fifth and final day of ascent was to end with us experiencing the sunrise at the peak, which meant after a full day of climbing to over fifteen thousand feet, we would hike the remaining four thousand feet through the night to reach the summit before dawn. We got to our final campsite, unloaded our packs, and prepared for dinner. As Navy and I ate our meal, we looked around at considerably more primitive conditions than we had seen when we started our trek. At 15,331 feet there were no animals, greenery, flowers, or other signs of life, other than a few mice and some large black ravens flying above our heads or invading our camp looking for food scraps. It was 7:00 p.m. and Attley came to tell us it was time for us to go to bed. He would wake us around midnight for the remaining seven miles to the summit, which he said would take us five or six hours.

I didn't understand why we had to go to bed so early and why we were only permitted to sleep for such a short time. Attley then explained to me that we were going to make the final ascent to the summit during the night, so we could arrive at the top for the sunrise. We changed into our pajamas, got into our sleeping bags, and both laid awake in our tent. The anticipation of what we were about to undertake made sleeping feel impossible. When Attley shook our tents, it was dark. There was a tension in the air as well as in our guides' movements and low voices. It had only been a couple of hours since we had gotten into our pajamas.

"Get dressed. Put your headlamps on," he instructed.

We sat up in our sleeping bags and felt around in the blackness for our headlamps. It was eerily quiet except for the rustling of other tents and the distressing sound of people all around us vomiting. The altitude was making people sick and I could overhear other hikers asking to be taken down the mountain.

Navy and I put on our warm coats, and when we opened the tent flap, we stepped out into a full-blown blizzard of whipping snow and frigid temperatures. I wasn't sure if this was normal, but as soon as Navy and I stood up straight, Attley pulled us close to him and to Thomas, who was standing to his left. We could see very little beyond the heavy white flakes in the beams from our headlamps.

"We need to pray," Attley said, and he gathered the four of us into a close huddle where we wrapped our arms around each other's shoulders. We bowed our heads and as I listened to the Swahili prayer wondering what he was saying, I felt I'd better say one of my own as well. I didn't know if he always said a prayer before summiting, but he and Thomas were behaving differently from what I had seen all week. He told me that because of the weather we needed to start our journey toward the summit much earlier. Even though we had hiked all day and had yet to sleep, we began trekking upward. Because of the heavy, wet snow, each step felt precarious, our feet backsliding a little every time we advanced.

Each of my legs felt like it weighed hundreds of pounds, and each step was so arduous that I wanted to pick them up with my hands and mechanically move them forward. Every few minutes I would break the icicles off the fur hood of my jacket so that the weight of the snow and ice didn't pull my hood over my eyes. Because of the steepness of the grade, we walked in small switchbacks left to right up the mountain so we didn't slide backwards. It was so black that I had no idea the pitch of the mountain, except when I bent my neck all the way back and saw small twinkling stars high in the sky, only to realize that they were the headlamps of other climbers. Navy and I had heavy coats and hats, but my mitts were completely insufficient. They were soaked within minutes. From my backpack, I pulled out a pair of wool socks to put on my hands, and then another, but they were soon all sodden as well. Seeing my alarm, Attley rolled his thin but waterproof gloves over his wrists and off of his hands, and handed them to me. I was hesitant to take them, hoping he had another pair, but took them gratefully. He remained bare-handed for the rest of the climb, tucking his fingers into the front of his pants when they got too cold.

Many people on the snow-covered trail were already suffering from altitude sickness, vomiting off to the side of the newly forged snowy path, and complaining of splitting headaches. Looking to the left and to the right, but only able to view what was in the scope of my headlamp, I saw climbers hunched over, groaning from what appeared to be abdominal pain or squatting in the frigid air from diarrhea, with their pants down in the snow.

Navy and I passed by one Scandinavian climber whom we'd seen all week, pulled off to the side in the deep snowbank. I shone my headlamp's beam on his face as I moved past him. Our eyes met for a small moment, and in the howling wind I heard him say, "It's heavy."

"Yes," I said, nodding.

Some climbers turned around and started going back down, unable to get warm, even seeing signs of frostbite on their limbs. One woman, a surgeon, said, "I can't lose my fingers," and quickly headed down the way we came. Attley and Thomas were checking our pupils regularly and asking us if we had a headache. They had instructed us at the start that if we had signs of altitude sickness we would have to descend immediately. We took frequent breaks to catch our breath and drink our icy water with our frozen lips. Attley continued to lead us. Along with his pack, he was now carrying mine, and Thomas was carrying Navy's. On one break, I asked Attley, shouting through the sound of the storm, how much farther we had to go.

"Many, many more hours," he shouted back through the wind.

Images were appearing in my mind of documentaries I'd seen of Mt. Everest expeditions. Men slowly walking up an icy mountain face, the snow from a blizzard pounding on them, their faces red and frozen. The difficulty they were experiencing seemed exaggerated when I watched it. My impression had been wrong. A few minutes later, we passed Robyn. She was leaning forward on her hiking poles trying to catch her breath. "I can't make it," she said, and waved goodbye as she started down.

Up ahead, I could see a large boulder where we could sit down and for the first time rest our legs. It had been six hours now and there were few of us left on the mountain. When I paused to rest on the boulder, I felt Navy sit down next to me. Then, I felt her entire weight collapse on me. I turned to find her slumped over and nearly unconscious from the altitude and the cold. I held onto her and looked through the blowing snow at Attley and Thomas for instruction. Immediately, I thought we would have to descend, and I was filled with relief at the thought of going down, my own body aching for oxygen and warmth. We were at eighteen thousand feet now and in the thinness of the air, everything in my mind and body was telling me to turn around. Attley checked my pupils and asked me if I had a headache. "No," I said. Thomas then walked toward me.

"Miss Elaine," he started. "You didn't come all the way from Canada to climb Mt. Kilimanjaro and to not make it to the top. I will look after Navy. We will make it," he promised.

I believed him. He supported Navy from behind, placing her feet on top of his, and pushed her along from behind, almost like a life-sized puppeteer. At our next break, he offered her some hot tea and it worked. A few minutes later, Navy passed me, walking on her own, waving at me, and telling me brightly that she'd see me at the top.

Before I reached the summit, the sky had lightened but with the storm still blowing the sun was nowhere to be found. I arrived at a large landing where the climbers who had made it through the night were collecting themselves to make the last ascent to the summit. I had been climbing for ten hours. I walked toward the base of the final hill and in the haze of the whiteout greeted one of the three Chilean men that we had been at camp with all week. He had a confused look on his face when he saw me. I asked him about his brothers.

"They didn't make it," he said sadly. He paused and looked up at me. "You're very strong," he said.

"Thank you," was all I could think of to say. *Am I?* I said to myself.

Navy was at the top, watching for me when I hoisted myself up to the summit of Mt. Kilimanjaro. She had waited for me. We had just a few moments to stand together, gazing at the terrain so far below us, to take in our incredible accomplishment. We were told that less than 10 percent of the people on the mountain had summited that day. We took two or three pictures, the storm still upon us. Soon, our guides were urging us to begin our descent and return to safety.

The climb down was tense and difficult. The blizzard had let up, but with so much snow we still had to watch our every step. We had been climbing for more than twenty-four hours and would now descend over nine thousand feet to our last camp. The storm was the talk of the mountain that day, the guides telling us it was the worst storm the mountain had seen in eighteen years. I thought about what Navy and I had just accomplished together, after so much time apart and after fighting through so many lies, heartaches, and dead ends. The mountain had not stood in our way, an obstacle to overcome. The mountain had given us its path to climb together, and it was the long-awaited turning point I had been praying for, beginning our journey back to each other.

Navy (in white) at the summit of Mt. Kilimanjaro

We hadn't slept yet and would arrive at our final camp that evening. We had spent another full day on the mountain and thirty-six hours later we finally got to bed. We looked forward to being reunited with my mom at the hotel the next day and to our first shower and change of clothes in almost a week. When we arrived to greet her, we looked like we'd been to war. We were sore, exhausted, wind-burned, and weathered. I had lost several toenails on the way down, including the nails on both of my big toes.

We spent the next two weeks on a wonderful safari together. Navy and I must have told the story of our climb a dozen times. We told it to everyone we met or had a meal with. Navy laughed, smiled, joked, and recounted the most harrowing parts of the climb to anyone who was interested, and even those who weren't. I watched her, and for a moment I was stricken with grief at the years I had missed, all the light in her eyes and all the smiles and laughter that I never got to see. But she was still there; she had been there all along.

Our grand adventure came to an end and we flew together to Toronto, where I tearfully parted ways with Navy and my mom. They would fly together to Calgary while I made my way back to Utah, to the fitness resort where my journey would continue. My heart was heavy as I let Navy go back to her dad, back to a life where I knew she was not happy or completely safe. On our last day in Tanzania, she had accidentally cracked the screen on her phone and had become almost hysterical with fear in anticipation at how angry Kevin would be at her. I couldn't protect her from this. I could no longer smooth things over, manage Kevin's reactions, or manipulate the situation so that she was protected from him. I had no control over these things, and I hadn't had for a long while. I texted Navy to see if her flight home was smooth. I realized how much I was changing when I noticed I wasn't entirely focused on our plans to stay in touch, arrange visits, or otherwise repair our relationship. Something had happened during our three weeks together; something was beginning to heal. I promised myself to follow the healing wherever it would take me, but to *allow* it to happen rather than trying to control it.

CHAPTER FOURTEEN

Once again at the fitness resort, I jumped back into the work of losing weight, increasing my strength, and finding emotional health. I had been doing more running since the new year and decided that since I had completed a half marathon, a 10K should be no big deal, so I entered myself in a local race. I was getting faster, and even managed to place first in my age group in the small community 5K race that I entered a few weeks later. I felt like my time at the resort was coming to a close, and I wanted to continue challenging myself physically. I had run all the distances except a full marathon, so it was the logical next distance to attempt, but I knew I would really have to step up my training to run forty-two kilometers. I didn't love running enough to enjoy the additional preparation it would take, so I thought a marathon in an interesting place might motivate me to intensify my effort.

I stumbled across something online called the Seven Continents Club. To join, competitors would have to complete seven runs, either all half marathons or all full marathons, on each of the seven continents. Not many had done it—and less than twenty of the runners who had completed it had been women. I was intrigued. I confirmed that my half-marathon in Utah had qualified, which meant that I would then need to find six more races. They could be of my own choosing as long as all the continents were represented, including Antarctica. I was very excited, and even more excited that I had found a good excuse to not have to train for a full marathon. I decided on the spot to do it. I had no idea what it would take or cost, but I said yes to the challenge anyway.

In late March, a month after returning from Mt. Kilimanjaro, I found myself running on a familiar treadmill. I had not yet reached my goal of 140 pounds. In fact, I weighed nearly 180 pounds after eight months at the resort. And yet, I was more fit and stronger than ever. I was, even at this higher weight, back to the same dress size I had been at 140 pounds. There were moments when I felt invincible in my new state of health and clarity, and deciding to compete in a foot race on every continent was one of those moments. I felt capable of anything and I couldn't set my sights high enough. With excitement and optimism, I wanted to say yes to whatever life would now hold for me. I felt like nineteen-year-old Elaine again, except with so much more wisdom.

That day on the treadmill, I looked out the same window I often did, and checked on the bird's nest I had been watching for weeks. The soft, delicate nest had been built amid the long spines of a cactus. Only one of the two eggs had hatched, and the parents had diligently fed and cared for the hatchling until, this very day I was watching from the treadmill, it was ready to fledge. As I pounded the revolving track, the little bird edged out of its nest and took off in the air. At that moment, I knew it was my time too. I knew that even the sharpest and most painful needles could be used to create a refuge, but every refuge is meant to be left behind after enough time and healing had passed. I had discovered a nest of safety and rebirth when I had most needed it. It had not made the needles disappear. It had made me ready to take off and go build my own nest.

I was only a few pounds away from my hundred-pound weight-loss goal, and I wanted to reach that milestone before I left. I continued to faithfully attend each of the fitness classes. I had graduated from the beginners hiking group and was now leading trail runs with the advanced hikers. But now, at the end of each day, rather than going to my room, I would go back to the gym and spend several more hours on the treadmill. I was determined to reach my goal in time. On the 19th of April, I checked out of the resort a hundred pounds and four ounces lighter than when I arrived, but having gained so much more.

I said a tearful goodbye to my family in Utah, the staff, who had been my biggest and best cheerleaders. I was given a huge send-off, a special video of my stay and a large 'graduation' ceremony. I had stayed longer than any guest in the resort's history and it had paid off. I loaded up my car and headed straight north to my mom's house.

Before   *After*
                            (9 months later, 100 pounds less)

A few days after I arrived, I was sitting in one of my mother's lounge chairs reading something on my phone and I looked up just in time to catch her taking a picture of me. I asked if I could see it and started swiping through her photos. I couldn't find it immediately so I looked through them again. It was then that I realized I had swiped past the picture she had taken. I stared at it for several seconds. I had been so focused on the work of looking after myself every day, that despite seeing myself in the mirror each morning, I hadn't truly seen what had happened to my body. It wasn't until I saw my transformation through a new lens that I knew I had achieved more than I imagined was possible.

Later that day, while I was packing my suitcase in preparation for my next big race, my mom expressed her apprehension about my decision to travel alone to every continent. She was concerned for my safety in some of the locations I had chosen, but I was undeterred. My first race would be in two weeks, near Beijing, for the Great Wall of China Half Marathon, the fifth-hardest race course in the world. On May 14, I arrived at my Beijing hotel and met the roommate I had been paired with by the race organizers. Oona, from Finland, was a student in her mid-twenties and we became friends quickly. She was the perfect companion while I was there. The tattoo on her arm fittingly read *Life is more than just staying alive*. I had spent far too much of my life just staying alive rather than living. *Never again*, I vowed.

Running atop such a magnificent artifact of ancient history was nothing short of incredible. My 2,600 steps on the Great Wall were delightfully enhanced by having to weave around a farmer herding his cows across the race route and small children from nearby villages running to high-five us as we ran by. Because of the erosion of the three-thousand-year-old brick and stone wall, several parts of the course were treacherous for us to walk, let alone run. There were even moments when we were forced to go single file, tightly gripping a constructed railing so that we didn't fall down the long and very steep crumbling steps. It was challenging, exhilarating, and thrilling. Three hours later, I successfully crossed the finish line, greeted by a large Chinese marching band aptly playing Beethoven's "Ode to Joy." My run on the Asian continent was now complete.

After China, I flew directly to Easter Island, the most isolated inhabited island in the world, famous for the ancient Moai statues belonging to the native Rapa Nui tribe, which our run took us right past. The island is a special territory of Chile, and therefore considered part of the South American continent. It was now early June, and I had completed my third continent by running on this obscure and charming island in the South Pacific.

Post-race, Easter Island, Chile

I had heard about the Camino de Santiago, a thousand-year-old pilgrimage from St. Jean Pied de Port, France, to Santiago, Spain, years earlier from my swim club friend Barb, who had walked it several times. Before deciding to go to Utah, it had been on the list of challenges I wanted to conquer one day. After Easter Island, I flew directly to France and spent eight days walking 125 miles of the five-hundred-mile trek. It included country roads and city streets, erratic weather, tall hills, incredible bread, cheese, and conversations with people from every place in the world and from every background. Each person's story about why they were walking "The Way" was as individual as they were themselves, and the customary greeting to each other and from the locals was "buen camino," Spanish for "good journey."

Camino de Santiago

In July, exactly one year after I had sold my house, quit my job, and checked into the fitness resort, I returned from Spain and my two continent runs, and settled into my mom's house once again. I began making plans for my remaining runs when Navy called— unexpectedly and only five days after my return home. We had texted occasionally since Kilimanjaro. Before I left for my run in China, I had visited the kids at their school and taken them out for meals. West had just graduated from high school and when I saw him, even though he was taller, older, and sounding more mature, those were the only things that felt different. He was happy, relaxed, and it strangely didn't feel like any time had passed. He seemed very excited to see me and, more than anyone else, was the most stunned by my physical transformation. Each time he looked at me he would repeat, "You look so different."

I'd had no contact with either Kevin or Karla that entire year. They didn't try to contact me, and as far as I know, didn't try to prevent the kids from seeing me.

"Mom," Navy began on the phone. Her voice was soft and a little hesitant. "Can I come and live with you?"

My heart stopped. Before I could respond, she added, "Just for a while?"

"Yes," I said quickly.

I had no idea how this would work, but my answer was yes, of course she could. We wouldn't all fit in my mom's house, so I told Navy I would start looking for a place for her and me, maybe a condo. She was relieved and happy.

"Great," she said. "Thank you."

I walked upstairs to my mom's bedroom where she was reading.

"Navy just called. She wants to live with me again," I told her. My mom looked stunned. "What? Why is she coming? For how long? Where are Kevin and Karla?" she asked, confused.

"I don't know," I said. "But I'm just so happy."

I had the same questions, but I didn't want to ask Navy. All that mattered was that my daughter was back in my life. The day I had hoped and prayed for for so long had actually come. *Navy had called and asked if she could live with me.* Navy came to my mom's house immediately. She and I would look for a place together, and while it was a little cramped, my mom and I were both thrilled to have Navy with us.

Within a few days, we had toured several condos and decided on one located not far from Cemetery Hill, the part of Calgary where I grew up. When I signed the lease, I texted West. *Hey, come by this afternoon and check out the place that Navy and I have rented.* He came by a few hours later. I took him downstairs to the fully finished basement. It had its own bathroom, a sitting area large enough for a sofa and coffee table, and a large space for a bed.

"If you find that you're looking for a change of scenery at some point, this space can be yours anytime," I told him. He looked around and seemed intrigued.

"Okay, thanks," he responded, cheerily.

A few days before we moved into the condo, Navy shared the reason she had asked to move in with me.

"My dad kicked me out," she said.

"What happened?" I asked.

"I was fighting a lot with Karla. Dad was fighting a lot with Karla too. She just hates me. After all that time of getting me to call her 'Mom,' and wanting me to change my last name to hers, she just changed. She couldn't stand me. I don't know why. Maybe it's because I look so much like you?" she said with an anxious look on her face. "I guess at some point, she told Dad he had to choose, her or me." She sighed heavily. "I'm here because he chose her."

I could only begin to guess the level of dysfunction in Kevin and Karla's relationship, but I was glad to have Navy in a safe place, away from the chaos of those two.

Two days later, I received a call from West at 2:00 a.m. I answered quickly because I was up, out on a date. I was alarmed when I saw his number flash on my phone so late at night.

"Is everything okay?" I asked.

"I'm in my truck," he said. "I have all my stuff in the back. I need a place to stay."

"Okay, no problem. Drive over to our condo," I instructed. "You remember the address? I'll meet you there."

Our new condo was still empty. Navy and I weren't scheduled to move in for another few days. When I met West, he was grabbing bags full of his things from his truck and his friend Adrian was helping him unload it. Adrian had been at Kevin's and Karla's with West. West's things smelled like a campfire.

"What happened?" I asked as soon as we were inside.

"Karla started a fire in the backyard," West said. "She got into a big fight with dad and started burning all his stuff. I smelled smoke and looked out the window and saw the flames. Then she started grabbing *my* stuff and headed towards the fire. That's when I called the police."

The fire department put out the fire and the police told West to take a few things and go somewhere safe for the night. Instead, West asked Adrian to help him, and he and West loaded every one of West's belongings into his truck as quickly as he could and called me. He had moved out. He had chosen to come to me.

I was reeling at what both kids had been through in the past few days and how little care they had been shown by their father. And I was so grateful that I had spent so much time getting myself well so that I could be completely there for them now. Though it had seemed the slimmest of possibilities such a short time ago, I always held onto the belief that they might someday return to me, and here they both were. Not just Navy, but now West was home too. A miracle had occurred. Had I not undergone a radical transformation to prioritize my own care and needs, I would have been in no condition to help them through these difficult days. But I was feeling healthy and stable. I had goals and ambitions of my own. I had a life I was proud to be living, with enough room and resources and love to welcome my children back with me.

The next month was wonderful, in that I was reunited with the children I had once thought were lost forever, but it was a big adjustment for me as their mom. They were no longer little kids. They were nearly sixteen and eighteen now. They had grown and changed and become young adults. I stifled my impulse to ask where they were going and with whom, or if they were eating well. I did my best to not get involved with whether or how they communicated with Kevin or Karla, although some days were easier than others and my curiosity would get the best of me. I struggled to not feel possessive of Navy and West after all the years I had lost with them, and would often feel threatened when they would mention their dad or Karla. But I couldn't make up for the lost time or will them to be twelve and fourteen years old again. I would have to meet them where they were and grieve the time we had all lost.

The kids and I resumed a favorite and very missed tradition of Sunday dinner at my mom's and I continued to train for my upcoming runs. What I didn't do, despite being overjoyed that we were all living under one roof again, was turn my whole being toward taking care of the kids. I was there for them and there for myself, too. I needed them to see me training and looking forward to meeting my goals, keeping my commitments to myself as much as the ones to them.

All their lives, I had seen myself as the strong one, so I had put myself on the bottom of the list of things I would care about. I had put them and Kevin ahead of me every time. I'd had to learn that caring for others doesn't have to come at the expense of caring for oneself, and that caring for myself was neither selfish nor wrong—it was necessary to make me able to care well for others. In my marriage, I had lost myself. As a mother, I had lost myself. Now that I had regained who I was, I was not going to let that go.

I made sure I had as little contact with Kevin and Karla as possible, but one of my few encounters with them was when Kevin dropped off

Navy's things at my condo. He'd somehow gotten my address, perhaps from one of the kids. Rather than letting Navy pack her things and move them to my place, he'd swept all the items left in her room into several huge garbage bags and dumped them on my doorstep. I saw him and stepped outside to face him.

"This is her stuff. You take it. I'm done raising her."

"What?" I asked. "Are you serious?"

"Yeah," he answered. "She's all yours now. I did my job."

With that, he turned and got back into his car and drove away. Maybe that's what Kevin needed to tell himself because it was easier to live with than knowing he was abandoning his sixteen-year-old daughter. Or knowing that he had made life so unbearable for West that prior to the night of the backyard bonfire when the police came, he had just spent several weeks staying at a friend's house to escape the chaos. After that point, neither West or Navy heard from Kevin for over a year. Even when Navy got into a car accident, Kevin wouldn't pick up when she called or return the message she'd left about what had happened. They likewise didn't hear from him on their birthdays or at Christmas.

That September, two months after the kids came to live with me full-time, they both had their birthdays. West was turning eighteen and Navy sixteen. They were milestone birthdays, and I wanted to celebrate what felt like a real new beginning for all three of us. Having always loved planning surprises, I decided to organize a scavenger hunt for them across the entire city. I created ten different clues and left them at ten different spots, coordinating with store managers to plant little surprises and clues for the kids to follow. It took me weeks to plan and set up, and it reminded me of all the times I had planned fun activities and special days for them when they were little.

I left the first clue in an envelope in our kitchen that sent them to a bakery for a set of custom cupcakes. Then, they went on to a drugstore, a gas station, and then to two of their favorite clothing stores at the mall—at each location they arrived to find a gift card to spend as they pleased, and a clue to their next location. Next they went on to a grocery store, and then to my mom's house for fresh cookies. The final clue sent them to the Cactus Club Café, a favorite restaurant, where I was waiting. It was a beautiful late summer day and I sat on the patio, facing the front doors so that I could watch them come in. They showed up, arms bursting with treats and faces beaming. They saw me and both grinned. On their faces I could see joy and excitement, but also love and pride. They were heading toward me quickly, ready for an embrace and a leisurely lunch, after which we would all return home together.

There was still so much healing and reconnecting to do, but we had time now and we had each other. I knew deep down that they weren't going anywhere, and neither was I. My plan was to finish all seven of my races on all seven continents and then settle down with a full-time job in travel and tourism. Until then, I would keep my time free and open for us. We had found our way out of a long darkness and back to each other, wounded and scarred, but not closed off to the possibility of our little family or the future. I smiled back at them as they approached our table. I opened my arms and said, "You found me."

EPILOGUE

It is beyond cold. It is pain. And I am running. Or at least, I think I'm running. It's hard to tell if my body is still moving forward through the sheer force of the Antarctic headwinds. I try to think about things, warm things—warm blankets, dark hot chocolate, the heater in my car turned on high—to take my mind off of the cold, but it's useless: I can only think of all things cold.

The land around me is like the moon—it is vast, empty, untouched, and I feel as though we, the runners, are the first people ever to set foot here. Where it isn't ice, the ground is black, a fine gravel that covers the whole land, and the stinging wind whips snow into my face so hard it hurts, and I can barely see. I feel as though my face will be frozen like this for the rest of my life, which at the moment seems like it might be considerably shorter than I'd previously expected.

As I boarded the plane to Antarctica with my fellow runners, I had thoughts similar to those that preceded my very first half-marathon, the one David House had convinced me to enter: *I have no business being here. These are real athletes. How did I get myself into this?* There were ninety of us who had come here for this purpose only: to run on the world's southernmost continent. It was an elite group of people, and several Guinness World Records were broken while we were there. Our group was the first in history to ever, in combination, camp and also run a marathon in Antarctica.

I'd arrived in this dry, windy, and bitterly cold place with few clothes or supplies because my luggage hadn't made it. Before we left Punta Arenas, Chile, I had bought a jacket, winter boots, and sleeping bag, and borrowed some of what I needed from people who had extra. It had been the coldest twenty-four hours of my life, but I became part of a little piece of history that day and my fourth continent was complete. My favorite part of visiting this desolate expanse was our only spectators, the penguins.

Antarctica, fourth continent completed

Two months later, in April, I flew to Vienna, Austria, and completed continent number five. My final two races, only six days apart, were in Victoria Falls, Zimbabwe, and Wellington, New Zealand, at the end of June. Returning to Africa someday had been a dream, but I hadn't anticipated it would be so soon after Mt. Kilimanjaro. I was one of very few non-African participants, and I got to know several of the locals along the race route and while mingling at the start line together. The perimeter of the race course was interspersed with men in uniforms holding rifles. Lions, elephants, cheetahs, hyenas, and leopards were roaming wild, and if these or any other wild animal came out of the trees, the gunmen were there to protect us.

Fortunately, the only wildlife I dodged that day was a family of wart-hogs crossing the road in front of me.

Zimbabweans are given wonderful names when they are born, often Western words. I met Freedom, Future, Progress, Knowledge, Welcome, Urgent, and Action. I spent most of that day running beside a thirty-two-year-old man from Victoria Falls named Challenge. When I came up behind Challenge, I noticed he had bandages wrapped around his left knee, and with each step he took he limped, appearing to be in pain. I decided to run beside him for a short while, hoping to help take his mind off of his knee. When he told me his name, I couldn't help but think about how fitting it was that Challenge and I ran together that day, considering the Seven Continents quest that I was undertaking. I was grateful for my unplanned running partner, and he and I cheered each other on almost all the way to the finish line.

That night, I flew to Wellington, New Zealand, part of the Oceania Continent. I would be running at sea level, where I was hoping to get a personal best. I crossed the finish line in a dead heat with my Easter Island time, equaling my fastest of the seven races. That day, I became only the thirty-fourth person in history, and nineteenth woman, to complete a half-marathon on each of the seven continents. I returned to Calgary, where I experienced my few minutes of fame, finding myself featured on my local evening news, and then in an article in *Women's Running* magazine. I received my Seven Continents Club medal a few weeks later.

I spent most of the next year going through a series of courses, both in-person and online, to become a professional executive and leadership coach. I opened my own practice where I worked one-on-one with business owners on effective leadership, marketing, best practices, team engagement, and how to improve profitability. Entrepreneurial by nature, I have always loved business. After several years of coaching, I returned to the travel industry and fulfilled my dream of leading a large hospitality-based organization. Serendipitously, it was as the general manager and COO of the very fitness resort where I had once been a guest for almost ten months. I guess my twelfth-grade career counselor had been right all along. A general manager at a hotel, despite the circuitous route getting there, was exactly what I was meant to be.

I helped dozens of people every week, who, like I had, arrived with their heads down, tired, discouraged, and out of alignment with who they knew themselves to be. My greatest joy was to see them leave with their shoulders back and heads held high, having closed the gap on the *who* that they knew themselves to be. I am now anxiously awaiting the opening of my own destination wellness resort: Redwood Fitness Retreat & Wellness Spa, near Banff, Alberta, in the majestic Canadian Rocky Mountains. It has been quite a round-trip. I will now get to be instrumental in the business and mission of helping people improve their health physically, mentally, and emotionally. There is nothing I'd rather do.

I've continued to make hiking a large part of my life, and being out in nature, challenging myself to get to the top of another peak, is exhilarating. The reality is that my weight journey will never be over. After losing a hundred pounds, I gained some of it back, and then lost it again. It's happened a few times since, but I continue to keep my health a top priority, and now travel that up-and-down weight journey less often.

West graduated from the University of Calgary with a degree in economics. He works as a successful account executive for a software company in Calgary and owns his own home. He also loves hiking and spending time with his friends climbing the mountains and rafting the rivers. He still wakes up happy every day. We continue to be very close and talk often.

Navy graduated from the University of Calgary with a combined Political Science and Law and Society degree. Just like when she was the fifth-grade team captain, she has never lost her passion for advocating for the underdog. Currently, she is attending law school in Europe, and aspires to work for the UN one day, to be able to help people on an international scale. She also loves to be in the mountains, especially climbing. Her most recent summer job was as a hiking guide for a health and fitness resort. We talk frequently.

My mom lives in Calgary and is enjoying retirement. We continue to be close and talk regularly. West and Navy are still the lights of her life, and she is theirs. We still enjoy Sunday night dinners together.

Nicole and her husband Doug continue to call Toronto home, where she is a homemaker with four children. Nicole and I are as close as we were when we were eleven. We talk weekly, and travel to see each other often.

Swizzle passed away at the age of fourteen and will always be one of the reasons I made it through the loss of West and Navy.

Kevin and Karla are still together. I have had no contact with either of them for many years. They live several thousand miles away in the Southwestern U.S. Both West and Navy have a relationship with them and speak on the phone or via text.

In 2018, I founded a support group for parents who have been alienated from their children. At my first meeting, four people attended. Within a year, we had over a hundred members. Unfortunately, the need is such that the group is growing at an extraordinary rate. While parental alienation is extremely common, it isn't widely understood and therefore an orphan amongst the many causes that our society gives funding and attention to. It is now almost as common for mothers to be alienated as it is for fathers.

The justice systems still commonly fail to recognize parental alienation. In our group, we offer much needed emotional support for each other—parents who have lost their children to this systematic brainwashing and campaigns of denigration. We hope to advocate for more awareness, and ultimately, change. If nothing else, I would like to bring attention to this: when a divorce is deemed high-conflict and involves a child who is demonstrating hatred toward only one of their parents, especially if the child is in adolescence, it is very often a case of alienation. Unless there are indications of physical or sexual abuse, alienation should always be a strong consideration. If every family court judge had this knowledge, there would be fewer cases of loving dads and moms being completely erased from their children's lives.

Since founding this group, the highlight for me was when West and Navy came and offered the parents an evening of Q&A. The group couldn't get their questions out fast enough, longing to hear about alienation from the perspective of the child. West and Navy were able to offer hope and insight for heartsick mothers and fathers aching for their children to be back in their lives. With other professional obligations now requiring my time, I have handed the group over to other members and the meeting continues to provide much needed support in the parental alienation community.

I now travel and speak at different engagements, coaching people in business and in life. With my personal stories, I talk about the connection between fear and courage, and how we can move through our fears, *because every one of us is already an expert*. Many of us have been to both the deepest valleys and highest mountains. But if we start by doing what is necessary, then what is possible, then suddenly we're doing the impossible. It has been important for me, however, to not be addicted to my story, nor do I feel any of us should be. My experiences helped guide who I am, and moved me to where I am now, but they don't define me. Who I am right now is who I am.

Naturally, it was a long while before I was interested in putting my feet back in the same water where I almost drowned. As I recalled in my memoir, I would often dream of what it would be like to be with a man who embodied all of those qualities that Kevin lacked; kindness, empathy, gentleness, thoughtfulness, and real, genuine love… the kind of relationships I had only seen in movies. At the time, it was hard to imagine that would ever materialize for me, but after many years of dating and other romantic misadventures, it actually happened. Finding that person feels like a miracle. But getting my kids back was also a miracle. *I believe in miracles.* To quote two of my favorite ecclesiastical leaders, "when every indication would say that hope was lost, hope is never lost,"[3] and "faith is the antidote for fear. Through faith, God will increase your ability to move the mountains in your life, even though personal challenges may loom as large as Mt. Everest."[4]

Or Mt. Kilimanjaro.

---

[3] Holland, Jeffrey R. (2013, October 2). Like a Broken Vessel.
https://www.churchofjesuschrist.org/study/general-conference/2013/10/like-a-broken-vessel

[4] Nelson, Russell M. (2021, April 4). *Christ Is Risen; Faith in Him Will Move Mountains.*
https://www.churchofjesuschrist.org/study/general-conference/2021/04/49nelson

SPECIAL THANKS

To my faithful (and patient!) Kickstarter backers, who endorsed me, supported me, and even insisted that I share my story.

Aleisha H	Connor S	Jessie M	Louise W	Shannon G
Allen C	Corne S	Jill A	Lulu H	Shauna O
Amanda W	Corrin & Tara R	Jocelyn G	Marlyn G	Shelley J
Amy E	Cynthia C	John F	Mary Lou S	Shellie M
Andrew K	Dan M	John P	Meena H	Sheri R
Angela F	Daniel	Julia S	Megan M	Sherry
Angie S	Danielle P	Julie P	Melody O	Silise L
Anne Margaret T	Darren & Maria D	Julie R	Mom	Sonja D
Anne Marie S	Dave Z	Julie S	Movara	Sonja M
Annie R	Don & Lisa S	Karen	Myanna K	Stéphane B & Karen C
Ariana K	Eliza K	Karen B	Nancy M	Stephanie
Arthur F	Elliot V	Karen J	Natalie Y	Stephanie L
Audrey A	Erin H	Karen V	Nicola M	Stephanie M
Barbara D	Erin S	Katherine H	Nicole	Stephanie V
Barbara K	Felipe C	Kathy H	Nicole L	Sue B
Becky S	Flora S	Katrina R	Pat H	Susan G
Brenda M	Fray	Kelly R	Pauline W	Susan S
Brenda S	Heather S	Kenda L	Rebecca C	Susanne S
Brent & Toni Y	Hegedus Masonry	Kendell R	Rebecca S	Tammy S
Brian H	Heidi G	Kenneth L	Renee P	Tanya W
Carol W	Holly C	Krista C	Robert W	Tara H
Carol-Ann M	Ina	Kristina A	Robin R	T Comessotti
Carolyn N	James H	Lalainia A	Roxanne A	Terri
Carolyn O	Jane B	Lauren L	Ryan & Jen R	Tina P
Carolyn R	Janet & Rick M	LaVaun & Garth B	Sandra M	Tonya N
Caryl O	Janet W	Leah C	Sandra S	Traci H
Cera E	Jan M	Leanne P	Sarah W	Tracy C
Cheri L	Janice M	Leslie S	Scott R	Tricia L
Chrissi S	Jeanette	Lindsay C	Scout	Trish M
Cindi G	Jeff M	Lisa	Serena G	Trish R
Colleen M	Jen Ann G	Lisa & Patrick H	Shannon	Valerie H
Connie H	Jennifer A	Lisa M	Shannon C	Valerie L
Connie M	Jessica C	Lori S		

WE BELIEVE YOU.
An Important Message to the Reader

I remember watching an interview with Elizabeth Smart a few years ago. She was the 14-year-old girl who was kidnapped at knifepoint in the middle of the night, held captive and chained to a tree by a man her family had hired to work on the roof of their house. She was starved and repeatedly raped and abused until she was finally rescued and reunited with her family nine months later.

During the interview, Elizabeth spoke candidly about the shame and embarrassment she felt about her rape and sexual assault. This shame was exacerbated by people, including the media, asking her questions like, "Why didn't you run? Why didn't you scream? He took you out into public, why didn't you *do* something?" But Elizabeth, like many victims of sexual assault and domestic violence, internalized these questions as, "You *should* have run; you *should* have screamed; you *should* have done something more. *You didn't do enough.* It's your own fault because you didn't do something."

It's experiences like these that keep abuse shrouded in secrecy because victims fear how they will be perceived, or fear that they won't be believed. In 2020, the Elizabeth Smart Foundation founded the movement *We Believe You*[5], recognizing the positive impact of believing survivors and bringing peace to victims.

---

[5] https://www.elizabethsmartfoundation.org/we-believe-you

It's all too frequent that victims of abuse experience re-victimization through victim-blaming or victim-shaming. The social and cultural norm of "might makes right" often leads to a person in a position of power not being held accountable, while the victims are viewed as being at fault for their own mistreatment. When victims aren't believed, the abuse cycle continues, not only by their perpetrator but also by society. Asking for help and then not being taken seriously is the deepest form of demoralizing pain because the victim already feels alone, and now also feels abandoned, instilling an even greater fear for their future. Disclosing the abuse is often a prolonged process, driven by fear and the need to make sense of their experience. If, after summoning the courage to confide in someone, they are not believed, the terrible risk is that they will never seek help again. Shockingly, studies reveal that two-thirds of sexual assaults remain unreported, largely due to a belief that their story will not be taken seriously.

> "This happened years ago and she's just talking about it now? Sounds like someone needs attention…"
>
> "She didn't even report it to the police. She's probably just making it up."
>
> "She only wants money."
>
> "I know him from work, he's a decent guy, there's no way he would do something like that."
>
> "If it was so bad, why didn't she leave? I would walk out the door the second a man hit me."

In some cases, a victim is believed, yet still subjected to judgment for "allowing" the abuse to occur. I'm still working through my own shame and embarrassment for choosing to stay with my abuser for as long as I did. It is hard for me to make sense of as I look in the rear-view mirror. But I also know that hope is an incredibly powerful force. Every day I hoped that my marriage would be different, and giving up on hope is difficult. It is, however, dehumanizing to assume that anyone is complicit or consenting to the abuse. Victim-shaming is rooted in the misguided belief that the person could have escaped or avoided the situation, but the reality is that everyone has the right to pursue their own wants and self-interests without fear of being abused. Everyone deserves to be treated with compassion, dignity, and respect, regardless of their circumstances.

According to Elise Lopez, a researcher in sexual and domestic violence at the University of Arizona, "Victim-blaming is at its core about self-preservation. A lot of people have a gut reaction to violence. It's emotionally charged. They think if somebody is being abused, they probably did something to incite it. In essence, if people can find a reason why abuse is the victim's fault, then abuse is something that can not only be controlled but prevented. And, in turn, it won't happen to them."[6]

Since the 2006 "Me Too" movement, it may seem that more people than ever have come forward with their stories of abuse and assault, but there is also a perception that there are more false accusations than ever before. However, studies show that false allegations of abuse or sexual assault are much less frequent than the problem of victims who aren't reporting the abuse at all.

My memoir reveals how the fear of not being believed was a major factor in my choice to remain in an abusive relationship. My fears were ultimately realized when I met with disbelief from friends, law enforcement, and the legal system. Some readers may also question details of my account, or assume it is exaggerated. Writing this memoir was not cathartic or therapeutic for me and required reliving painful memories. I didn't need, or particularly want, to write it. However, I have gone

---

[6] Lopez, Elise. Why We Blame Victims for Domestic Violence.
https://newchoicesinc.org/2017/08/26/why-we-blame-victims-for-domestic-violence/

through difficult experiences and I want them to serve a greater purpose than just being personal hardships. I believe it is my duty to use my experiences to correct myths about violence and parental alienation and provide hope to others who have also suffered abuse, addiction, trauma, or loss.

Domestic violence affects one in every three women and one in every four men. The abuser may not fit the typical stereotype; they can be anyone, from your next-door neighbor to your CEO, your child's teacher, your brother. The victim is also not always who you may expect. It's crucial to remember that victims are not broken people, but individuals who have been *broken upon*. They need to know that it's not their fault, that they did not do anything wrong. Victims often make every effort to avoid self-blame but find it challenging to not hold themselves responsible for remaining in the situation, and may experience feelings of guilt, embarrassment, and shame for staying. They should not be blamed by others either. Instead, they should be told that they are *supported, loved, and believed.*

These principles also apply to parents who have lost their children to parental alienation. They feel shame and embarrassment, and they are in excruciating pain mourning the loss of children, while also facing a lack of understanding that they didn't do something to make their child hate them. They should instead be told that they are *supported, loved, and believed.*

If you are a victim of domestic violence, reach out to someone. Don't stop looking for someone who believes you. There are support groups and organizations that can help you. Don't be afraid to ask for help, and don't be discouraged if someone doesn't believe you. Keep searching until you find someone who does.

We believe you!

–Elaine Hartrick

RESOURCES

Domestic Violence

https://www.domesticshelters.org/
https://www.crisistextline.org/
https://www.awhl.org/ (Assaulted Women's Helpline)

US:

National Domestic Violence Hotline: 1-800-799-7233 (US)
Additional information and resources can be found at:
https://www.acf.hhs.gov/fysb/programs/family-violence-prevention-services/programs/ndvh

Canada:

https://sheltersafe.ca/
https://menandfamilies.org/trauma-services/ (Domestic Abuse Support for Men)

Local hotlines and resources specific
to your city and province can be found at:
https://www.canada.ca/en/public-health/services/health-promotion/stop-family-violence/services.html

Parental Alienation

https://www.warshak.com/divorce-poison/
https://nationalassociationofparentalalienationspecialists.com/resources/

ABOUT THE AUTHOR

Lest the foregoing gives you the impression that our author is nothing more than a grim and humorless survivor defined by her trauma, you should know that couldn't be further from the wild and playful truth.

Elaine Hartrick is ... easily excited. Especially about people, places, or things that inspire her, which is a lot of people, a lot of places, and a lot of things. One thing that really excites her is living in Calgary, Canada, near her beloved Canadian Rocky Mountains. She also gets excited about spending time in distant places, especially developing countries.

She over-thinks and over-feels, (but only over-shares when she's writing a memoir).

Elaine regrets that her memoir didn't allow more room for humor. (Sorry her life wasn't funnier for you!) Elaine herself is easy to make laugh, which is one of the reasons she's so fun to hang out with. If you think Elaine is someone you could be friends with, you're probably right.

Connect with Elaine on Facebook (facebook.com/elainehartrick) or Instagram (@elaine_hartrick), or visit her website elainehartrick.com for upcoming speaking engagements and other events.

You can also reach Elaine at:
Redwood Fitness Retreat & Wellness Spa (redwoodfitnessretreat.com) located near Banff National Park, Canada.

Nine months later, Easter Island.

Manufactured by Amazon.ca
Acheson, AB